BLOCKHEADS, BEAGLES, AND SWEET BABBOOS

BLOCKHEADS, BEAGLES, AND SWEET BABBOOS

New Perspectives on
Charles M. Schulz's *Peanuts*

Michelle Ann Abate

University Press of Mississippi / Jackson

The University Press of Mississippi is the scholarly publishing agency of the Mississippi Institutions of Higher Learning: Alcorn State University, Delta State University, Jackson State University, Mississippi State University, Mississippi University for Women, Mississippi Valley State University, University of Mississippi, and University of Southern Mississippi.

www.upress.state.ms.us

The University Press of Mississippi is a member of the Association of University Presses.

Copyright © 2023 by Michelle Ann Abate
All rights reserved

First printing 2023

∞

Library of Congress Cataloging-in-Publication Data

Names: Abate, Michelle Ann, 1975– author.
Title: Blockheads, beagles, and sweet babboos : new perspectives on Charles M. Schulz's Peanuts / Michelle Ann Abate.
Description: Jackson : University Press of Mississippi, 2023. | Includes bibliographical references and index.
Identifiers: LCCN 2022047685 (print) | LCCN 2022047686 (ebook) | ISBN 9781496844170 (hardback) | ISBN 9781496844187 (trade paperback) | ISBN 9781496844194 (epub) | ISBN 9781496844200 (epub) | ISBN 9781496844217 (pdf) | ISBN 9781496844224 (pdf)
Subjects: LCSH: Schulz, Charles M. (Charles Monroe), 1922–2000—Criticism and interpretation. | Comic books, strips, etc.—United States—20th century.
Classification: LCC PS6728.P4 A33 2023 (print) | LCC PS6728.P4 (ebook) | DDC 813/.6—dc23
LC record available at https://lccn.loc.gov/2022047685
LC ebook record available at https://lccn.loc.gov/2022047686

British Library Cataloging-in-Publication Data available

CONTENTS

ACKNOWLEDGMENTS
- vii -

INTRODUCTION. CHARACTER STUDIES
The *Peanuts* Gang, Reconsidered
- 3 -

Chapter 1.
"SOMETIMES MY HAND SHAKES SO MUCH I HAVE TO HOLD MY WRIST TO DRAW"
Charles M. Schulz and Disability
- 14 -

Chapter 2.
WHAT'S THE FREQUENCY, CHARLIE BROWN?
Sound Waves, Music, and the Zigzag Shirt
- 33 -

Chapter 3.
"WHY CAN'T I HAVE A NORMAL DOG LIKE EVERYONE ELSE?"
Snoopy as Canine—and Feline
- 57 -

Chapter 4.
I LOVE LUCY
The Fussbudget and the First Lady of Sitcoms
- 81 -

Chapter 5.
FRANKLIN AND PIG-PEN
The Aesthetics of Blackness and Dirt
- 106 -

Chapter 6.
CHIRPING 'BOUT MY GENERATION
Woodstock, Youth Culture, and Innocence
- 130 -

Epilogue.
PEANUTS TO WATCH OUT FOR
Linus Van Pelt, Alison Bechdel, and
the Legacy of Charles M. Schulz
- 152 -

NOTES
- 174 -

WORKS CITED
- 182 -

INDEX
- 199 -

ACKNOWLEDGMENTS

Happiness is . . . having so many wonderful people to thank.

The *Peanuts* comic that appeared on November 2, 1974, presents Snoopy in a familiar setting: sitting atop his doghouse with his typewriter (fig. A.1). Unlike the many other comics that depict the World Famous Author, he is not diligently writing. Instead, in the opening panel, Snoopy is turned away from his typewriter. His paw is on his chin, his head is tilted upward in contemplation, and his expression looks anxious and even worried. In the next panel, the situation has not improved. Snoopy now appears completely distraught: his eyes are clamped shut, his face is grimacing, and beads of sweat are emanating from his brow. After all this anguish, however, Snoopy

Figure A.1. *Peanuts* comic strip, November 2, 1974. PEANUTS © Peanuts Worldwide LLC. Dist. by ANDREWS MCMEEL SYNDICATION. Reprinted with permission. All rights reserved.

finally finds some relief. The third panel presents the beagle working at his typewriter once again. The text above him reveals what he has typed: one solitary word, "The." The fourth and final panel relays the strip's punch line. "A great writer will sometimes search hours for just the right word," Snoopy says sagely.

Happily, the process of researching and writing this book went more smoothly (most of the time) than Snoopy's experience in this strip. Nonetheless, I am indebted to many individuals who provided invaluable assistance as I searched for just the right words. First and foremost, I wish to thank Benjamin Clark, the director of the Charles M. Schulz Museum and Research Center. He responded to numerous research queries with insight, detail, and good humor, including during the pandemic.

I am likewise exceedingly grateful to Katie Keene, my editor at University Press of Mississippi, for her interest, enthusiasm, and support of this project. I am also indebted to the anonymous outside readers of my manuscript. Their many helpful suggestions sharpened my ideas and enhanced my analysis.

I likewise owe a great debt, literally, to Peanuts Worldwide and Reagan Carmona, who allowed me to reproduce the many Schulz comics that appear in this book without needing to take out a second mortgage on my house, doghouse, and Sopwith Camel. I am thankful for their support, kindness, and generosity.

While this book has been a professional endeavor, it has also been a deeply personal one. Like many other individuals born in the second half of the twentieth century, I spent my childhood immersed in *Peanuts*, from the newspaper comics and the animated television specials to the paperback reprints and, of course, the bonanza of merchandising. When I was growing up, my plush Snoopy dog was my most treasured possession, next to my security blanket, of course. I took Snoopy everywhere, even to school on a number of occasions, where he spent the day clandestinely in my book bag. I wasn't much of a reader as a young child, but I devoured the *Peanuts* paperbacks. Whenever we visited the neighborhood public library, I would borrow tall stacks of these titles, often as many as the lending limit would allow—or that I could find in the spinner rack.

Since beginning work on this project, I have discovered that *Peanuts* and I are connected in a number of other, more unexpected, and even uncanny, ways. Charlie Brown and I share the same birthday: October 30. Similarly, Schulz was born on the same day as my paternal grandmother, November 26; the two were just one year apart in age. Moreover, the cartoonist and I have many similar personality traits: enjoying our daily routines, heading to our work space faithfully every morning, eating the same thing for breakfast all the time. Although Schulz enjoyed an English muffin with grape jelly, when he was asked to contribute a recipe for a celebrity cookbook, his submission was for how to make my favorite dish: a bowl of cereal. Finally, but far from insignificantly, Schulz and I are connected by another, more heartrending experience: the loss of our mothers. Schulz's mother died when he was in his early twenties. This event affected him profoundly, becoming what Schulz's biographer David Michaelis argued was the defining moment of the cartoonist's life. I also lost my mother from my life when I was in my early twenties. Although death was not the cause, the impact was the same. Then, a few months after sending the first full draft of this manuscript to my editor, my mother passed away. My relationship with her was far different from the one Schulz had with his mom, but—akin to the cartoonist—both her presence in my life and her absence from it affected me profoundly. She also loved *Peanuts* and especially Snoopy. Even before she died, I often thought about her as I was working on these pages. This link, in fact, is perhaps what kept me from writing about Schulz for so many years.

Peanuts has shaped so many aspects of my personality and played such a large role in my experiences that it is difficult to imagine what my life would be like if the comic had not existed. Surely I am not alone in this sentiment. American popular culture as a whole would be far different without Charles M. Schulz.

Portions of some chapters have appeared previously. A version of chapter 1 was published in *Inks: The Journal of the Comics Studies Society* 5, no. 2 (2021): 135–54. A modified version of chapter 3 was also published in *Inks: The Journal of the Comics Studies Society* 3, no. 3 (2019): 227–48. Finally, an earlier take on the epilogue appeared in *The Comics of Alison Bechdel: From the Inside Out*, edited by Janine Utell (University Press of Mississippi, 2019), 68–88. I am grateful to the publishers for their permission to reprint. I am equally indebted to the editors—Qiana Whitted, Jared Gardner, and Janine Utell—as well as anonymous outside readers who evaluated these versions; their feedback made my discussion stronger and my arguments more insightful.

The novelist Ann Patchett, in an essay about her childhood love for *Peanuts* and its influence on her adult life, wrote: "Even when I was old enough to know better, I was more inclined toward 'To the Doghouse' than *To the Lighthouse*. I was more beagle than Woolf. I did the happy dance, and it has served me well." I was born in the Year of the Rabbit. Moreover, the day of my birth places me under the astrological sign of Scorpio. These details notwithstanding, akin to Ann Patchett and countless others, my Patronus has always been a beagle.

BLOCKHEADS,
BEAGLES, AND
SWEET BABBOOS

INTRODUCTION

CHARACTER STUDIES

The *Peanuts* Gang, Reconsidered

The critical acclaim, commercial success, and cultural impact of Charles M. Schulz's *Peanuts* is difficult to overstate. Making its debut on October 2, 1950, in a mere seven newspapers, the series quickly became a national sensation. As Chip Kidd has written, "At its peak, the comic strip ran in over 2,600 newspapers, with a readership of 355 million in seventy-five countries, translated into twenty-one languages" (n.p.). These figures are astounding on their own, but they represent just one facet of the comic's presence in US print culture. Beginning in 1952, *Peanuts* strips were collected and reprinted in paperback editions. By 1966, no fewer than twenty different titles had been released, collectively "selling four and a half million copies—or one [book] every thirty seconds" (Michaelis 339). The success of the paperback volumes inspired the release of new material, including Robert L. Short's *The Gospel according to Peanuts* (1964) and Schulz's *Happiness Is a Warm Puppy* (1962). The former title became a "national best seller in hardback, snapped up at the rate of four thousand copies a week, with more than ten million of its paperback editions eventually scattered throughout the world" (Michaelis 352). Meanwhile, by 1967, *Happiness Is a Warm Puppy* "would sell 1,350,000 copies in three languages" (Michaelis 339). Additionally, it spawned a series of spin-off volumes, each with "hefty seven-figure sales, and unprecedented stints on the bestseller lists" (Kidd, n.p.).

The success of *Peanuts* in American print culture caused it to migrate to other cultural platforms and media venues. On December 9, 1965, the animated television special *A Charlie Brown Christmas* premiered on CBS. As David Michaelis has relayed, "Almost half the people watching television in the United States tuned in—some fifteen and a half million households" (359). The program would go on to win both a Peabody Award and an Emmy for Outstanding Individual Achievement. Over Schulz's lifetime, an additional

3

forty-four animated *Peanuts* television specials would be released. The programs would earn Schulz a second Peabody Award and a second Emmy Award, along with five more Emmy nominations. Furthermore, several of the episodes, including *It's the Great Pumpkin, Charlie Brown* (1966) and *A Charlie Brown Thanksgiving* (1973), would become instant classics, airing annually and becoming a seasonal viewing tradition for countless adults and children alike.

The *Peanuts* gang also appeared onstage. On March 7, 1967, the off-Broadway musical *You're a Good Man, Charlie Brown* debuted in New York City. Like the animated Christmas special, the show was an immediate hit, enjoying a four-year run in New York alone. Moreover, as Schulz reflected in an interview in 1992, *You're a Good Man, Charlie Brown* became "the most performed musical in the history of American theatre. . . . Every school and church and high school and grade school and kindergarten you can think of has put this thing on" ("Timeline").

Schulz's creation likewise found its way to the radio airwaves. In November 1966, the Royal Guardsmen released the song "Snoopy vs. the Red Baron." The tune would eventually reach number two on the Hot 100 list. Moreover, the song's success would inspire the Royal Guardsmen—with Schulz's approval—to create a full-length album, *Snoopy and His Friends* (1967). The record launched several additional radio hits, including "The Return of the Red Baron" and "Snoopy's Christmas."

By 1970, it seemed that no facet of US print, visual, or material culture was untouched by *Peanuts*. The characters appeared in the feature-length film *A Boy Named Charlie Brown* (1969), as balloons in the annual Macy's Thanksgiving Day parade, and as the official mascot for NASA's Apollo 10 mission (Kidd, n.p.). Arguably overshadowing all these elements, however, was the veritable bonanza of *Peanuts* merchandise. In a campaign spearheaded by Connie Boucher at Determined Productions during the 1960s, Schulz's characters would be licensed to seemingly every conceivable consumer product imaginable: toys, clothes, home decor, jewelry, school supplies, greeting cards, sporting goods, stationary, health and beauty products, figurines, holiday decorations, bedding, cookbooks, and games (Michaelis 337–39). In a powerful indication of both the success and the esteem of these items, in 1988, a fashion show featuring outfits created for plush versions of Snoopy and his sister Belle begin touring the United States. The show eventually reached the Louvre Museum in 1990, where it "was a smash hit" ("Charles M. Schulz at the Louvre"). The opening in Paris was timed to mark the comic strip's fortieth anniversary and "featured 300 Snoopy and Belle plush dolls dressed in fashions created by more than 15 world famous designers." Moreover,

"Snoopy in Fashion" represented "the only time that an American comic strip artist was honored with a retrospective at the Louvre" ("Charles M. Schulz at the Louvre").

Over the decades, Schulz's characters have also appeared in both print and television advertisements for entities ranging from MetLife insurance and Ford automobiles to Rock the Vote drives and Dolly Madison snacks. Taken collectively, the sales of *Peanuts*-themed products, licenses, and merchandise made Schulz one of the most successful cartoonists not just of his time but of all time. As James E. Caron has documented, "Schulz reached his income zenith from everything *Peanuts* in 1989: $1 billion total revenue and $62 million personally" (149)—an amount that exceeded the salaries of many movie stars, corporate executives, and media moguls.

Schulz's work has been as critically acclaimed as it has been commercially successful. Together with his Peabody and Emmy awards, the cartoonist received "Congressional Gold Medal honors, along with two honorary doctorates" (Lind x). He was also feted by his peers. Schulz was given the top honor by the National Cartoonists Society—the Reuben Award for Outstanding Cartoonist of the Year—not merely once but twice: in 1955 and again in 1964. Additionally, he was named Humorist of the Year by the organization in 1958, and *Peanuts* was selected as Best Humor Comic Strip in 1962 (Caron 148–49). Such esteem was anything but short-lived. As Eileen Daspin points out, even today—more than two decades after the strip ended—*Peanuts* "regularly makes the lists of best comics ever" (5).

By the time of Schulz's death on February 12, 2000, he had created, drawn, and published nearly eighteen thousand comic strips—an astounding output. Moreover, David Michaelis has speculated that Schulz's work had "reached a larger readership and audience than any other artist in American history" (442). Many of the strip's ideas and expressions—such as the concept "security blanket," the term of endearment "Sweet Babboo," and the insult "You Blockhead!"—have entered the popular lexicon. Given this influence, Claire Catterall has asserted that "*Peanuts*' influence on culture and society is nothing short of seismic" (qtd. in Laux). This statement is far from hyperbole. Seemingly no aspect of American visual, commercial, or popular life has been untouched or unaffected by the strip. Eileen Daspin referred to *Peanuts* as "a cultural touchstone" (5). Few would disagree. Peter Shore, United Feature Syndicate's vice president for marketing and licensing in the United States, said about Schulz's creation: "The characters are embedded in worldwide culture, they are part of your life" (qtd. in Johnson 227). In 2021, a special issue of *Life* magazine dedicated to *Peanuts* called it nothing less than "the world's greatest comic strip."

Despite the massive success of and widespread acclaim for *Peanuts*, it has not received comparable levels of critical analysis. In a detail that is surprising given how popular Schulz's comic has been for so many decades, "the number of peer-reviewed academic volumes and scholarly essays dedicated to *Peanuts* over the past twenty years can likely be counted on two hands" (Gardner and Gordon 4). By contrast, the scholarly attention given to other long-standing characters and lucrative brands—*Star Wars*, *The Simpsons*, and the Marvel Universe all come to mind—has been formidable, with dozens of books, essays, and journal articles.

The reasons fueling the critical neglect of *Peanuts* are multifold—and multifaceted. First, and perhaps most powerfully, "newspaper comics more broadly have suffered considerable academic neglect" (Gardner and Gordon 4). Although the field of comics studies has become more prominent in recent decades, the resulting scholarship has largely focused on other modes of sequential art: namely, comic books and graphic novels. Comic strips that appeared in daily newspapers remain on the margins of the field. Exacerbating the critical neglect of *Peanuts* is Schulz's own insistence that he was not an artist and his strip was not important art. In comments that typify ones that he made throughout his career, Schulz asserted in an essay from 1975, "There are several factors that work against comic strips, preventing them from being a true art form" (Schulz, "My Life and Art" 4). Whether this viewpoint can be attributed simply to Schulz's midwestern modesty, or whether it arose from his sincere belief that his strip was mere ephemera, it nonetheless did not encourage critical engagement.

Finally, but not insignificantly, the vast quantity of *Peanuts* material has also served as an impediment over the years. In the words of Gardner and Gordon once again, "we have here an archive whose primary text alone is made up of almost eighteen thousand individual strips" (6). Of course, coupled with the already massive print collection are the forty-five animated television specials, five feature-length films, multiple theatrical productions, and a veritable mountain of merchandise. The sheer number of cultural venues in which the *Peanuts* comic and its characters have circulated make working on it daunting and even overwhelming. For these reasons, a powerful paradox quickly emerged. On the one hand, *Peanuts* was—in the apt words of Geraldine DeLuca—"the most successful comic strip in newspaper history" (308). At the same time, however, it was also arguably the most critically neglected.

Ironically, it was only after Schulz's death when this trend began to change. In September 2000, M. Thomas Inge released *Charles M. Schulz: Conversations*. The book reprinted a variety of interviews that Schulz had given over the years as well as reflections about his life, craft, and career written by critics like Leonard Maltin and Gary Groth, along with fellow cartoonists Bill Watterson and Garry Trudeau. Then, in 2004, an even more significant development occurred: Fantagraphics began republishing the full run of *Peanuts*, making the comics more accessible to contemporary readers. The final volume of the twenty-five-book series was released in 2014. Furthermore, in 2007, the publication of David Michaelis's epic six-hundred-plus-page tome, *Schulz and Peanuts: A Biography*, sparked new interest in both the cartoonist and his work. The book received not simply national but international attention, with reviews in the *New York Times*, *Newsweek*, the *Los Angeles Times*, the *New Yorker*, *The Guardian*, *The Telegraph*, and Reuters. Then, in 2010, M. Thomas Inge released *Charles M. Schulz: My Life with Charlie Brown*. Although the title suggests another biography, the book is a collection of more than two dozen of Schulz's essays, articles, interviews, and speeches, organized into three categories: Schulz's life, his profession, and his art.

With the full run of the *Peanuts* comics released, an epic biography of the cartoonist available, and two volumes collecting many of the commentaries that he made throughout his career published, the past five years have seen a surge in Schulz scholarship. In 2015, Stephen J. Lind released *A Charlie Brown Religion: Exploring the Spiritual Life and Work of Charles M. Schulz*. In many ways, the book is an extension of Michaelis's biography, building on it, expanding it, nuancing it. Together with renewed interest in the cartoonist's life, the second decade of the twenty-first century also saw the release of the first collections of critical essays about his comic strip. Jared Gardner and Ian Gordon's *The Comics of Charles Schulz: The Good Grief of Modern Life* appeared in 2017. The volume contains thirteen chapters that examine everything from the strip's depiction of sports and its evocation of Christianity to its exploration of sincerity and the connections between Schulz's artwork and the sublime. Two years later, in 2019, a collection titled *Peanuts and American Culture* was released; edited by Peter W. Y. Lee, the book features nine essays that tackle tropics ranging from Snoopy's role in the Space Race to gender, professionalism, and power in Lucy's psychiatric booth. Also in 2019, Andrew Blauner published *The Peanuts Papers: Writers and Cartoonists on Charlie Brown, Snoopy and the Gang, and the Meaning of Life*. The book reprints more than thirty short essays that have been published over the decades about Schulz's comic and characters, including pieces by notables ranging from Umberto Eco and Ira Glass to Chris Ware and Jonathan Franzen. In a telling index of the ongoing professional esteem for Schulz and his work, *The Peanuts Papers* was nominated for an Eisner Award in the category of Best Academic/Scholarly Work. Most recently,

Blake Scott Ball's *Charlie Brown's America: The Popular Politics of Peanuts* (2021) hit library catalogs—and bookstore shelves. As the title implies, the project examines Schulz's strip from a historical perspective, exploring both the political climate in which the series was created and the sociocultural commentary it contained.

Blockheads, Beagles, and Sweet Babboos adds to the growing critical interest in *Peanuts*. This project sheds new light on the past importance, ongoing significance, and future relevance of Charles M. Schulz's series. To do so, I examine a fundamental feature of *Peanuts*: its core cast of characters. While previous critics have rightly called attention to features such as the striking aesthetic style, compelling narrative plotlines, and savvy licensing deals in discussions about the attraction and appeal of Schulz's strip, the unique, distinctive, and memorable characters were essential ingredients. From Charlie Brown and Linus to Snoopy and Woodstock, these figures became not simply household names but national icons, readily recognizable even to individuals who have never read the newspaper strip.

Blockheads, Beagles, and Sweet Babboos examines the main characters who made Schulz's strip so successful, so influential, and—above all—so beloved. In so doing, it gives these figures the in-depth critical attention that they deserve and for which they are long overdue. Each chapter spotlights a different well-known member of Schulz's core cast: Charlie Brown, Snoopy, Lucy, Franklin, Pig-Pen, Woodstock, and Linus, respectively. That said, I consider these exceedingly familiar figures in markedly unfamiliar ways. From suggesting a new way of viewing the zigzag pattern on Charlie Brown's iconic shirt and identifying unforeseen links between Woodstock and his music festival namesake to exploring Snoopy's feline side and placing the debut of Lucy back within the context of the massively popular television sitcom with which she shares her name, I revisit, reexamine, and rethink characters from *Peanuts* that most of us believe we already know. During this process, I demonstrate not only how Schulz's comic remains a subject of acute critical interest more than twenty years after the final strip appeared, but also how it embodies a rich and fertile site of social, cultural, and political meaning.

The character studies in *Blockheads, Beagles, and Sweet Babboos* begin, quite appropriately, with the character behind it all, Charles M. Schulz himself. While countless individuals know the cartoonist's tremendous commercial success and ongoing cultural impact, most do not know that he struggled with a health condition for the final two decades of his life: essential tremor (ET), a neurological disorder that causes parts of the body to shake uncontrollably. First diagnosed in 1981, Schulz's essential tremor is visible in his cartooning. In many comics, we see a discernible waviness to his lines.

As the cartoonist aged and the condition worsened, this feature became more pronounced. Chapter 1 reexamines the life and career of Charles M. Schulz by moving his essential tremor from the background to the forefront of consideration. For more than half of its run, not only was *Peanuts* drawn by an artist with an impairment, but this condition was also a highly visible aspect of his cartooning. Accordingly, the first chapter explores both the importance and the implications of viewing Charles M. Schulz through the context of essential tremor. Doing so yields new critical insights about the composition as well as the aesthetics of *Peanuts*. At the same time, it adds to ongoing discussions about disability in comics.

Chapter 2 examines a feature of *Peanuts* that is arguably the most famous and simultaneously the most critically neglected: Charlie Brown's iconic shirt. While the pattern on the well-known garment has long been described as a zigzag, I view the wavy lines in an alternative way—as a triangle wave. Triangle waves play a role in a variety of fields, such as electronic power transmission, radio technology, and sound engineering. In the realm of music, a triangle wave is the graph formed by the frequencies of odd harmonics. Sound in general and music in particular form a core component to *Peanuts*. The triangle wave that can be identified on Charlie Brown's shirt adds a new facet to these features. Ultimately, seeing Charlie Brown's zigzag shirt as a triangle wave calls attention to innovative ways that sound can be incorporated into visually based forms of sequential art.

Chapter 3 shifts from Charlie Brown to his pet pooch, Snoopy. Although Schulz's star character is both drawn and identified as a beagle, I make a case that he exhibits a variety of traits that are more stereotypically associated with felines than with canines. In examples ranging from his refusal to play fetch and his grandiose views of himself to his finicky palate and his penchant for sleeping on top of his doghouse rather than inside it, Snoopy is far more catlike than doglike in many respects. Exploring Snoopy's feline qualities not only adds a new dimension to this exceedingly popular character but also adds a new facet to a common theme in *Peanuts*: failure.

Chapter 4 examines the self-proclaimed "fussbudget" of *Peanuts*, Lucy Van Pelt. When this figure made her first appearance in Schulz's comic strip on March 3, 1952, another character named Lucy already permeated American popular culture: Lucy Ricardo from the television show *I Love Lucy*. In a historical detail that has long been overlooked, Lucy Van Pelt was created and introduced against the backdrop of the *I Love Lucy* craze. However unexpected and even unlikely, the initial portrayal of Schulz's fussbudget exhibits a variety of areas of overlap with the figure who is commonly remembered as the First Lady of Sitcoms. Exploring the suggestive echoes between Lucy

Van Pelt and Lucy Ricardo locates *Peanuts* within one of the most significant events taking place in American popular culture during the postwar years while simultaneously calling attention to another long-overlooked area of cultural cross-pollination: the one between television sitcoms and newspaper comics.

Chapter 5 examines the comics life and cultural legacy of the character Franklin. Since his debut in July 1968, Franklin's introduction to the strip has long been praised as a landmark moment when a white cartoonist broke the color line to introduce a Black character to his all-white cast. While the appearance of Franklin was an important event in US comics, it was not without complications and even problems. In a heretofore overlooked detail, the shading technique that Schulz used to signify the race of his new Black character mirrors the one that the artist used to shade another long-established figure from the strip: Pig-Pen. As his name implies, Pig-Pen is known for being filthy: his face is dirty, his clothes are soiled, and his body is surrounded by an ever-present cloud of dust. Schulz uses a similar hatching method to indicate that Pig-Pen's skin is dirty as he does to indicate that Franklin's is black. In so doing, *Peanuts* connects itself with the long history in American popular culture of likening blackness with dirt. The visual links or aesthetic connections that occur between Franklin and Pig-Pen not only complicate celebratory views of Franklin as a progressive character but also add to recent discussions about the importance of paying attention to the line in comics.

Chapter 6 spotlights Snoopy's comedic sidekick and feathered friend, Woodstock. More specifically, it ponders his most stubbornly elusive feature: his name. While previous critics have concluded that there is no clear, direct, or obvious reason that Schulz chose to name his little yellow bird after the historic musical festival that took place in upstate New York in August 1969, I make a case that the moniker is highly resonant. By naming the character after the well-known event, Schulz invites his readers to see the bird as a metaphor or even metonym for the concert. At the same time, and perhaps even more importantly, the cartoonist is also encouraging readers to see Woodstock as an embodiment of the era's young people, the Woodstock Generation. Reexamining Schulz's Woodstock through this lens changes our perception of the character along with his role in the comic. The little bird is Snoopy's best friend and comedic sidekick, but he is also a conduit for sociopolitical issues. When *Peanuts* debuted on October 2, 1950, the comic strip offered a pointed commentary on US children and childhood. Twenty years later, in June 1970, when Schulz named his little bird Woodstock, he revisited this interest for a new generation of young people. With the decision to name a character Woodstock, the comic strip took up questions of youth and youth culture once again.

Finally, the epilogue examines the legacy of Charles M. Schulz. To the already impressive array of people and pop culture phenomena that the cartoonist has influenced, my closing discussion adds another, perhaps less expected, cartoonist and comics series to the list: Alison Bechdel's *Dykes to Watch Out For*. For decades, Mo Testa, the beloved protagonist of the strip, has been seen as an autobiographically inflected representation of the cartoonist herself. Mo certainly functions as Bechdel's alter ego, but I make a case that she may also have her roots or origins in a figure from *Peanuts*: Linus Van Pelt. Linus is perhaps best known as Charlie Brown's best friend, but he is also known for being the most contemplative, introspective, and—with his beloved blue blanket—insecure character in the comic, traits that also typify Bechdel's Mo. Exploring the similarities between Mo and Linus extends the reach of Schulz's work into a new realm while simultaneously revealing a compelling kinship between Bechdel's work and one of the most well-known strips in the history of American comics.

As anyone familiar with *Peanuts* can attest, Charles M. Schulz populated his comic with a wide array of distinctive personalities. From the bossy Lucy and philosophical Linus to the perpetually filthy Pig-Pen and the lovable loser Charlie Brown, Schulz's characters possessed strikingly different habits, interests, and traits. Accordingly, it is only fitting that *Blockheads, Beagles, and Sweet Babboos* employs a similarly wide array of eclectic critical perspectives. The chapters that follow draw on disability studies, sound waves, television sitcoms, animal studies, critical race theory, and 1960s music festivals—among other topics. For some, this diverse slate of approaches might seem too dissimilar, too unrelated, and even too disparate to form a cohesive book. After all, monographs are expected to contain not merely a clear focus but a unified perspective—as the prefix *mono-* suggests. Rather than seeing the heterogeneous lenses employed here as detracting from the homogeneous focus of my project, I see them as necessary components of it. Schulz's characters are far from monolithic, and thus discussions about them cannot be either. Instead of striving to fit all these distinct and different individuals into the same critical, cultural, or theoretical mold, my chapters meet them where they are and—even more importantly—as who they are. I examine characters from *Peanuts* in ways that are the most critically illuminating, rather than the ones that would be the most thematically unifying. The catholic nature of each chapter mirrors the catholic nature of Schulz's comics cast. No two of the cartoonist's figures are the same, and thus no two chapters in this book use the same approach, framework, or lens.

All of that said, readers will notice a variety of thematic, methodological, and even interpretive connections among the seemingly disconnected approaches. First and foremost, as the summaries earlier reveal, many chapters are concerned with the aesthetics of Schulz's drawing style in general and the role that his line work plays in his work in particular. This issue forms the jumping-off point for my discussion of Schulz's essential tremor in chapter 1, as well as for my consideration of the connections between Franklin and Pig-Pen in chapter 5. In many respects, paying attention to the nature, shape, and possible meaning of a line also forms the basis for my analysis of Charlie Brown and the zigzag shirt in chapter 2. In the same way that several chapters have a shared focus on the drawn line, others possess a shared focus on lineage. Chapter 4 about Lucy and chapter 6 about Woodstock both explore alternative ways of understanding these characters' names. Moreover, the discussions do so by placing their names back within the context of events in the era's popular culture. Given these features, the character studies that constitute *Blockheads, Beagles, and Sweet Babboos* are united by more than simply their focus on Schulz's core comics cast. They are also united by a shared critical end point. Whatever character I am examining and whatever claim I am making about that specific figure, all of the chapters share the same interpretive goal: to get readers to look at Schulz's core characters and, by extension, his comic strip in new, alternative, and even unexpected ways.

One final word about organization and methodology. The chapters that follow move through figures from *Peanuts* in a specific and intentional way. I begin with the cartoonist himself and then progress through his comics characters in descending order of their prominence in the strip: first the protagonist, Charlie Brown; then his sidekick, Snoopy; from there, Charlie Brown's foil and nemesis, Lucy; and so on. My intent was not to establish (or affirm) a hierarchy of characters in *Peanuts*; all these figures occupy an undeniably significant place in the series. Instead my arrangement is simply a pragmatic means of arranging them. That said, the chapters of *Blockheads, Beagles, and Sweet Babboos* can be read out of order as well as independently from each other. I have done my best not to repeat information: about the start date of *Peanuts*, its tremendous commercial and critical success, the total number of strips, the animated television specials, and the licensing, branding, and merchandising. However, I am also aware that not every person who picks up the book will read it from cover to cover. Accordingly, I have tried to strike a balance between avoiding repetition and supporting different readers along with different readings of the text. Surely I have missed this mark in some places, including too much background information for some and not enough for others. I take comfort in the fact that these failures only place me in closer kinship with Charlie Brown.

The *Peanuts* strip that appeared on November 28, 1955, presents a scene that is simultaneously familiar and unexpected. The opening panel shows Schroeder sitting at his beloved toy piano, playing an unknown musical piece. In the background, Lucy stands quietly by, watching him. This situation repeats, with slight variation, in the next two panels: Schroeder continues to play—his hands moving vigorously up and down the keyboard—while Lucy continues to silently observe him from different vantage points around the room. In contrast to her usual conduct while visiting Schroeder, the young girl doesn't lean against the instrument, nor does she chatter on about banal topics while he is trying to practice. Instead Lucy simply watches him, wordlessly and attentively, her arms folded behind her back. In the fourth and final panel, however, she can restrain herself no longer. Climbing onto the piano and leaning closely into Schroeder's face, Lucy tells the virtuoso, "You fascinate me!"

Lucy is not alone in this sentiment. For more than seventy years, not merely Schroeder but all the characters of Charles M. Schulz's comic strip have fascinated untold millions in the United States. The chapters that follow examine some the most beloved *Peanuts* personalities, further indulging our interest while simultaneously unpacking the reasons why we remain so captivated by them.

CHAPTER 1

"SOMETIMES MY HAND SHAKES SO MUCH I HAVE TO HOLD MY WRIST TO DRAW"

Charles M. Schulz and Disability

Given the tremendous commercial success of *Peanuts*, along with its lasting cultural impact, Charles M. Schulz is "widely regarded as one of the most influential cartoonists of all time" ("Famous Cartoonists"). He is certainly among the most famous from the twentieth century. Even individuals who have never read the newspaper strip recognize Schulz's name, his image, and, of course, his characters.

As with other famous figures, many fans know details about Schulz's personal life in addition to his professional work. For example, readers might be aware that the cartoonist came from the Midwest. Or they might realize that Schulz had a passion for ice hockey. Finally, they might remember that he was a World War II veteran. As the biographer Beverly Gherman noted, in the same way that *Peanuts* fans felt they knew Schulz's characters, they also felt they knew the cartoonist (9). Unlike other celebrities who cultivate an air or mystery or create a professional persona that is very different from their private personality, Schulz was—akin to his comics characters—a straightforward person who did not engage in artifice.

In spite of how well-known Charles M. Schulz has been for generations, one aspect of his life and career remains widely unknown: the fact that he had a disability. While individuals may think about the cartoonist's midwestern roots, his commercial success, and his cultural impact, they do not think of him as struggling with a health condition for much of his life. In 1981, Schulz was diagnosed with essential tremor (ET), a neurological disorder that causes an individual's extremities to quiver uncontrollably. Schulz's hands were especially affected; they often trembled in a rhythmic fashion. By the

Figure 1.1. Final panel from *Peanuts* comic strip, February 17, 1995. Reprinted in *The Complete Peanuts, 1995 to 1996*, by Charles M. Schulz (Fantagraphics Books, 2015), 21. PEANUTS © Peanuts Worldwide LLC. Dist. by ANDREWS MCMEEL SYNDICATION. Reprinted with permission. All rights reserved.

late 1980s, the condition had become so pronounced that the cartoonist revealed, "Sometimes my hand shakes so much I have to hold my wrist to draw" (Phoenix).

Schulz's essential tremor is visible in his cartooning. In many comics, we see a discernible waviness to his lines; this feature is most typically noticeable in his speech balloons (fig. 1.1). As the cartoonist aged and the condition worsened, this feature became more pronounced (fig. 1.2). In various strips from the final few years of the series, in fact, Schulz's hand is so shaky that the rendering of his beloved characters is noticeably affected (fig. 1.3).

Despite the many decades that Schulz lived with ET, as well as the clear impact that it had on his work, few past or present discussions of the cartoonist address his condition. The obituaries about Schulz that appeared on the front page of many major national newspapers—such as the *Washington Post* and *Los Angeles Times*—never mention it. And when other critics discuss Schulz's essential tremor, they usually do so briefly and only in passing—often as an "I bet you didn't know this about him" piece of trivia.

This chapter reexamines the work of Charles M. Schulz in light of his possession of essential tremor. In so doing, it inaugurates one of the core themes of *Blockheads, Beagles, and Sweet Babboos*: how the line is rendered in the

Figure 1.2. Detail from *Peanuts* comic strip, September 12, 1999. Reprinted in *The Complete Peanuts, 1999 to 2000*, by Charles M. Schulz (Fantagraphics Books, 2016), 110. PEANUTS © Peanuts Worldwide LLC. Dist. by ANDREWS MCMEEL SYNDICATION. Reprinted with permission. All rights reserved.

Figure 1.3. Side-by-side comparison of two *Peanuts* comics panels. The image on the left is from a strip that appeared on July 12, 1970; the image on the right is from September 12, 1999. Reprinted in *The Complete Peanuts, 1969 to 1970*, by Charles M. Schulz (Fantagraphics Books, 2008), 240; and *The Complete Peanuts, 1999 to 2000*, by Charles M. Schulz (Fantagraphics Books, 2016), 110. PEANUTS © Peanuts Worldwide LLC. Dist. by ANDREWS MCMEEL SYNDICATION. Reprinted with permission. All rights reserved.

cartoonist's work. For decades, critics and fans have discussed Schulz's distinctive aesthetic style. From the curl of hair on Charlie Brown's forehead to the marks that constitute Woodstock's speech, line work forms a central and highly recognizable part of *Peanuts*. Essential tremor exerted a significant, but long-overlooked, influence on Schulz's drawing style. Acknowledging and foregrounding the cartoonist's ET provides a fuller and more accurate portrait of his life while simultaneously changing the way we think about his comics and career. For more than half of its run, *Peanuts* was drawn by an artist with an impairment. Moreover, the condition is also a highly visible aspect of his cartooning. Rather than being peripheral, it is central. Far from being undetectable, it is evident. Instead of being inconsequential, it is—like the name of the tremor itself—essential. Accordingly, this chapter explores both the importance and the implications of viewing Charles M. Schulz through the context of essential tremor. Doing so yields new critical insights about the composition as well as the aesthetics of *Peanuts*. At the same time, it adds to ongoing discussions about disability in comics.

THE DOCTOR IS IN: DEVELOPING AND DRAWING WITH ET

Schulz's diagnosis with essential tremor came on the heels of another problem with his health. In September 1981, the cartoonist underwent heart surgery to repair a series of obstructed arteries (Michaelis 520). Just as his quadruple bypass solved one medical problem, another one arose. While recovering in the hospital, Schulz began experiencing trembling in his hands. Given the sequence of these events, many biographers have linked the two conditions, seeing Schulz's development of essential tremor as a complication or, at least, side effect of his bypass surgery. David Michaelis—who in his six-hundred-plus-page biography never actually names Schulz's condition as essential tremor—accounts for it in this way: "The operation left [Schulz] with pronounced tremors in his drawing hand" (Michaelis 521). However, essential tremor is connected to the nervous system, not the cardiac one. As the official international foundation for the disorder explains, "ET is a neurological condition" ("About Essential Tremor"). The Mayo Clinic, in its overview of ET, states flatly: "Other conditions don't cause essential tremor" ("Essential Tremor"). While the precise origins of the disorder remain unknown, genetics play a key role. "About half of essential tremor cases appear to result from a genetic mutation," the Mayo Clinic explains. Age is another contributing factor, with ET appearing more commonly in individuals who are over forty years old ("Essential Tremor").

ET is not a fatal condition, but it does become more pronounced over time, and this happened with Schulz. As Rheta Grimsley Johnson noted, the tremors in the cartoonist's hands "worsened with each succeeding month" (225). Eventually, many individuals with ET have difficulty performing basic daily tasks like drinking from a glass without spilling, shaving, putting on makeup, and writing legibly ("Essential Tremor"). As Johnson commented after meeting the cartoonist, "It is startling to see the coffee cup waggling wildly in the artist's unsteady hand" (225). While the cartoonist never made ET part of his public identity—in the way that he did being a midwesterner or a World War II veteran—he also was not reticent about it. As Beverly Gherman discussed in *Sparky: The Life and Art of Charles Schulz*, "He didn't like having a tremor in his drawing hand," and he commented on, as well as complained about, it during her many conversations with him (114).

In *The New Disability History*, Paul K. Longmore and Lauri Umansky explore conceptions about bodily difference in the twenty-first century. Echoing the long-standing rejection of what is known as "the medical model," they assert that disability "is not simply located in the bodies of individuals" (19). Phrased in a different way, disability is far more than merely a clinical diagnosis or a physical condition. It is also "a socially and culturally constructed identity. Public policy, professional practices, societal arrangements, and cultural values all shape its meaning" (19). That said, Longmore and Umansky go on to note that disability cannot be wholly disconnected from corporeality. After all, different somatic states, bodily experiences, and modes of functioning play a tangible role in the lives of individuals. Ignoring or minimizing occurrences such as the experience of pain, feelings of fatigue, or the frustrations of taking medication misrepresents the lives of people with disabilities. Given this reality, "disability historians must grapple with the significance in the lives of their historical subjects of physiological states that depart from typical human experience" (19). In a pointed critique of the social model of disability that has dominated thinking for the past few decades, Longmore and Umansky call for a methodology that "recognizes the corporeal dimensions of human experience and its consequences for daily functioning, while striving continually to understand the contingencies that shape, reflect, express, and result from that dimension" (20). Simi Linton has termed this new approach the "socio-somatic model," and it combines the physical with the personal, exploring how the two realms intersect, interlock, and interact (n.p.).

Essential tremor is most productively viewed from a socio-somatic perspective. While the condition is not considered "serious" from a medical standpoint—it is not fatal, it is not contagious, and it does respond to treatment—it is significant from a personal and social one. Essential tremor affects far more than the physical parts of the body in which the tremors are present; it affects the whole person. The condition may not be life-threatening, but it does greatly affect an individual's life.

Charles M. Schulz was undeniably affected by ET. Developing the condition in September 1981, he lived and worked with it until his death on February 12, 2000. Schulz could not stop his hands from shaking, so he developed strategies to cope with the problem. As Johnson revealed in her biography, to be able to draw on many days, Schulz had to steady his "hand by propping it against the surface of the table" (226). Additionally, as Woodrow Phoenix notes, Schulz also accommodated his ET by "using varied sizes of pen nibs for different kinds of inking" (n.p.). Especially as the cartoonist aged and his condition worsened, these materials became vital for the continuation of his work. When a company stopped making a certain size pen tip, Schulz famously bought out its entire stock (Thielman).

Together with modifying the physical setup and material supplies in his studio, Schulz made changes to his drawing style after developing ET. Sam Thielman has commented, "By the late 1980s, Schulz had incorporated his affliction as fully as possible into his line-work" (n.p.). The heads of characters are rendered via one quick continuous line in an effort to minimize evidence of his hand tremor. Even so, every ink stroke contains a slight "wobble like a football on a seismograph" (Thielman, n.p.). From the speech balloons and lettering to the bodies of his characters and the background details, Schulz's lines possess a faint waviness. Indeed, once you notice this feature, you can't stop seeing it. When comics from the 1960s or 1970s are placed alongside those from the 1980s or 1990s, the difference in the line work is striking (see fig. 1.3). By the end of Schulz's career, in fact, this detail is "probably one of the most recognizable characteristics of his style" (Thielman, n.p.).

Schulz's essential tremor affected more than simply the way he rendered his lines. It also played a role in the format or layout of his comic strip. In 1988, Schulz moved away from the strict four-panel sequence in which *Peanuts* had appeared since debuting in 1950. While the cartoonist sought more creative flexibility with this change, this decision was also fueled by his development of ET. As the Diann Shaddox Foundation has commented, on days when the trembling in his hands was especially acute, "he then could do some one-panel strips, which took less time to draw than four-panel ones" ("Charles Schulz").

Rheta Grimsley Johnson, who wrote the first biography of Charles M. Schulz, commented about his distinctive form of cartooning: "It would be impossible to narrow down three or two or even one direct influence on [Schulz's] personal drawing style. The uniqueness of 'Peanuts' has set it apart for years.... That one-of-a-kind quality permeates every aspect of the strip and very clearly extends to the drawing" (68). Certainly, no newspaper comic that appeared before, or no daily strip that has debuted since, has even come close to matching the magic that was *Peanuts*. However, I would argue that, whoever and whatever can be identified as forming Schulz's influences, essential tremor is among them. For almost twenty years, the cartoonist's possession of this condition directly and demonstrably shaped the strip's appearance, its style, and even its format.

"HE DOES IT ALL. AND ALONE": SCHULZ AS SUPERCRIP

Given that Schulz not only had essential tremor but continued cartooning for more than twenty years after developing the condition, it is tempting to view his life and career as an inspirational story about triumph over adversity. Being a cartoonist in general, and creating a daily newspaper strip in particular, is a notoriously demanding profession. Rheta Grimsley Johnson commented on "the relentless press of it.... Cartoonists have no vacations so long as newspapers publish seven days a week, every day of the year" (41). Although Schulz loved what he did, he also lamented the unyielding schedule that accompanied it. "Unfortunately," he noted in an article from 1975, "it is a little like running up a glass hill, for no sooner does one arrive at the top when he slides rapidly down to the beginning" (Schulz, "Creativity" 97). Far from indulging in hyperbole, Johnson rightly noted that newspaper cartooning is "a competitive, brutally demanding industry that accepts no excuses, offers no sick days" (254). Even so, Schulz never fell behind. "Unlike many peers whose hair-raising tales of deadline production are legend," the cartoonist was never late in submitting work to his syndicate (Johnson 64).

In a detail about his career that has become even more idolized and mythologized, Schulz made the already grueling schedule that accompanied being a newspaper cartoonist more arduous. As Johnson relayed in her biography, "He does it all. And alone" (258). For the entire fifty-year run of his comic strip, the cartoonist insisted on "lettering every word, drawing every line, birthing every idea for every *Peanuts* strip ever done" (Johnson 41). Discussing why he refused to hire an assistant or take any vacations, he remarked: "You don't work all of your life to get to do something so that you can have time not to do it"—or so that you can hire other people to do it for you (41). And work on *Peanuts* is what he did. For nearly five decades, "Schulz wrote, penciled, inked, and lettered by hand every single one of the daily and Sunday strips to leave his studio, 17,897 in all" (Inge x). M. Thomas Inge has commented, "No other single cartoonist has matched this achievement" (x).

Schulz's accomplishments are impressive for an able-bodied cartoonist. The sheer number of daily newspaper strips that he created over the course of his career, combined with their consistently high quality, is astounding for an individual with no physical limitations. When an awareness that, for nearly half of this period, Schulz struggled with a neurological condition that caused his drawing hand to tremble, making the already strenuous task of creating a daily newspaper strip even more arduous, Schulz's achievement is nothing less than astonishing. Given these details, it is tempting to see the cartoonist as a type of superhero—or, in the lexicon of disability studies, what is known as the "supercrip." Jeffrey J. Martin summarizes this identity as "someone who overcomes their disability in ways that are often seen by the public as inspiring" (139). Examples of such figures range from the magnificent to the mundane: a boy with polio walking with leg braces, a woman in a wheelchair traversing the Appalachian Trail, a young adult with cerebral palsy living independently, and so on. Regardless of the precise nature of the accomplishment, the individual is cast as an uplifting example for achieving it.

As Rosemarie Garland-Thompson, Tobin Siebers, and Simi Linton have all written, while the supercrip identity might be inspirational for the able-bodied, it is a damaging and even dangerous one for those with disabilities. In the words of Linton, "The idea that someone can overcome a disability has not been generated within the community; it is a wish fulfillment generated from the outside. It is a demand that you be plucky and resolute, and not let the obstacles get in your way" (18; italics in original). The supercrip identity simultaneously praises while it panders. The admiration bestowed on these figures is not actually sincere and complimentary; it can more accurately be framed as patronizing and belittling.

Such critiques of the supercrip largely emerged from the modern disability rights movement. In another important but commonly overlooked aspect of the cultural context for *Peanuts*, Schulz's life and career took place against the backdrop of some of the most significant events in the fight for disability rights in the United States. In 1962—the same year that the cartoonist's phenomenally successful book *Happiness Is a Warm Puppy* was published—Ed Roberts, a young man whose limbs were paralyzed after contracting polio as a child, enrolled at the University of California at Berkeley. His admission is widely considered "a pivotal moment in the history of the disability rights movement" (Baird, Rosenbaum, and Toombs 138). As Baird, Rosenbaum, and Toombs have documented, "Within a short period of time, several other men and women with disabilities joined him on campus. Dubbing themselves the 'rolling quads,' they banded together to fight for better services and for permission to live independently rather than at the hospital" (138). The group obtained a grant from the US Department of Education and created the "Physically Disabled Students Program, the first of its kind on a college campus. It was, in effect, the beginning of the independent living movement" (138).

Six years later, in 1968—when Snoopy served as the official mascot for NASA's Apollo 10 space mission—another milestone in the fight for disability rights took place: the passage of the Architectural Barriers Act. The congressional legislation required that all federal structures be designed, constructed, or modified for accessibility. Kim E. Nielsen has written, "The chairman of the PCEH [President's Committee on Employment of the Handicapped] characterized the measure as 'the Declaration of Independence for the Handicapped'" (165). Efforts to eliminate physical barriers for individuals with disabilities were strengthened in 1973—the year that Schulz received an Emmy for *A Charlie Brown Thanksgiving*. In the words of Baird, Rosenbaum, and Toombs, "In 1973, the legislature passed the revised Rehabilitation Act. Its most important aspect was Section 504, a one-sentence paragraph prohibiting any program or activity receiving US government financial assistance from discriminating against qualified individuals with disabilities" (139).

Just two years later, in 1975—the year that *Peanuts* celebrated its twenty-fifth anniversary with a new animated television special, along with "a special birthday note to Charlie Brown from then President Gerald Ford" ("Timeline")—another landmark piece of disability rights legislation was passed: the Education for All Handicapped Children Act. The act "ensured equal access to public education for such students. Renamed the Individuals with Disabilities Education Act (IDEA) in 1990, it called for a free and appropriate public education for every child with a disability, to be delivered in the least restrictive environment" (Baird, Rosenbaum, and Toombs 139). These measures changed the life trajectories of untold numbers of young people with physical, developmental, emotional, and intellectual disabilities. "IDEA promotes the concept of inclusion, requiring that students with disabilities be educated in general education settings, alongside students without disabilities, to the greatest extent possible" (139).

In 1988—the year the *Snoopy in Fashion* show traveled the world, displaying the numerous outfits "created for Snoopy and Belle by many high-end contemporary fashion designers" ("Timeline")—protests at Gallaudet University made national news. Longmore and Umansky summarized the events: "For five days in March of 1988 the entire world watched as Deaf students at Gallaudet University in Washington, D.C., backed by the Deaf community, seized their campus to protest the appointment of yet another hearing person as president of the premier institution of education for deaf people. They demanded a 'Deaf President Now!' and they won" (11).

Of the many important milestones in the fight for disability rights that occurred during the span of *Peanuts*, however, arguably none was more significant than the passage of the Americans with Disabilities Act (ADA) in 1990. "Modeled after the Civil Rights Act of 1964, this landmark US Government antidiscrimination law ensures equal access to employment opportunities and public accommodations for people with disabilities" (Baird, Rosenbaum, and Toombs 139). Going far beyond merely providing access, the ADA sought nothing less than to achieve "the full participation, inclusion, and integration of people with disabilities into society as a national goal" (139). Kim Nielsen has observed that when the ADA was signed into law on July 26, 1990, it became "the best-known civil rights legislation for those with disabilities—impacting an estimated 43 million people at the time of its passage" (180).

While *Peanuts* is not commonly remembered as a strip that offered sociopolitical commentary, it did engage with cultural issues and respond to current events. In July 1968, for example, Schulz famously defied the long-standing racial dynamics of newspaper comic strips by introducing an African American character, Franklin Armstrong, to his all-white cast. The move was in direct response both to the resistance to school desegregation and to the recent assassination of Martin Luther King Jr. ("Timeline"). Additionally, in 1979, *Peanuts* discussed another topical issue: feminism and women's rights. After meeting Billie Jean King, the cartoonist included a multiday story line about women's participation in sports in general and the importance of Title IX in particular ("Timeline").

Despite Schulz's engagement with various sociocultural events and political issues, disability was not among them. The cartoonist never included a recurring character in his newspaper strip who was directly or explicitly associated with any type of impairment.[1] Perhaps even more surprising, *Peanuts* never alluded to any of the events happening in the burgeoning disability rights movement. Not only is this omission remarkable, given the historical era in which *Peanuts* was created and published, but it seems especially astounding in light of Schulz's own struggles with essential tremor. As various biographers and critics have noted, many of the *Peanuts* comics and characters draw on facets of the cartoonist's life and experiences. Eileen Daspin, in fact, recently asserted that "there are hundreds if not thousands of biographical references in the strip" (6). This statement was not hyperbole. For example, Schulz had a childhood dog named Spike, and his mother suggested that they name their next pooch Snoopy (Gherman 39). Additionally, his stepdaughter Meredith formed the original basis for Lucy Van Pelt; later, his first wife Joyce would serve as the model for this character's personality (Michaelis 228, 231, 300–308, 368–69, 428, 446–47, 480). Finally, when a fire destroyed Schulz's studio in 1966, he created a story line in which Snoopy's doghouse is engulfed by a blaze ("Timeline"). Although Schulz included numerous autobiographical elements in his strip, essential tremor or any type of physical impairment is not among them.

This detail invites speculation about the possible reasons for this omission as well as the implications that it has for the strip's legacy. Given that Schulz included elements from both his personal life and American sociopolitical culture in his comic, why did he neglect issues related to disability? Did the cartoonist not feature any direct discussion about disability in *Peanuts* because he was embarrassed or even ashamed about having essential tremor? In other words, can the omission be seen as a type of internalized ableism? Was Schulz concerned—either consciously or unconsciously—that, by including a *Peanuts* character who had a disability, he would call (unwanted) attention to his own possession of ET? Whatever factors fueled Schulz's decision to avoid engaging with non-able-bodiedness, what social, cultural, and even ethical ramifications does this absence have? *Peanuts* has long been regarded as a comic that broke new ground with regard to the subject matter that newspaper strips could and even should contain. As Jared Gardner and Ian Gordon have written, most mainstream comics, especially those showcasing child characters during the mid-twentieth century when *Peanuts* made its debut, featured playful antics, humorous hijinks, and comedic calamities (3–9). In examples ranging from *Skippy* (1923–45) and *Nancy* (1938–present) to *Dennis the Menace* (1951–present) and *Archie* (1946–2011), these strips took their subject matter from the fun adventures, humorous escapades, and merry mischief that transpired during childhood. From the debut strip of *Peanuts* with its punch line of "Good ol' Charlie Brown. / How I hate him," Schulz's comic focused on different topics and unexpected themes. His strip spotlighted the insecurities, disappointments, frustrations, annoyances, and setbacks that individuals experience: Charlie Brown never kicks the football, Linus never meets the Great Pumpkin, Snoopy never gets his novel published, and so on. The strip's silence about matters related to disability seems out of step with its otherwise frank treatment of the challenges and complexities of life.

This situation is complicated further by the fact that at least two *Peanuts* television specials feature characters who are not able-bodied. In *Snoopy, Come Home* (1972), Snoopy is reunited with his original owner, Lila, who has been hospitalized for a lengthy period of time by a condition that is never named. Additionally, a character in *Why, Charlie Brown, Why?* (1990) is struggling with a serious illness. As the Charles M. Schulz Museum and Research Center summarizes, "The Emmy nominated special deals with a new character named Janice who is diagnosed with cancer. Schulz would go on to receive an award from the American Cancer Society for bringing hope and understanding to children with cancer" ("Timeline"). That said, *Peanuts* addresses these issues only in the animated specials, not in the daily newspaper comic strip. Moreover—like Lila from *Snoopy, Come Home*—Janice is a one-time character, not a recurring member of the *Peanuts* gang.

Disability has been characterized as the "majority minority." Lennard Davis, in the opening commentary to his book about the history of the ADA, reveals: "One out of five people have disabilities" (xi). The importance of seeing, recognizing, and engaging with disability, however, goes far beyond the sheer number of individuals who populate this category. Disability also cuts across other vectors of identity like race, class, gender, sexuality, region, and religion. Moreover, it is also a taxonomy to which all of us—to some extent, for some duration—will likely belong. Mariah Crilley has aptly noted, "No one can be healthy and whole forever" (83). At some point, we all become ill, get injured, or—at the least—age.

Charles M. Schulz provides a vivid demonstration of the need to see, recognize, and acknowledge disability. Continuing to overlook the cartoonist's possession of essential tremor and the physical, material, and aesthetic ways in which ET shaped his comic strip erases an important facet of his life and career. Even more problematically, it perpetuates ableist assumptions about Schulz—and newspaper cartooning in general. For two decades, Schulz created *Peanuts* with an impairment that affected nothing less than his drawing hand. Ignoring or omitting this detail not only ignores or omits an important aspect of *Peanuts* but also buoys and sustains what Robert McRuer has termed "compulsory ablebodiedness" (89). Notions of normalcy are so commonly regarded as the default that they have become naturalized. Borrowing from Adrienne Rich's famous essay "Compulsory Heterosexuality and Lesbian Existence," McRuer points out that in the same way that heterosexual identity is culturally produced and the lived experience of this sexuality is widely variable, so too is the widespread belief that ablebodiedness is the norm (89). The somatic profile of most individuals does not conform to such rigid, strict, and limiting notions. Whether in possessing a physical trait, a cognitive quality, or a psychological characteristic, most individuals deviate in some way (if not in multiple ways) from what is considered "normal." Thus, while conformity to normality is expected and even required, it is elusive and even unrealistic. Great variation exists within the human species. For this reason, we should view bodily diversity, rather than normality, as the default position.

Viewing Charles M. Schulz's life and career in light of his possession of ET challenges compulsory able-bodiedness and normalizes corporeal difference. Given the way in which Schulz's essential tremor is literally written into many of the comics that he created during the second half of his career, it also invites us to reexamine his work through the lens of disability, looking for details, events, and elements that could or even should be viewed in this way but have not been before. While none of the protagonists from *Peanuts* are overtly associated with an impairment, several can be placed in this context. Charlie Brown, for example, commonly says that he is depressed, a statement that places him in dialogue with mental health. Along the same lines, Snoopy's fantasies about being a World War I flying ace or his perception that he is on the brink of being a famous novelist might be seen as megalomania, delusions of grandeur, or even a type of psychosis. Woodstock's wobbly flight patterns and his speech balloons—which are inscrutable to everyone but Snoopy—suggest possible neurodivergence.[2] Peppermint Patty's struggles in school—with processing language while reading, remembering multistep instructions, and computing numbers during math class—could be indicators of an undiagnosed learning disability. Finally, Lucy's frequent assertion that Charlie Brown is a "blockhead" raises issues about intellectual ability—as well as limitations. Lucy also commonly calls other characters—especially Snoopy and her younger brother Linus—"stupid." Given both the harsh and often inaccurate nature of Lucy's assessments, her use of insults like "blockhead" and "stupid" invites reconsiderations about ableism and discrimination.

Reexamining *Peanuts* through the lens of disability likewise changes the way we view some of the animated television specials. In several of these programs, but perhaps most noticeably in *A Charlie Brown Christmas* (1973), the character of Linus speaks with a lisp. This speech disorder, which is likely the by-product of the character's penchant for sucking his thumb, is a core facet of his character. The trait also forms a key element in the delivery, impact, and memory of his now-classic speech about the true meaning of Christmas. When audiences recount this scene, they recall not only the content of Linus's comments—"For unto you is born this day in the city of David a Savior"—but also the manner in which he speaks: namely, with a childlike lisp. In an equally well-known feature of the animated television specials, all the adults speak in unintelligible ways—as muffled utterances.[3] While the *Peanuts* characters can understand what the grownups are saying, viewers of the specials cannot. This feature can be viewed as another potential instance of corporeal difference in *Peanuts*.

Of course, disability is not the only feature that has a coded or clandestine presence in *Peanuts*. As Ben Saunders, Vikki Reich, and Heather Hogan have pointed out, queerness does as well. While Peppermint Patty can be viewed as possessing an undiagnosed learning disability, she is more commonly seen as possessing an unspoken lesbian identity. From the time of her debut on August 22, 1966, "her queer potentiality has attracted plenty of attention in the culture at large" (Saunders 14). Patty claims to have to crush on Charlie Brown, but she embodies a variety of personal, behavioral, and sartorial traits that had long been associated with lesbians, from wearing Birkenstocks to playing softball. Patty's connection with queerness only strengthened when the character Marcie debuted on July 20, 1971. A shy, nerdy intellectual, Marcie shadows Peppermint Patty wherever she goes, calling her "Sir"—a trait that places their interactions in dialogue with butch/femme role play that emerged in lesbian bar culture during the twentieth century (Faderman 159–87). Peppermint Patty and Marcie quickly became icons of lesbian culture during the 1970s and 1980s (Reich, par. 3). Many queer women read the two characters as a same-sex couple or, at the least, as occupying a place on Adrienne Rich's "lesbian continuum" (Hogan, n.p.). Saunders notes, "A cursory Google search, for example, turns up examples of femslash fanfic devoted to the exploration of Patty's relationship with Marcie" (14). Of course, nonheteronormativity and non-able-bodiedness are neither interchangeable nor analogous states of identity. An individual's sexual orientation and corporeal condition are separate and distinct. That said, as Robert McRuer—whose work is quoted earlier—and, more recently, figures like Alison Kafer have pointed out, a variety of areas of social, cultural, and political overlap exist between "crips" and "queers." Both the disabled community and the LGBTQ one, Kafer notes, are often "yearning for an elsewhere—and, perhaps, an 'elsewhen'—in which [their identities are] understood otherwise: as political, as valuable, as integral," rather than as tragic, burdensome, and problematic (3). In comments that further locate Peppermint Patty as a rich site of alterity in *Peanuts*, Kafer calls attention to the points of sociopolitical intersection between these communities, including "the ways in which compulsory able-bodiedness/able-mindedness and compulsory heterosexuality intertwine in the service of normativity," as well as "how terms such as 'defective,' 'deviant,' and 'sick' have been used to justify discrimination against people whose bodies, minds, desires, and practices differ from the unmarked norm" (Kafer 17). For decades, queerness has been seen as possessing a tacit but traceable presence in *Peanuts*. Moving forward, we need to view disability in the same way. From the cartoonist to his creations, this issue permeates *Peanuts* in ways that have not previously been seen or critically analyzed.

Rosemarie Garland-Thompson aptly noted: "Disabled people have variously been objects of awe, scorn, terror, delight, inspiration, pity, laughter, and fascination" (348). Foregrounding Schulz's essential tremor has the potential to disrupt or at least destabilize this phenomenon. Viewing the cartoonist through the lens of disability invites us to see him and his work in a different way. Just as importantly, doing so challenges us to view disability from a new perspective as well. Rather than regarding the cartoonist's ET as an inspirational story, a cause for pity, or an obscure factoid, this approach encourages us to view it as he did: as a straightforward, matter-of-fact aspect of his life.

Charles M. Schulz lived with a disability and—in a statement that should not come as a revelation in the second decade of the twenty-first century—so do many other individuals as well.

DRAWING DISABILITY: *PEANUTS* AND NEW MODES OF REPRESENTATION

Peanuts may not have engaged explicitly with the issue of disability, but many other comics and cartoonists over the decades have done so. During the past few years, in fact, discussions about disability in sequential art have increased exponentially. In examples ranging from José Aleniz's groundbreaking book *Death, Disability, and the Superhero* (2012) to Chris Foss, Jonathan W. Gray, and Zach Whalen's compelling collection of critical essays *Disability in Comic Books and Graphic Narratives* (2016), this topic has become one of the field's most vibrant areas of critical inquiry.

That said, discussions about comics and disability tend to take one of two forms.[4] First, and most commonly, these analyses explore the depiction of disability in general and the portrayal of disabled characters in particular in works of sequential art. From Alaniz's study of Silver Age superheroes like Daredevil, the Fantastic Four, and the X-Men to Margaret Galvan's essay in *Disability in Comic Books and Graphic Narratives* about the inclusion of Thea in Alison Bechdel's *Dykes to Watch Out For* series, they explore the politics of representation. Accordingly, their discussions pivot around questions such as the following: How has disability been portrayed in sequential art? What roles do characters with disabilities play in comics and graphic novels? In what ways does the inclusion of disability either affirm or challenge ableist stereotypes? How have comics served as a progressive medium for the advancement of disability rights—and in which ways have comics served as a regressive or reactionary medium that hinders that advancement?

The second category of discussion about disability in sequential art concerns the growing new subgenre of what has come to be known as "graphic medicine": works that profile the life and experiences a disabled friend, family member, or the cartoonist themselves. Christina Maria Koch has commented, "The evolution of American autobiographical comics over the past decades has been increasingly accompanied by a strong trend toward subject matters of illness, disability, or more generally physical or psychological traits perceived as deviations from the norm" (Koch 29). Examples range from David B's *Epileptic* (2002, English translation), Paul and Judy Karasik's *The Ride Together* (2003), and Steven T. Seagle's *It's a Bird . . .* (2004)

to David Small's *Stitches* (2009), Ellen Forney's *Marbles* (2012), and Cece Bell's *El Deafo* (2013). These titles engage with a wide array of conditions: epilepsy, autism, Huntington's disease, cancer, mental health, and deafness, respectively. Furthermore, they have become some of the most commercially successful and critically acclaimed works of sequential art in recent years. In so doing, graphic medicine not only adds to the historical depiction of bodily difference in comics—moving from titles that are *about* people with disabilities to ones that are created *by* them—but also raises the question of how sequential art can be seen as a unique medium to address these issues. As Jay Dolmage and Dale Jacobs put it, "We see the potential of comics to go beyond the use of disability as narrative prosthesis—a kind of multimodal, narrative shorthand—and to *become a form of prosthesis themselves*, an additional tool in making meaning accessible and for intervening in and interrogating disability as what Rosemarie Garland-Thompson calls a 'representation system'" (14).

Recognizing and foregrounding Schulz's essential tremor adds a new facet to the way in which disability has been—and can continue to be—presented in sequential art. Although the cartoonist never directly addressed the condition in his newspaper strip, it appears anyway, with the presence of his wavy line. Given this situation, even though none of the thousands of comics that he created over the second half of *Peanuts* explicitly engage with disability, all of them implicitly do. Schulz's essential tremor is literally written in every inked detail of every comic for two decades. Additionally, in strips that are shorter than four panels, it can also be reflected in the format. When an awareness of these details is moved from the background to the forefront of *Peanuts*, they change the way we view and interpret the comic. Beginning in late 1981 when Schulz was diagnosed with essential tremor, his strip becomes tacitly but also inextricably about disability. This issue permeates every facet of the comic, from the cartoonist's panel sequencing and his line work to his lettering and choice of layout. Although disability is never directly enunciated, it is also not erased. In so doing, *Peanuts* can be placed in dialogue with Jacques Derrida's notion of "the trace." In *Of Grammatology*, Derrida explains: "The trace is not only the disappearance of origin"; instead "it means that the origin did not even disappear, that it was never constituted except reciprocally by a non-origin" (Derrida 90, 71). As a consequence, the trace becomes spectral, apparitional, and deeply evocative. It signifies "the origin of the origin" (61). As Gayatri Chakravorty Spivak has said about this concept, it is the "mark of the absence of a presence, an always-already absent present" (xvii). The same observation applies to the existence of disability in the final two decades of *Peanuts*. Although ostensibly absent, it is always already present.

The way in which Schulz's essential tremor influenced his cartooning has implications that extend beyond *Peanuts*. Given the pervasiveness of disability in the population and the likelihood that individuals will experience some type of impairment during their lifetime, Schulz was not the only cartoonist whose work can be viewed through this lens. Surely many other graphic artists have struggled with some type of health-related issue—an injury, an illness, a period of depression or anxiety—at some point during their careers, whether they directly engaged with it in their work or not. In so doing, their cartooning during this period can likewise be viewed through the lens of disability or, at least, corporeal difference. Moving an artist's experience with ill health from the background to the forefront does more than simply provide additional context for their cartooning; it also often changes the content of their work. Akin to Schulz, knowing that they were dealing with a physical, emotional, or cognitive condition while creating a work changes the way that we view, engage, and interpret it. By inviting us to view their cartooning through the lens of disability, this perspective adds new themes, introduces new topics, and alters existing analyses.

In the same way that Schulz's possession of essential tremor calls attention to a new mode of representation for disability in comics, it also calls attention to a new element in the realm of comics theory. Jared Gardner has written about the multifaceted importance of the line in sequential art. Not only is the type of line that a cartoonist uses—its shape, size, thickness, appearance, and so on—a rich site of aesthetic, literary, and semiotic meaning, but it is also an important feature of this mode of storytelling. Text-only narratives "render the hand of the [creator] invisible" (Gardner 54). Even if these works are written with pen and paper, they are certainly not published in this way. Sequential art, on the other hand, "has not effaced the [physical presence] of the artist" (56). The lines drawn on the page "make us cognizant of an embodied *graphateur* at all times" (65). Initially referring to these elements as "the handprint of the storyteller," Gardner later argues they can more accurately be called a "voicepoint" (56, 66). A cartoonist's choice of line is akin to "the human voice of oral storytelling, of song, or performance" (66).

Hillary Chute has built on these observations, commenting how sequential art "has a multivalent and complex relation to embodiment" (112). The form "resurrects and materializes" corporeality in ways that are as inevitable as they are unintentional (112). As she asserts, "Comics is a largely a hand-drawn form that registers the subjective bodily mark on the page" (112). From the lettering to the line work, "its marks are an index of the body" (112).

The role that Schulz's essential tremor played in the production of *Peanuts* adds a new facet to observations about the inherent corporality of comics.

Comics are a medium that undeniably and even unavoidably reveal the body.⁵ More than simply revealing the "hand" or—to use Gardner's term—"voice" of the cartoonist, comics imprint information about the person's entire constitution: their physical condition, emotional state, and—in the case of Schulz—neurological functions. Consequently, even when a cartoonist does not realize that they are revealing their corporeality, it appears. Schulz's body of work in *Peanuts* cannot be separated from his actual physical body. One corpus leads to the other. The same observation, of course, is equally true of all other cartoonists.

Thierry Groensteen, in his influential book *The System of Comics*, uses the term "arthrology" to classify the "linear semantic relationships that govern" sequential art (103). As he explains, "Comics is not only an art of fragments, of scattering, of distribution; it is also an art of conjunction, of repetition, of linking together" (Groensteen 22). Arthrology encapsulates this complex "spatio-topical operation," allowing us first to name this important phenomenon and then to identify the specific processes within it, such as braiding (22). When Groensteen first introduces arthrology, he frames it as a "generic term with a very broad meaning . . . from the Greek *arthron*: articulation" (21). The meaning of this word, however, is actually far more specific and specialized. As any dictionary will reveal, "Arthrology is the science concerned with the study of anatomy, function, dysfunction and treatment of joints and articulations" ("arthrology"). It is a medical word, or at least one connected with human physiology.

Peanuts gives new meaning or, at least, added significance to Groensteen's concept of arthrology. Although Groensteen did not intend this term to retain its connection to the corporeal, such meanings resonate throughout Schulz's strip. Two simultaneous and palimpsestic modes of arthrology can be traced in *Peanuts*: the "linear semantic relationships that govern" each daily strip (Groensteen 103), and the "function, dysfunction and treatment of joints and articulations" of the cartoonist ("arthrology"). Moreover, given the central and even inextricable role that corporeality plays in comics as a whole, arthrology is a far more appropriate term than Groensteen intended—or even realized. As Jared Gardner first pointed out, and *Peanuts* expands and elaborates, sequential art is inherently about the hands, limbs, and bodies of its creators. The aesthetic articulation of comics panels cannot be separated from the physical articulation of the cartoonist's body, be it that of Charles M. Schulz or any other artist. After all, it is their joints, muscles, and nerves that create the frames, images, and text.

Kim Nielsen, in the closing comments to her book *A Disability History of the United States*, asserts that "disability history is at the core of the American story" (182). As she explains, "The experience of people with disabilities is pivotal to US history, just as the concept of disability is at the core of US citizenship, contested explorations of rights, racial and gender hierarchies, concepts of sexual deviance, economic inequalities, and the process of industrialization" (182). Douglas Baynton, in an essay that appeared in *The New Disability History*, echoes this observation: "Disability is everywhere in history, once you begin looking for it, but conspicuously absent in the histories we write" (52).

While both Nielsen and Baynton were referencing American sociopolitical history, their observations apply equally to the realm of US comics. During the past few decades, disability has emerged as an important issue in American sequential art. An awareness of Charles M. Schulz's essential tremor adds to this rich, vibrant, and growing body of inquiry while simultaneously challenging its place in comics studies. As *Peanuts* demonstrates, disability is not a specialized topic in the genre; it forms a core facet of many of the most commercially successful, critically acclaimed, and historically important strips. The time has come to move this issue from the background to the forefront of *Peanuts* and US comics as a whole.

The next chapter examines Charles M. Schulz's alter ego, Charlie Brown. Perhaps appropriately, given the way in which this *Peanuts* protagonist was the cartoonist's comics avatar in many ways, the discussion follows in the footsteps of this one. Although it does not examine Charlie Brown through the lens of disability, it shares the same core premise: namely, what the shape, nature, and especially bends of a line can reveal. Rather than examining the subtle waviness of Schulz's inked line, chapter 2 examines the overt waviness of the zigzag across Charlie Brown's iconic shirt. In the same way that audiences have overlooked the meaning embedded in the wobbliness of Schulz's drawing style, they have likewise overlooked a possible meaning encoded by the zigzag. As my discussion asserts, far from simply being a fashion design, the pattern across Charlie Brown's shirt might be a rich, resonant, and long-neglected symbol.

CHAPTER 2

WHAT'S THE FREQUENCY, CHARLIE BROWN?

Sound Waves, Music, and the Zigzag Shirt

Many of the characters in *Peanuts* are associated with a signature possession. Linus, for example, has his beloved security blanket; Schroeder has his treasured toy piano; Snoopy has his distinctive doghouse.

Of all the material items that are linked with characters in *Peanuts*, perhaps none is more famous than Charlie Brown's shirt. As Caren Pilgrim has discussed, although the main color of the garment has changed over the years—it has been "red, orange, green, blue, and yellow" (Pilgrim)—one aspect of it has remained the same: the black zigzag around the middle. Rheta Grimsley Johnson, in fact, deems this feature nothing less than "Charlie Brown's trademark" (160). Few would disagree. The zigzag shirt has become a powerful symbol of this specific character and—given his prominence in *Peanuts*—for the strip as a whole. Moreover, in light of the tremendous popularity of Schulz's work, the pattern is nothing less than iconic, both in the United States and in countries around the world.

Despite the power and pervasiveness of Charlie Brown's zigzag shirt, this item has largely escaped critical attention. While past and present critics recognize the pattern as a core feature of *Peanuts*, few have examined its origins, contemplated its meaning, or probed its significance. This situation has caused Charlie Brown's zigzag shirt to become arguably the most famous and simultaneously the most neglected aspect of *Peanuts*.

This chapter offers a corrective to this trend. In the pages that follow, I give Charlie Brown's iconic garment the critical attention that it deserves, and for which it is long overdue. While the pattern on the shirt is commonly described as a zigzag, I view it in an alternative way: as a triangle wave (fig. 2.1). This waveform gets its name because its crests and troughs form a

TRIANGLE WAVE

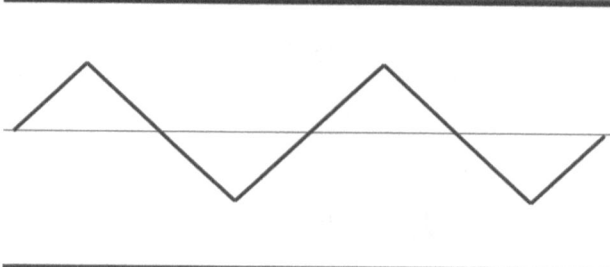

Figure 2.1. Triangle wave. Graph by the DAW Studio, January 9, 2013. Image available at https://www.thedawstudio.com/triangle-wave/.

triangle shape that repeats horizontally. From a mathematical standpoint, a triangle wave is a "non-sinusoidal waveform" that is the product of a "periodic, piecewise linear, continuous real function" (Prathapani). Triangle waves play a role in a variety of fields, including electronic power transmission, radio technology, and sound engineering. In the realm of music, a triangle wave is the graph created by the frequencies of odd harmonics. The distortion of harmonics is a common aspect of sound mixing in a recording studio. Amplifying or minimizing the odd harmonics represented by the triangle wave alters the sound to generate a desired auditory effect.

    Admittedly, this chapter's focus on Charlie Brown's shirt and the triangle wave might seem like a radical and even jarring departure from my previous discussion about Schulz and disability. However, the two analyses are connected. My examination of the zigzag continues my consideration of the meaning and significance of the line in Schulz's cartooning. The previous discussion spotlighted the wobbliness of Schulz's drawing as an unexplored sign of his essential tremor. This chapter examines Schulz's comics avatar, Charlie Brown, and makes a case that the zigzag across his iconic shirt can be seen as its own semiotic sign filled with rich and unexplored meanings. Chapter 1 called attention to the importance of the unintentional bends, wiggles, and curves in Schulz's work; this chapter extends the same consideration to a well-known example of an intentional jagged line.

    Seeing Charlie Brown's zigzag shirt as a triangle wave not only changes the way that we view this iconic aspect of this specific character but also changes the way that we view Schulz's comic strip as a whole. Sound in general and music in particular form a core component of *Peanuts*. The triangle wave that can be identified on Charlie Brown's shirt adds a new facet to these features. It connects this figure who is not commonly linked with auditory elements directly to them. In so doing, it invites us to reconsider the role that Charlie Brown plays in the presence, use, and function of sound in the comic. In the same way that Schroeder is routinely shown with his toy piano, Charlie Brown can also be seen as outfitted in a garment whose pattern is connected with the production of music. Ultimately, seeing Charlie Brown's zigzag shirt as a triangle wave adds a new facet to the way that sound can be incorporated into sequential art.

CLOTHES MAKE THE MAN: CHARLIE BROWN'S FASHION STYLE AND CHARLES SCHULZ'S MINIMALIST STYLE

Ironically, given how firmly Charlie Brown is associated with the zigzag shirt, it may come as a surprise to learn that he has not always worn this garment. When *Peanuts* first appeared on October 2, 1950, Schulz's core character was dressed in a plain white T-shirt. In subsequent strips, Charlie Brown's outfit would occasionally change. For example, he donned a necktie for a series of gag strips later that month. Additionally, he put on a hat and coat to play outside as autumn turned to winter. In the bulk of these early comics, however, Charlie Brown wears a collarless shirt that has no pattern or design.

It was not until December 21, 1950—nearly three months after *Peanuts* began—that Charlie Brown appeared in the now-iconic zigzag shirt (fig. 2.2). The pattern is not part of the gag of the strip. Although one can imagine a character commenting on the zigzag—asking him what it means, wondering why he is wearing a shirt like that, and so on—this does not happen. Instead the pattern appears seemingly for no reason. Readers are meant to regard it as an innocuous detail or, at least, inconsequential fashion choice.

Although Charlie Brown returns to the plain white T-shirt in the strip that appears the next day, the zigzag returns in the comic that followed, on December 23, 1950. From that strip forward, Charlie Brown is most

Figure 2.2. *Peanuts* comic strip, December 21, 1950. Reprinted in *The Complete Peanuts, 1950 to 1952*, by Charles M. Schulz (Fantagraphics, 2004), 24. PEANUTS © Peanuts Worldwide LLC. Dist. by ANDREWS MCMEEL SYNDICATION. Reprinted with permission. All rights reserved.

commonly depicted in this garment. Whether he is indoors or outdoors, at home or at school, in summer or in winter, he wears the zigzag shirt. That said, Schulz would make one final tweak to Charlie Brown's attire: he would add a collar, changing it from a T-shirt to a polo, on December 29, 1950. Other than this minor detail, the shirt would remain the same—and remain in view. Unless Charlie Brown dons a coat that covers the shirt, he wears it in strips for the next fifty years. Fashion trends would change dramatically over the five decades that spanned the comic's run. However, his outfit remained the same.[1]

In many ways, Charlie Brown's distinctive shirt seems unusual, unexpected, and even out of character. After all, this *Peanuts* figure longs to fit in, not stand out. Indeed, one could more easily see the opinionated Lucy or the nonconformist Peppermint Patty wearing this shirt than the milquetoast Charlie Brown. Schulz's protagonist generally avoids calling attention to himself, something that a shirt with a big black zigzag across the middle does.

Together with the zigzag shirt being an unlikely fashion choice for Charlie Brown, it is also an unlikely addition to the comic strip as a whole. In what has become an oft-cited detail, Schulz said about his aesthetic for *Peanuts*:

> Each cartoonist fights for attention on the comics page. Some get it easily by being given more space than others, and some try for attention by using thick black borders around their panels. . . . I was forced to present a strip that was the tiniest on the page, so I had to fight back by using white space. On a page crammed with comic strips, a small feature with lots of white space attracted attention. (Schulz, "Creativity" 101)

Far from an exaggeration, many *Peanuts* panels are wholly devoid of background details—these areas are made up of negative space. Meanwhile, the foregrounds to Schulz's drawings are equally sparse: they contain little more than a simple ground line and a few characters, usually only the ones directly involved in the gag.

The minimalism of Schulz's drawing style would persist throughout the strip's fifty-year run. As the cartoonist reflected decades later, "I have discovered that, because of the type of humor in Charlie Brown, the drawings must remain very simple. And I rarely do any backgrounds. Keeping it all very simple is the key here" (Schulz qtd. in Kidd, n.p.).

The cartoonist was not alone in recognizing this aspect of *Peanuts*. While critics have disagreed about various facets of Schulz's comic over the decades—such as the expanding presence of Snoopy and the tokenism of Franklin—none have questioned the strip's minimalism. Commentaries written by figures ranging from biographers and fans to critics and fellow cartoonists have all noted the sparse, spare, and simple style of *Peanuts*. As the biographer Beverly Gherman noted, "*Peanuts* was not cluttered with details" (61). Jared Gardner and Ian Gordon echo this observation, noting how "*Peanuts* is drawn with a flowing clean line against a spare background dominated by negative space and minimalist details" (7). Finally, and perhaps most vividly of all, fellow cartoonist Jeff Kinney praised the spare aesthetic of *Peanuts*, writing how "Schulz understood how to make every line count. Nothing extraneous, no waste. Only what's necessary" (Kinney, n.p.). Kinney's final statement, "Only what's necessary," serves as the title for Chip Kidd's 2015 coffee-table book about the cartoon art of Charles M. Schulz. As Schulz's widow Jean wrote in the foreword to the volume, "The title *Only What's Necessary* refers to Sparky's spare comics panels, which tell a story with a minimal number of pen lines." In the words of Kinney once again, "Less space meant making every line count. Every word of dialogue. Every gesture" (Kinney, n.p.).

Of course, one could make a case that every line, detail, and gesture in every comic is deliberate and thus significant. The sparse nature of *Peanuts*, however, makes this truism even more apt. As Kinney observed, "Nobody got more out of fewer lines than Charles Schulz did with *Peanuts*" (Kinney, n.p.). Given the paucity of detail in the strip, Schulz's decision to add the zigzag to Charlie Brown's shirt assumes added importance. Not only was this feature a deliberate choice, but it was an especially significant one in light of the comic's commitment to minimalism. If Schulz was—as his critics, biographers, and widow affirm—committed to including "only what's necessary," it raises the question of what was necessary about this pattern.

WALK THE LINE: FROM ZIGZAG TO TRIANGLE WAVE

Charles M. Schulz was anything but reticent when it came to Charlie Brown. In numerous articles, essays, and interviews over the course of his career, he discussed issues ranging from the character's autobiographical basis and his love of sports to his penchant for failing and his philosophy on life. By the time of Schulz's death on February 12, 2000, in fact, his comments about Charlie Brown were as numerous as they were voluminous. Over the previous fifty years, he had spoken both frequently and at length about him.

Of the many comments that Schulz made about Charlie Brown, however, he never discussed his attire. The cartoonist never explained why he outfitted his character in a zigzag shirt. He never spoke about why he chose this pattern. Furthermore, he never addressed why he decided to add this feature to his strip in the first place.

Although Schulz never articulated his rationale for placing Charlie Brown in a zigzag shirt, remarks made by Harry Gilburt, the sales manager at United Feature Syndicate when *Peanuts* debuted, provide some possible insight. In the first biography about Schulz, Gilburt discussed the strip's slow commercial start. Although the syndicate was confident that *Peanuts* would be a hit, "it just didn't seem to catch on" (qtd. in Johnson 27). In Gilburt's view, the problem was obvious. "I felt there were too many characters," he opined, "and people had trouble remembering who was who" (27). Given this situation, Schulz may have added the zigzag to Charlie Brown's shirt for a purely pragmatic reason: the pattern allowed readers to quickly identify the character and easily differentiate him from the others in the cast. Indeed, as the cartoonist said about Charlie Brown, "He's still the backbone of the strip. . . . No matter what happens, I still like to have it come back around to him somehow" (qtd. in Johnson 174). Given Charlie Brown's centrality, it would be prudent to make him more prominent.

Charlie Brown was not simply the protagonist of *Peanuts*; he was also the most autobiographical figure. While Schulz acknowledged that all the characters reflected some aspect of his personality, this principal character was the most directly patterned after himself and his life (Schulz, "My Life and Art" 3–19). After all, the two share the same first name, they both have fathers who work as barbers, they enjoy many of the same hobbies (baseball, ice hockey), and they are known for being melancholy (3–19). Thus, when Schulz changed the style of Charlie Brown's shirt, it is not surprising that he might model this new garment after an item in his own wardrobe. In a detail that also appears in the first biography of the cartoonist, Schulz had a zigzag shirt—several of them, in fact. Donna Johnson Wold, the woman whom Schulz courted in the years preceding the appearance of *Peanuts*—and who famously became the basis for the Little Red-Haired Girl when she turned down his marriage proposal in the summer of 1950—commented on this fact. "He came calling frequently during those intense few months," Donna relayed, "sometimes wearing a pale gray shirt with a black zigzag around it not unlike Charlie Brown's trademark shirt" (qtd. in Johnson 88). Indeed, she went on to remark about this garment: "It was his favorite. . . . He has another one just like it, except different colors. Pale green with a dark green zigzag, I want to say" (88). Given this biographical link, when the time came to give Charlie Brown a more distinctive outfit, the cartoonist may have looked no farther than his own closet. Schulz may have chosen the distinctive pattern for his principal character because he had shirts like it himself.

All of this said, there is one more possible influence on Schulz's decision to adorn Charlie Brown's shirt with a zigzag: George Herriman's newspaper strip *Krazy Kat* (1913–44). Schulz was a lifelong fan of Herriman's comic, commenting at numerous points throughout his career about how he personally read and professionally admired it (Michaelis 75–77). As Michael Tisserand noted, "Herriman traveled extensively throughout northern Arizona, and among the many ideas he adapted from Navajo artists were bold zigzag stripes, symbols of lightning" (116). Tisserand speculates that the zigzag across Charlie Brown's shirt might be a nod to *Krazy Kat*. Patrick McDonnell, who is the cartoonist of the strip *Mutts*, "recalled a conversation in which they discussed Charlie Brown's shirt. Although Schulz said it hadn't been a conscious homage, he acknowledged that it appeared to be the kind of influence that results from one artist deeply admiring and studying the other" (Tisserand 116).

These sources of possible influence notwithstanding, it is just as feasible to see the pattern across Charlie Brown's shirt as a triangle wave as it is to view a zigzag—and, in some regards, perhaps more so. The symmetry between the crests and the troughs, along with how the pattern repeats continuously around the front and back of the garment, is arguably more indicative of the graph that is generated by the frequencies of odd harmonics than it is of the linear depiction of a person or object periodically altering direction. While there is no rigidly prescriptive way that a zigzag must be rendered to be classified in this category, the lines that make it up are often uneven, with a crest drawn higher than a trough—or vice versa. Additionally, while zigzag patterns can encompass any number of crests and troughs, they are commonly associated with two: a "zig" going one direction, and a "zag" in the other; hence the name "zigzag." Of course, this situation need not be either/or; it can be both/and. Seeing the zigzag pattern on Charlie Brown's shirt as a triangle wave adds a new facet to our understanding of this detail, this character, and Schulz's comic as a whole.

A triangle wave might seem like a phenomenon far afield from the world of *Peanuts*. However, Schulz's strip routinely included elements of music as well as musical notation. As Tom Zlabinger has written, more than six hundred comics featured characters making music, listening to music, or discussing music (49). Schroeder, of course, plays his beloved toy piano. Marcie and Peppermint Patty attend a variety of "Tiny Tots" concerts. At repeated points throughout the strip, all the characters sing. From well-known tunes like "Happy Birthday" (December 19, 1957; December 16, 1959) and "It's Raining, It's Pouring" (July 3, 1957) to lesser-known songs like "Rally 'round the Flag" (July 8, 1961) and "Just before the Battle, Mother" (March 28, 1961), the performance and enjoyment of music are an important part of *Peanuts*.

More than simply including references to music and depictions of characters as musicians, Schulz also includes musical notes and notation in his strips. For example, rather than merely showing Lucy belting out the well-known lyrics to "Happy Birthday" in the comic from December 19, 1957, the cartoonist drew a few eighth notes in her speech balloons to further indicate that she is singing. Such features reach their greatest level of sophistication in strips involving Schroeder. Once again, Schulz rarely shows the young boy merely seated at his toy piano with his fingers on the keys, a scenario that, for most readers, would be sufficient to demonstrate that he is playing. Instead, to further convey both the style of music and the character's skill at the piano, Schulz commonly draws a musical score—featuring measures of both treble and bass clef—at the top of a few panels. From time signatures, staves, and rests to key signatures, notes, and dynamics (forte, allegro, staccato, etc.), these snippets of sheet music are detailed renderings. Moreover, they are also legitimate ones. As William Meredith, Roy T. Cook, and Tom Zlabinger have all discussed, most are faithful transcriptions of actual classical pieces by Bach, Rachmaninoff, and, of course, Beethoven, who is Schroeder's idol. That said, Schulz rarely identifies either the musical composition or its composer, "thereby playfully setting up a game of 'name that tune' for his readers" (Meredith, "Greatest Hits"). As Meredith goes on to reveal, however, doing so is far from a fruitless exercise. Identifying the pieces of music depicted in *Peanuts*, listening to them, and understanding their themes lead to a "richer appreciation of the strips' meanings."

The comic that appeared on June 9, 1968, offers an excellent case in point. The opening sequence features Schroeder fervidly playing his piano while Lucy prattles on about an array of quotidian hypotheticals: what would she make Schroeder for breakfast if they got married, what would happen if she got tired of cooking for him, what would he do if she decided to sleep in, and so on (Schulz, *1967 to 1968* 226). Unable to listen to this banal banter any longer, an exasperated Schroeder exclaims, "I can't stand it" and leaves (226). Snoopy walks over and takes his place at the piano. Lucy is so self-absorbed, however, that she is completely unaware that either of these events has taken place. She just keeps chattering away. Akin to most strips featuring the *Peanuts* pianist, several measures of music appear at the top of one of the first few panels. As Meredith points out, "You really don't understand what's happening until you know what that little piece of music is right there" (qtd. in Scheinin). These measures reveal that the composition that Schroeder is playing is Beethoven's Piano Sonata no. 8 in C Minor. However, this piece is more commonly and colloquially known as the *Sonata Pathétique* (Scheinin). While the events of the comic are humorous on their own without knowing this information, these details give them added resonance: Schroeder is playing the *Pathétique* while being subjected to Lucy's equally pathetic chatter. Then, when Schroeder is unable to endure the situation, another equally pathetic scenario emerges: a dog begins playing the piano, and Lucy doesn't even notice (Schulz, *1967 to 1968* 226). As the work of William Meredith has documented, nearly all the comics that include snippets of sheet music function in this way.[2] These strips acquire added meaning or additional resonance when the reader knows the musical composition that is being referenced.

Just as significant as Schulz's reproduction of musical scores is his deconstruction of them. As Roy T. Cook has written, "*Peanuts* is chock-full of strips . . . in which musical notation is transferred from a nonpictorial indication of the presence of music (and hence the encoding of the prescription to imagine that we, and the characters, are hearing music) to a pictorial representation of the presence of musical-notation-shaped physical objects that are" (52). Indeed, characters routinely touch, walk on, trip over, and get tangled in musical notes, notations, and measures. For example, in the comic from May 10, 1980, Snoopy shoves the measures off the top of Schroeder's piano so that he can lie down on it and take a nap (fig. 2.3). When Woodstock attempts to land on Schroeder's piano in the comic from December 21, 1981, he gets stuck in the treble clef. The final panel shows the bird trapped inside the opening measure, the lines of the staff resembling the bars of a cage (fig. 2.4).

Figure 2.3. *Peanuts* comic strip, May 10, 1980. Reprinted in *The Complete Peanuts, 1979 to 1980*, by Charles M. Schulz (Fantagraphics, 2011), 212. PEANUTS © Peanuts Worldwide LLC. Dist. by ANDREWS MCMEEL SYNDICATION. Reprinted with permission. All rights reserved.

Figure 2.4. *Peanuts* comic strip, December 21, 1981. PEANUTS © Peanuts Worldwide LLC. Dist. by ANDREWS MCMEEL SYNDICATION. Reprinted with permission. All rights reserved.

These elements go beyond merely clever and comedic facets of Schulz's strips. They also reveal the cartoonist's interest in depicting, experimenting with, and even manipulating the visual representation of sound. As Roy T. Cook observed, "Schulz was well aware of the pictorial role that various textural or text-like notations can and do play in comics, and how that role can be manipulated in order to draw attention to the nature of comics, the nature of text or other notations in comics, and aspect of the nature of art itself" (42). Music is heard, but it is also printed, seen, and read. It is both auditory and visual. How sound is drawn can influence what is heard, how it is heard, and—perhaps most importantly—why it is heard. Schulz illustrated this point repeatedly in *Peanuts*. In his drawings of music and musical notation, the cartoonist experimented with the representation, distortion, and manipulation of sound.

Given these features, seeing Charlie Brown's zigzag shirt as a triangle wave is neither bizarre nor out of place in *Peanuts*. On the contrary, it is wholly in keeping with the strip's long-standing interests, central themes, and recurring subtext. Reading and interpreting the iconic pattern in this way adds another facet to the comic's complex engagement with the visual representation of music. Since 1950, Charlie Brown's shirt has been viewed as a design feature on a garment of clothing; it is just as accurate and arguably more fruitful to view it as another means by which *Peanuts* depicts and deconstructs sound.

RIDE THE WAVE: CHARLIE BROWN AS ODDBALL— AND AS AMPLIFIER OF ODD HARMONICS

The sounds we hear travel to our ears via different types of waveforms. As Scott Rise has noted, "A sine wave sounds different from a square wave, which sounds different than the waveform that comes out of an accordion." The reason for this situation is simple: "All these waves have unique timbres because they have different harmonic content." At its most basic level, a harmonic is "a multiple of a fundamental frequency." To make this abstract concept more concrete, Rise explains, "Let's say you're playing a note with a frequency of 100Hz. That would be the 1st harmonic." Along the same lines, "The second harmonic would be twice that frequency, or 200Hz," and so on: the third harmonic is 300 Hz, the fourth is 400 Hz, and so on. Different waveforms have different sounds because they comprise different frequencies. A sine wave, for example, has a single spike, at 100 Hz. By contrast, a sawtooth wave "not only gives us spikes at the fundamental frequency, [but] there are also some smaller spikes at each harmonic frequency going up (200Hz, 300Hz, 400Hz etc.)" (Rise).

Triangle waves are likewise formed by distinct frequencies. Like the sawtooth, the triangle waveform possesses multiple spikes. What makes this wave unique, however, is that the crests occur "only at the odd-numbered harmonics (3rd = 300Hz, 5th = 500Hz, etc.)" (Rise). The difference between odd-numbered harmonics and even-numbered ones is more than merely mathematical. It is also auditory. Even harmonics contain different timbres that sound different to our ears. Kieran Whitehouse explains this distinction: "Let's say we are cranking our tube amplifier on a high gain channel, tube distortion is synonymous with warmth and clarity. This is because the tubes create EVEN harmonics which sound more pleasant to the ear." By contrast, if we use a solid-state amplifier instead of a tube one, "the distortion will produce ODD harmonics which (you guessed it) are not as pleasant to listen to" (Whitehouse). Odd harmonics "sound rather brassy" (Thain); their tones are sharp and harsh as opposed to full and round.

All of that said, even harmonics are not necessarily more desirable than odd ones. In the words of Whitehouse, "Our ears naturally pick up on even order harmonics, we're able to interpret them as more musical than odd order harmonics but that doesn't mean that odd order harmonic distortion doesn't have its place." Indeed, most closed-tube musical instruments—such as the clarinet, trumpet, and trombone—generate sounds in which the odd harmonics are more pronounced (Whitehouse). Of course, every individual has their own musical tastes and auditory preferences. However, few would argue that brass instruments are categorically inferior to stringed ones—like the guitar, bass, or violin—where the sounds of even-frequency harmonics are more pronounced. On the contrary, there are musical compositions where the sounds produced by brass instruments are preferable.

In the realm of audio engineering, triangle waves and the odd harmonics that they represent play an important role. Sound mixing involves the isolation, amplification, and distortion of multiple frequencies, both those that we find pleasing and those that are dissonant. In many cases, the deliberate use of cacophony—such as the screech that interrupts Beck's "Beercan" (1994) around the 2:30 mark or the dissonance that is a common feature in songs by Björk and Wilco—can add to the musical effect.[3] At a minimum, these sounds serve a specific auditory purpose.

Charlie Brown has long been regarded as an oddball. Try as he might, he just doesn't fit in: not at home, not at school, and certainly not among his peers. While children commonly struggle as well as routinely fail when they try new things, Charlie Brown blunders even the most basic and mundane tasks. Schulz's principal character can't fly a kite, kick a football (or at least avoid being duped into repeatedly trying), or lead his baseball team to a single victory. Lest these examples do not suffice to demonstrate Charlie Brown's odd nature, a strip that appeared on June 30, 1987, provides an even more vivid example. While leaning on the brick wall, Linus muses about the emotional butterflies that you feel when you spot the girl of your dreams across a crowded room. In the final panel, Charlie Brown makes an unusual confession: "I've never been invited into a crowded room."

Charlie Brown's odd nature can be extended to include his iconic shirt. The triangle wave pattern introduces an additional and alternative type of oddness to this character: that of odd harmonics. Every time that Charlie Brown appears in the comic, his shirt can be seen as inserting an element of sound. A strip that otherwise does not contain harmonic elements now possesses these qualities. Moreover, this situation applies even to strips that are devoid of dialogue, music, or background noise. *Peanuts* comics that might formerly have been regarded as wholly silent can now be seen as possessing sound.

In so doing, this feature forms another area of overlap with my analysis in the previous chapter about Schulz and disability. The intentionally curvy line across Charlie Brown's shirt functions in a similar semiotic manner as the unintentional wobbliness of the cartoonist's overall drawing style after developing essential tremor. In the same way that the waviness of Schulz's line introduces elements of disability into strips that do not explicitly address this issue, the triangle wave pattern on Charlie Brown's iconic shirt adds an element of sound and even music to strips that do not explicitly engage with these phenomena.

Together with introducing auditory elements to comics that are otherwise quiet, the triangle wave that adorns Charlie Brown's shirt affects sound in more specific ways. When this character appears, his iconic garment mixes, alters, and distorts the auditory balance. Charlie Brown's presence introduces odd harmonics, frequencies that are dissonant and even discordant to the human ear. Rather than delight, odd harmonics unsettle. Instead of being enjoyable, these tones can be unpleasant and often even uncomfortable.

Charlie Brown, of course, has long been seen as having a similar effect in *Peanuts*. Akin to the auditory traits of the triangle wave, he is odd, uncomfortable, and inharmonious. Rather than blending in, he stands out. Far from pleasing, he often disappoints. Instead of helping to bring harmony to the *Peanuts* gang, his presence—on the baseball team, in a school activity, at a social event—more often sows discord. Given these traits, it seems acutely appropriate that the pattern on his iconic shirt resembles a triangle wave.

Far from being known for zigging and zagging, Charlie Brown is known for disrupting the harmony, altering the balance, and changing the frequency.

The *Peanuts* strip that appeared on February 28, 1951, offers an excellent example of the way that the triangle wave on Charlie Brown's shirt amplifies the character's personality, experiences, and impact. In the opening panels, Shermy and Patty are arguing about some unknown issue. "I'll bet you a million dollars," Shermy tells her, confident that his position is correct (Schulz, *1950 to 1952* 43). Unshaken in her own conviction that she is right, Patty ups the ante, vowing: "I'll bet you a million billion trillion dollars" (43). The third panel cuts away from their dispute to show Charlie Brown announcing some good news about a stroke of good fortune. "Hey, Shermy! Patty! Look!! I found a penny!" he gleefully says (43). While both Shermy and Patty marvel at the coin in the final panel—saying, respectively, "A penny! Wow!" and "Boy, are you lucky!" (43)—this scene is filled with irony. After all, the penny that Charlie Brown found is a pittance compared to the "million billion trillion dollars" that Shermy and Patty were just discussing. Seeing the pattern on Charlie Brown's shirt as a triangle wave provides a soundtrack or, at least, a sound effect that enhances these events. Odd harmonics are more pronounced in brass instruments, and the dissonant tones represented by Charlie Brown's iconic garment can be seen as adding something akin to the "wah-wah-wah" of a sad trombone.

Countless other *Peanuts* comics can be viewed in a similar way. The message, theme, or humor of these strips is augmented by seeing Charlie Brown's shirt as a representation of odd harmonics. As with the snippets of unidentified sheet music that accompany Schroeder's piano playing, it is not essential that readers realize that the zigzag shirt can also be a triangle wave. However, akin to those mystery measures of treble and bass clef above Schroeder's piano, doing so augments their understanding, experience, and enjoyment of the comic.

The implications for noticing the presence of Charlie Brown's shirt likewise prompt us to pay closer attention to the rendering of the pattern itself. In some comics, for example, the black line that encircles the garment is bold and thick, suggesting a louder or at least amplified sound (fig. 2.5). In other strips, the zigzag is thinner, and the distance between the crests and the troughs is greater, perhaps signaling a shift in both the volume and the register (fig. 2.6). Finally, especially in strips from later in the series as Schulz aged and his essential tremor worsened, the zigzag becomes scribbly, made up of fainter as well as more irregular lines (fig. 2.7). The rendering of the zigzag in this way could indicate the presence of static or even feedback to an already dissonant tone. Whatever the precise pattern and its specific meaning,

Figure 2.5. Third panel from *Peanuts* comic strip, April 17, 1962. Reprinted in *The Complete Peanuts, 1950 to 1952*, by Charles M. Schulz (Fantagraphics, 2004), 11. PEANUTS © Peanuts Worldwide LLC. Dist. by ANDREWS MCMEEL SYNDICATION. Reprinted with permission. All rights reserved.

Figure 2.6. Final panel from *Peanuts* comic strip, March 27, 1954. Reprinted in *The Complete Peanuts, 1950 to 1952*, by Charles M. Schulz (Fantagraphics, 2004), 40. PEANUTS © Peanuts Worldwide LLC. Dist. by ANDREWS MCMEEL SYNDICATION. Reprinted with permission. All rights reserved.

Figure 2.7. Second panel from *Peanuts* comic strip, March 27, 1988. PEANUTS © Peanuts Worldwide LLC. Dist. by ANDREWS MCMEEL SYNDICATION. Reprinted with permission. All rights reserved.

one thing is clear: Charlie Brown's shirt is not an inconsequential feature. The pattern on the garment embodies a rich site of potential meaning.

In an article about the fundamentals of sound mixing, Kieran Whitehouse makes the following comment about the unadulterated sound frequencies of sine waves: "They are clear, constant notes which in musical terms are pretty boring to listen to." He explains that "the more distortion we add (or the more saturated the sound becomes) the more harmonics are produced," and the more interesting the sound becomes to our ear. Adding distortion in the form of amplification or muting adds to the complexity of the sound and thus adds to our engagement with it.

The same observation applies to the portrayal of life in *Peanuts*. In various articles and interviews, Charles M. Schulz often noted, "There is nothing funny about being happy. Sadness creates humor" (Schulz, "On Staying Power" 125). Few would likely view a young boy flying a kite on a sunny day amusing. However, the kite repeatedly getting caught in a tree despite the character's best efforts to avoid it is humorous. If happiness is a warm puppy—as the title of the best-selling *Peanuts* book from 1962 made famous—then failure is a triangle wave. The odd harmonics that this wave represents add dissonance, but they also add complexity, making the production more interesting. That this waveform can be identified on Charlie Brown's shirt might be unintentional, but it does not make it any less apt. The repeating triangle pattern hits the right note, in more ways than one.

MUSIC MAN: LISTENING TO CHARLIE BROWN

Seeing the pattern of Charlie Brown's iconic shirt as a triangle wave does more than simply introduce a new aspect of sound to *Peanuts*. It also invites us to reexamine this character's relationship to music as a whole. After all, the isolation, amplification, or distortion of the odd harmonics represented by triangle waves is a common operation in the production of music. Very few songs are released exactly as they are recorded. Even live versions usually undergo some type of audio engineering: background noise might be reduced, a note that the lead singer hit slightly off pitch might be brought back into tune, or the sound balance among the various instruments might be adjusted—perhaps the lead guitar is made more prominent, or the sound of the bass is reduced. Whatever the precise nature of these modifications, musicians and their producers commonly make alterations to a recording before it is released.

Given the way that Charlie Brown's shirt links him to harmonics, it is perhaps unsurprising that this figure also has strong links to music. Forming another overlooked aspect of Schulz's principal character, in the months directly preceding as well as immediately following his acquisition of the zigzag shirt, Charlie Brown was a dedicated and multifaceted musician who has a penchant for classical composers. Recouping and reexamining Charlie Brown's involvement with music adds a new dimension to the presence

Figure 2.8. *Peanuts* comic strip, November 8, 1950. Reprinted in *The Complete Peanuts, 1950 to 1952*, by Charles M. Schulz (Fantagraphics, 2004), 103. PEANUTS © Peanuts Worldwide LLC. Dist. by ANDREWS MCMEEL SYNDICATION. Reprinted with permission. All rights reserved.

of this theme in *Peanuts* while simultaneously adding a new facet to his relationship with the character who is most commonly associated with this element: Schroeder.

Schroeder is widely known as the musician in *Peanuts*, but few realize that Charlie Brown was the first figure in the series to pick up an instrument. In the strip that originally appeared on November 8, 1950, Charlie Brown is walking along and playing a snare drum as if he is in a marching band (fig. 2.8). Far from banging on the instrument haphazardly, as many youngsters would do if given a drum and drumsticks, he does so confidently and competently, as if he has either taken lessons or—like Schroeder—has natural talent. In the opening panel, the musical eighth notes on both sides of Charlie Brown along with the words "Bum Biddedy Bum! Biddey Bum Bum Bum!" reveal that he is playing the drum in a rhythmic way (Schulz, *1950 to 1952* 11). Indeed, the strip's central gag is not the character's ineptitude as a drummer, his inability to keep the beat, or his failure to play a musical instrument. On the contrary, the central gag arises from Charlie Brown's insufficient solution to playing more quietly, not more competently. In the second panel, Patty says to him angrily, "Don't you know how annoying that is!" After he concedes that she might be correct, the fourth and final panel presents his solution: Charlie Brown has resumed his rhythmic "Bum Biddedy Bum! Biddey Bum Bum Bum!"—only now he is wearing earmuffs.

The next *Peanuts* comic that presents a character making music is also one that features Charlie Brown. In the strip from February 16, 1951, Schulz's principal figure is now playing the violin (fig. 2.9). In details that can be regarded as interrelated, Charlie Brown has picked up a new musical instrument and has simultaneously forgone his zigzag shirt. This comic is one of few in which he is not wearing his new signature garment; instead he wears a plain collared shirt. Although Charlie Brown would often be accused of being "wishy-washy" and doing things halfheartedly, he plays the violin passionately. The opening panel, for example, shows him looking at the instrument

Figure 2.9. *Peanuts* comic strip, February 16, 1951. Reprinted in *The Complete Peanuts, 1950 to 1952*, by Charles M. Schulz (Fantagraphics, 2004), 107. PEANUTS © Peanuts Worldwide LLC. Dist. by ANDREWS MCMEEL SYNDICATION. Reprinted with permission. All rights reserved.

in a focused way. Emanata marks around his left foot reveal that he is tapping it to keep time; likewise, those that appear beside his right arm indicate that he is moving the bow vigorously. This effort and determination aside, Charlie Brown is a far less talented violinist than he is a drummer. The musical notes that appear in the white space above the instrument are squiggly and broken, suggesting that the sounds are screechy, mangled, and not in tune. In case these details are overlooked, or the way they are rendered is not understood, the reaction of Snoopy, who is seated in the background, is unmistakable. Instead of enjoying the beautiful music of the violin, Snoopy finds it unpleasant: he is scowling in the first panel and covering his ears in the second one (Schulz, *1950 to 1952* 40). Charlie Brown is aware that his violin playing is abysmal. The manner that he chooses to describe this situation, however, is as amusing as it is telling. In the final panel, Charlie Brown turns to Snoopy and asks: "Do you think that I could have anything to do with the death of Beethoven?" (40). The humor of this comment arises from both its absurdity and its anachronistic nature. Of course, no matter how poorly someone might play a song, their performance will not cause the death of the music's composer. Furthermore, they certainly cannot be responsible for the death of a figure who lived—and died—almost two hundred ago. That said, the fact that Charlie Brown compares his playing not simply to a classical composer but to Beethoven is noteworthy, given the role that this genre of music and specific figure will come to occupy in *Peanuts* in the coming years.

Charlie Brown is not discouraged by his initial experience on the violin. Undaunted, he plays the instrument again in the comic from March 20, 1951 (fig. 2.10). Once more, the opening panel shows him looking determined, tapping his foot, and moving the bow vigorously. In the second panel, his facial expression and body language shift from being merely focused to being impassioned. His eyebrows are slanted downward, giving his face a fierce intensity. Moreover, emanata lines now appear beside his head and torso, indicating that he is throwing his whole body into playing. By the time

Figure 2.10. *Peanuts* comic strip, March 20, 1951. Reprinted in *The Complete Peanuts, 1950 to 1952*, by Charles M. Schulz (Fantagraphics, 2004), 121. PEANUTS © Peanuts Worldwide LLC. Dist. by ANDREWS MCMEEL SYNDICATION. Reprinted with permission. All rights reserved.

Shermy interrupts him, beads of sweat are flying off both sides of his head, and his tongue his hanging out (Schulz, *1950 to 1952* 49). The punch line to this comic is strikingly similar to the previous one. Shermy inquires how violin practice is going, and Charlie Brown tells him, "Not too good. In fact, last night, I dreamed that Beethoven strangled me!" (49). Once again, of all the musicians that Charlie Brown could have named, he chooses this classical composer. In the coming years, of course, Beethoven will be referenced by another character in *Peanuts* who is known for his love of music: Schroeder.

Reexamining the relationship that Charlie Brown has with music, however, yields more than merely his overlooked history as a musician. It also unveils the significant, but equally neglected, role that he had in encouraging and even mentoring the strip's more well-known musician, Schroeder. This character made his debut on May 30, 1951, and Charlie Brown quickly expressed a strong connection to him. In the comic that appeared on June 2, 1951, for example, Charlie Brown successfully coaxes the toddler-aged boy to smile and exclaims: "Gee! I feel like a father!" (Schulz, *1950 to 1952* 70).

Of course, Charlie Brown is not Schroeder's father—or even a member of his family. That said, he can be seen as his musical patriarch. In details that have not been explored in previous discussions about *Peanuts*, Charlie Brown is the individual who introduces Schroeder to music. In the strip that appeared on September 24, 1951, Schulz's principal character gives Schroeder his first toy piano and—just as significantly—encourages him to play it (fig. 2.11). Admittedly, this interaction is presented for laughs. In the comic's first two panels, Charlie Brown taps out notes on the keyboard while saying encouraging things like "See how easy it is, Schroeder?" and "The piano is a beautiful instrument if played properly" (Schulz, *1950 to 1952* 103). Charlie Brown is not playing a complicated musical composition. Rather, in keeping with the piano's status as a toy suitable for a toddler, he is having fun pressing individual keys. To illustrate this fact, the words "plink plink plink" appear beside the piano in both scenes, along with the drawing of a solitary musical note. When Charlie Brown turns the piano over the Schroeder, however, the

Figure 2.11. *Peanuts* comic strip, September 24, 1951. PEANUTS © Peanuts Worldwide LLC. Dist. by ANDREWS MCMEEL SYNDICATION. Reprinted with permission. All rights reserved.

toddler surprises as well as embarrasses him: he sits down at the instrument and—as the measures of music that appear in the sound balloon coming from the instrument indicate—plays a highly complicated and challenging piece (103). As William Meredith has identified, it is nothing less than Sergei Rachmaninoff's Prelude in G Minor (*Schulz's Beethoven*).

Charlie Brown shares not only his interest in music with Schroeder, but also his interest in Beethoven. In the comic that appeared on October 10, 1951, Charlie Brown is sitting on a low stool and reading a book to Schroeder (fig. 2.12). "Now on the very next day," he narrates in the opening panel to a happily smiling Schroeder (Schulz, *1950 to 1952* 107). When Patty walks by and asks if they are reading a fairy tale, young Schroeder is incensed. His face, both in the panel where Patty asks this question and in the one where Charlie Brown answers her, has a sour grimace. Likewise, in each image, young Schroeder utters the grouchy interjection "Humph!" Charlie Brown informs Patty, "Schroeder's not interested in fairy tales. . . . This is the life of Beethoven!" Lest Patty or the reader disbelieve this assertion, one glimpse at the young boy affirms its veracity: his grimace has changed to a blissful grin. Likewise, a speech balloon above his head advertises his utterance of a contented "sigh!"

The way in which Charlie Brown instills, inspires, or at least supports Schroeder's love of Beethoven does not end there. Roughly a month later, in the comic that appeared on November 26, 1951, Schulz's principal character continues in this vein (fig. 2.13). The strip's opening panel shows young

Figure 2.12. *Peanuts* comic strip, October 10, 1951. PEANUTS © Peanuts Worldwide LLC. Dist. by ANDREWS MCMEEL SYNDICATION. Reprinted with permission. All rights reserved.

Figure 2.13. *Peanuts* comic strip, November 26, 1951. PEANUTS © Peanuts Worldwide LLC. Dist. by ANDREWS MCMEEL SYNDICATION. Reprinted with permission. All rights reserved.

Schroeder sitting at his piano. In the background, Charlie Brown is holding a large cardboard box and exclaiming, "I got it, Schroeder!" (Schulz, *1950 to 1952* 121). The next panel reverses the arrangement of the two characters: Charlie Brown now occupies the foreground, and Schroeder has been moved to the background. Regardless, their shared interest in the arrival of the box remains unchanged. "Boy, is it ever heavy," Charlie Brown says in second panel while panting and sweating. Schroeder is so excited that he is literally jumping up and down. In the third panel, Charlie Brown has cut the twine around the box and opened the flaps. He asks Schroeder, "Where do you want it? On top of your piano?" The final panel breaks the suspense: it shows a large bust of an older male figure perched atop Schroeder's toy piano. Below the sculpture, in all caps, is the name "Beethoven." Schroeder is elated: his face bears a big smile, and his hands are clasped gleefully in front of him. Although Schroeder is too young to be able to read the inscription, he knows the identity of this figure. In the speech balloon above Schroeder's head, he exclaims, "Beethoven!!!" and then lets out a dreamy "*sigh*."

Charlie Brown and Schroeder would continue to have a special relationship throughout *Peanuts*. In a possible acknowledgment of the fact that Schulz's principal character gave him his first toy piano, Charlie Brown is the only character whom the young virtuoso allows to lean against his beloved instrument without being annoyed or getting angry. When Violet, Snoopy, and especially Lucy do so, Schroeder rebuffs them in some way: he tells them to go away, he gives them the cold shoulder, or he outright yells at them. As the *Peanuts* Wiki notes, however, Charlie Brown is the sole character who can lounge against Schroeder's piano without being reprimanded and even without Schroeder getting annoyed.

Charlie Brown and Schroeder also have a special connection on the baseball field: Schroeder serves as the catcher to Charlie Brown's pitching. Given how closely pitchers and catchers work together, teammates who hold these two positions are known for having a strong bond. Schulz's characters are no different. Schroeder is one of the few characters who respect Charlie Brown either as a position player or as team manager: "He also often encourages Charlie Brown during a baseball game, whereas the rest of the team says, 'Don't let us down by showing up!'" ("Schroeder"). Finally, and just as significantly, Schroeder also comes to Charlie Brown's defense off the baseball field. In an oft-mentioned incident, Schroeder "once angrily denounced Violet for giving Charlie Brown a used valentine" ("Schroeder"). Given these dynamics, next to Linus, "Schroeder is probably Charlie Brown's closest friend" ("Schroeder").

For more than fifty years, Schroeder has been regarded as the musician of Schulz's comic. Ludwig van Beethoven has been identified as his inspiration. Seeing Charlie Brown's zigzag shirt as a triangle wave complicates these perceptions. The alternative way of viewing the well-known pattern becomes an access point to Charlie Brown's early interest in music and his multifaceted activities as a musician while simultaneously changing his relationship to Schroeder and his involvement with music. Schroeder is an undeniable virtuoso on the piano. However, in an important but long forgotten detail, it was Charlie Brown who introduced him to this instrument and also shared his love for the classical composer who would become his favorite. Beethoven may be Schroeder's muse, but Charlie Brown is his long-overlooked musical mentor.

STOP, CHILDREN, WHAT'S THAT SOUND: *PEANUTS* AND NEW WAYS OF INCORPORATING AUDITORY ELEMENTS IN PRINT COMICS

Although print comics are technically a nonauditory medium—asking us to look at them with our eyes, not listen to them with our ears[4]—they have always included elements of sound. As Joshua Abraham Kopin noted, the newspaper series that is often seen as the first comic strip, Richard Outcault's *Hogan's Alley*, contained a myriad of both melodious and cacophonous features. Not only did characters like the protagonist the Yellow Kid speak via speech balloons, but he and his fellow gang of ragamuffins also sang, shouted, and screamed. Furthermore, the entire cast was immersed in a sound-saturated environment: namely, the Lower East Side of Manhattan at the turn of the twentieth century. Horse-drawn carts rattled down the cobblestone streets, policemen blew their whistles, dogs barked, and neighbors yelled from their apartment windows to people below. Given this situation, Kopin asserts, "sound becomes a defining characteristic of the emerging comic strip." Moreover, as the decades passed and the genre grew, comics would "only get louder" (Kopin).

While it is now commonplace to think of the role that sound plays in print-based comics, the presence of auditory elements tends be divided into two main categories. First, and most commonly, are textual features like the use of speech balloons and the inclusion of onomatopoeia. Speech balloons are one of the genre's hallmarks, and they also serve an important pragmatic purpose: they allow a cartoonist to quickly and clearly demonstrate which figure in the panel is speaking. Catherine Khordoc, in an essay about speech balloons, describes them as "visual sound effects" (156). Greg Uyeno has expanded on these observations. Readers not only "hear" the words that are being uttered inside the balloon, but also "listen" to the balloon itself—its size, shape, font, and outline can convey volume, tone, and timbre. A speech balloon where the words appear in bold and underlining is "louder" than one where the lettering lacks any emphasis. Likewise, a balloon that is formed by jagged, uneven lines is "heard" differently from one that is formed by a smooth oval: the jagged lines might convey radio static, auditory feedback, or the signal from some type of electronic transmission, like a telegraph.

In the same way that speech balloons form a core component of the use of sound in comics, so too does onomatopoeia. Words like "Pow!," "Bang!," and "Thunk!" are used to relay the sound of all manner of noise-producing activity, from characters fighting to objects falling. As K. J. Stewart has noted, "Onomatopoeia is a staple part of comic book lore." As a result, over the decades, "a canon of onomatopoeia has developed," signaling which utterances denote various actions or events (Uyeno). Given both their long-standing importance and their prominence, "comics really wouldn't be the same without these words" (Stewart). Brian Cronin calls onomatopoeia nothing less than "the most iconic sound effects" in comics. Indeed, words like "Pow!" and "Bam!" are often used in magazine and newspaper articles, on items of clothing, or on stickers, posters, or stationary as a synecdoche to signify the genre.

Print-based comics can incorporate sound in another way: they can be about music or musicians, they can include references to songs or bands, and they can also present musical compositions, notes, or notation. As Camilo Díaz Pino has written, "Comics have found themselves regularly immersed within cultures of music—be it in the bubblegum pop world of *Archie*, the psychedelia of California's alternative comics movement, the introspective jazz-centeredness of Harvey Pekar's work, or the punk counter-culture inhabited by the characters of Jaime Hernandez's Locas comics" (86). This list, of course, is neither exhaustive nor all-inclusive. Keir Keightley, for example, has examined the "numerous depictions of sheet music" in Outcault's *Hogan's Alley* (Keightley 29). In a variety of vignettes, characters are holding songbooks, looking at musical scores, or standing on streets where sheet music is scattered on the ground (29–31). Likewise, both Camilo Díaz Pino and Kieron Michael Brown have explored the presentation of garage bands in the *Scott Pilgrim* series. As they note, the comic not only includes many scenes of musicians playing but also includes guitar chord charts, lyrics, and tablature (Pino 98–100). Finally, and most recently, Qiana J. Whitted has explored the function of music in an array of graphic texts about the civil rights movement, such as blues, jazz, and soul in Jeremy Love's *Bayou*, songs by Otis Redding in Jim Demonakos and Mark Long's *The Silence of Our Friends*, and religious spirituals in John Lewis's *March* trilogy. As Whitted asserts, the inclusion of lyrics and even musical notes in these works does more than simply establish the historical setting or provide a soundtrack for the events. Instead, music in these texts forms "critical instruments of contemplation and mourning" (Whitted).

Charles M. Schulz's *Peanuts* participates in both of these modes for incorporating sound in print-based comics. The newspaper strip, of course, is filled with speech balloons that relay the comments and conversations of various characters. Additionally, *Peanuts* commonly uses onomatopoetic words, such as "AAUGH!" when a character is frustrated, "SMAK!" when Snoopy kisses Lucy, or "WHOMP!" when Charlie Brown hits the ground after Lucy pulls the football away. Furthermore, as discussed earlier, *Peanuts* also incorporates elements of music: characters sing songs, play instruments, and interact with snippets of actual sheet music.

Seeing the pattern on Charlie Brown's iconic shirt as a triangle wave adds to the visual vocabulary of sound in *Peanuts*—and in comics as a whole. The zigzag line embodies a new way of incorporating auditory elements into a print-based medium. Together with speech balloons and musical notes, this feature allows us to "see sound." The triangle wave is a pictorial depiction of wavelengths that comprise odd harmonics. It is literally a graph of sound. Comics, of course, are often referred to as graphic art. The triangle wave that we see on Charlie Brown's shirt bridges these elements; it brings together graphic art and sound graphs.

Comics are often characterized by their combination of word and image. The interplay of written text and visual drawings, in fact, is so essential to sequential art that it is regarded as one of the signature aspects of the genre. Scott McCloud, in his seminal *Understanding Comics* (1993), for example, dedicates an entire chapter to identifying and discussing the various types of word-image relationships (138–61). At least when it comes to the presentation of Charlie Brown in *Peanuts*, a third element might need to be added to this feature. Given how the zigzag pattern on his shirt can also be viewed as a triangle wave, this comics character can perhaps most accurately be seen as merging not merely word and image but also word, image, and sound.

Osvaldo Oyola, writing about auditory elements in print-based comics, reflected: "The transparency of sound can make its presence and function easy to overlook." Comics audiences, be they fans or critics, routinely take elements of sound for granted. They read the speech balloons but don't listen to them. They see the onomatopoetic utterances but don't hear them. In light of this situation, Oyola asserts: "There is still a lot to consider when it comes to sound in comics—not just the rhetoric of sound or sound as a signifier of time, but sound as identity." The same observations apply to Charlie Brown and the zigzag shirt in *Peanuts*. Since Schulz's character first donned this article of clothing on December 21, 1950, countless millions have seen it. The time is long overdue for us to begin listening to this iconic garment as well.

The next chapter continues my interest in presenting familiar characters from *Peanuts* in unfamiliar ways. To do so, I examine another one of Charlie Brown's iconic accoutrements: his dog Snoopy. Next to his zigzag shirt, in fact, this canine creature is arguably Charlie Brown's most recognizable possession. Numerous *Peanuts* strips show Charlie Brown in the company of Snoopy. The *Peanuts* protagonist brings Snoopy his supper dish, has numerous conversations with him at his doghouse, and even coaches him as the shortstop on the baseball team. Over the course of the strip, Snoopy embodies many things to Charlie Brown: he is his pet, his friend, his teammate, his confidant, and occasionally even his foil. Regardless of the specific role that Snoopy plays in Charlie Brown's life at a given moment, one underlying fact remains true: Snoopy is his dog. This past chapter made a case that the zigzag on Charlie Brown's shirt may not be a zigzag, and the next chapter makes an even bolder claim: it suggests that Snoopy may not be viewed exclusively as a dog. Previous critics have commented how, especially as *Peanuts* progressed, Charlie Brown's pet pooch displayed an array of human qualities. The following chapter argues that, from the beginning of Schulz's strip, Snoopy also possessed an array of feline ones.

CHAPTER 3

"WHY CAN'T I HAVE A NORMAL DOG LIKE EVERYONE ELSE?"

Snoopy as Canine—and Feline

Charlie Brown may be the principal character in Charles M. Schulz's *Peanuts*, but Snoopy has long been its star. Making his debut on October 4, 1950, in the third comic of the series, the beagle would soon become "the strip's most popular character" (Flagg 60). By the early 1960s, growing numbers of *Peanuts* comics centered on Snoopy, documenting his exploits in his World War I Flying Ace persona, his interactions with his sidekick Woodstock, and his efforts to write and publish a novel. Together with moving to the forefront of the newspaper strip, Snoopy also moved to the forefront of its fandom. In 1968, Snoopy—rather than his owner and human, Charlie Brown—was a write-in candidate for president of the United States. The "Snoopy for President" campaign resurfaced in 1972, receiving such strong support that California passed a law making it "illegal to enter the name of a fictional character on the ballot" ("Snoopy for President").

While Schulz made licensing deals for all his characters from *Peanuts*, Snoopy quickly emerged as a commercial standout. From figurines, stationary, and clothing to housewares, school supplies, and toys, he permeated seemingly every facet of American material culture by the mid-1970s. As the journalist Sarah Boxer has written, Snoopy plush dolls with their changeable outfits were a staple among young people from her generation. Snoopy continued to be the public face of Schulz's strip in the decades that followed. In 1983, the California-based amusement park Knott's Berry Farm opened a *Peanuts*-themed area dubbed "Camp Snoopy." Additional venues would follow, including a seven-acre Camp Snoopy at the Mall of America in Schulz's home state of Minnesota in 1992, and a Camp Snoopy featuring ten rides at Cedar Point amusement park in Ohio in 1999. Snoopy has also long been the character who represents *Peanuts* in the Macy's Thanksgiving Day parade. The beagle balloon debuted in 1968, the first time that Schulz's creation participated in the event. Over the decades, the canine character has made more appearances as well as been revamped more times—Snoopy as an astronaut, Snoopy with Woodstock, Snoopy wearing ice skates, Snoopy as the Flying Ace, and so on—than any other balloon figure in the parade ("Snoopy").

Snoopy has been just as prominent outside of the United States. "In parts of Europe *Peanuts* came to be licensed as *Snoopy*," Sarah Boxer has documented. Meanwhile, "in Tokyo, the floor of the vast toy store Kiddy Land that is devoted to *Peanuts* is called Snoopy Town" (Boxer). Not surprisingly, given his long-standing visibility, Snoopy is the only figure from Schulz's strip to have his own star on the Hollywood Walk of Fame. The plaque was unveiled in November 2015—just before the release of *The Peanuts Movie*—and it appears next to the one honoring the cartoonist himself (Rivett-Carnac). As even this brief overview suggests, for decades now, Snoopy has been "the most beloved of Schulz's creations" (Wong). The novelist Jonathan Franzen, in a foreword to one of the volumes of the complete *Peanuts*, said unequivocally, "What launched the strip to its heights was, above all, the character of Snoopy" (xiii).

Of the many factors contributing to Snoopy's popularity, chief among them is his active imagination and expansive sense of self. Over the years, Snoopy adopted a plethora of personae: World War I Flying Ace, Joe Cool, World Famous Author, Easter Beagle, and so on. These identities range from the silly to the serious. Regardless, they all form a core aspect of Snoopy's character along with his role in the comic strip. Moreover, they contribute to his mass appeal: there is a side of Snoopy for everyone.

This chapter makes a case that Snoopy channels an additional and wholly unexpected mode of being: one that is more feline than canine. Although Schulz's star character is both drawn and identified as a beagle, he exhibits a variety of behaviors, traits, and sentiments that are more stereotypically associated with cats than dogs. From his refusal to play fetch and his grandiose views of himself to his finicky palate and his penchant for sleeping on top of his doghouse rather than inside it, Snoopy is often more catlike than doglike in many respects. Moreover, far from embodying occasional or isolated elements, Snoopy's feline features are among his signature traits and even beloved qualities.

Exploring Snoopy's catlike qualities adds a new dimension to this exceedingly popular character while simultaneously adding a new facet to a common theme in *Peanuts*: failure. In what has become an oft-mentioned aspect of the comic, characters routinely have their hopes dashed, their efforts spoiled, and their dreams unfulfilled. To the long list of failures that permeate *Peanuts*, Snoopy satisfying the role of a dog could be added. His promotion to the rank of "Head Beagle" notwithstanding, the character's actions, personality, and interests are often more feline than canine.

THE DOG DAYS ARE OVER: SEEING JOE COOL AS JOE FELINE

Snoopy may be the most popular character in *Peanuts*, but he has also been the most controversial in many ways. During the same time that Charlie Brown's pet pooch was taking over the strip, he was also widely regarded as ruining it. Echoing the sentiments of many other critics, Kevin Wong has written: "As legendary as *Peanuts* is, it was only 'great' for a 15–20 year period—from about the mid-50s to the early 70s. And even by the 70s, there was a slow, but definite drop-off in quality. By the 80s, with the exception of a few notable story lines, the strip was essentially dead. The 90s was just more of the same" (Wong). Rather than seeing this decline as arising from a constellation of factors—such as changing sociopolitical times, creative fatigue, and so on—Wong attributes it to a specific source. "Much of the blame for this can be traced back to Snoopy," Wong asserts. "As the strip progressed, the beagle hogged more and more of the spotlight in increasingly negative ways. And the intelligence and darkness of the strip, which once made it so distinctive on the comics landscape, was replaced by more mainstream, cutesy humor." The expanding role of Snoopy exemplified, if not wholly precipitated, this shift. *Peanuts* went from tackling weighty subjects like "the cruelties and hardship of being a child" (Wong) to having strips where the main plotline was Snoopy leaning against his doghouse as "Joe Cool."

Significantly, the more that Snoopy moved away from being a conventional dog, the more he was seen as detracting from Schulz's strip. In the words of Wong once again, "Snoopy began walking on his hind legs and using his hands, and that was the beginning of the end for the strip." Starting in the 1960s and accelerating rapidly in the 1970s, Snoopy "was technically still a dog, but in a very substantial way.... His opposable thumbs and upward positioning meant that for all intents and purposes, he was now a human in a dog costume" (Wong). Sarah Boxer has echoed these sentiments. In an essay that appeared in *The Atlantic*, she argued that by the 1980s, Snoopy had ceased being Charlie Brown's pet dog and instead became another child character in the strip—only with floppy ears and a tail. In a powerful illustration of this shift, Snoopy "didn't need any of the other characters in order to be what he was.... More and more often he appeared alone on his doghouse, sleeping or typing a novel or a love letter" (Boxer). Not only did Snoopy's different personae generate different images that could be marketed (and merchandized) to different consumers, but nearly all of them were also human identities: college student, fighter pilot, author, tennis player, attorney, hockey player, and so on. Given this situation, Gordon Flagg notes that "Snoopy grew more anthropomorphic," and his role in the comic became more "humanlike" (60).

The discussion that follows both builds on and breaks from these observations. Snoopy did become less canine as *Peanuts* progressed, but he did not simply become more human; I contend that he became more feline in many ways as well. From the beginning, Snoopy exhibited a variety of traits that—however unexpected and even unlikely—were more in keeping with a cat than a dog. Over the course of the strip, these qualities grew both more numerous and more pronounced. Snoopy first donned his black sunglasses as Joe Cool in the *Peanuts* strip that appeared on May 27, 1971. Decades before he would adopt this persona, however, he embodied another even more prominent identity: Joe Feline.

Snoopy's possession of traits, behaviors, and qualities that can be viewed as catlike begin with his origins in *Peanuts*. First and foremost, for the first full year of his existence, Snoopy has no clear owner. In a trait that is more in keeping with the stalwart independence associated with cats rather than the desire to belong to a pack that is commonly exhibited by dogs, Snoopy roams into and out of the lives of the characters on his own. It is not until the comic that appeared on September 19, 1951, that Schulz alludes to Snoopy's possible master—who it is not Charlie Brown. Instead, it is Shermy. Although Charlie Brown takes care of Snoopy in strips from the opening days of November 1955, it was not until the comic on September 1, 1958—nearly eight years after Snoopy debuted—that Schulz's principal character is finally identified as Snoopy's owner. Once again, these traits of autonomy, independence, and even aloofness are more typically associated with cats than dogs.

Snoopy is largely reticent during the first few months of the comic, but he soon begins expressing himself via speech balloons that are later replaced by thought balloons. For the most part, however, these comments are both limited and largely nonverbal, consisting of an exclamation point to denote surprise, a black scribble to signify disgust, or a question mark to indicate confusion. Significantly, Snoopy's first complete sentence in *Peanuts* is also an utterance that is exceedingly catlike. In the comic that appeared on May 27, 1952, Charlie Brown walks by Snoopy on a beautiful spring day, picks

Figure 3.1. *Peanuts* comic strip, May 27, 1952. PEANUTS © Peanuts Worldwide LLC. Dist. by ANDREWS MCMEEL SYNDICATION. Reprinted with permission. All rights reserved.

up one of his ears, and jokes, "Kind of warm today for ear muffs, isn't it?" (Schulz, *1950 to 1952* 194). The final panel shows Snoopy walking away in a huff; the thought balloon above his head reads: "Why do I have to suffer such indignities!?" (fig. 3.1). The resentment that Snoopy feels about being treated in a manner that he regards as disrespectful is more stereotypically associated with the ego of a cat than the personality of a dog. Furthermore, like a cat, when Snoopy is unhappy, he is not shy about saying so. Given the nature of Snoopy's first complete sentence in *Peanuts*, in fact, one might argue that he does not acquire the ability to communicate so that he can do doglike things like ask for treats or tell his owner how much he adores him. Instead, he learns how to speak so that he can complain about not being treated with the proper decorum.

Together with not acting like a dog in many early strips, Snoopy also paradoxically resents being identified as one. In the comic that appeared on October 21, 1952, Snoopy trots behind Charlie Brown as he strolls down the sidewalk (fig. 3.2). Annoyed by being shadowed, Charlie Brown stops abruptly, turns around, and snaps at him: "Stop following me!! All day long you've been following me around like a dog!" (Schulz, *1950 to 1952* 257). Snoopy is not simply surprised by Charlie Brown's rebuff; he is bizarrely insulted by it. "Whoops! What have I said?!" Schulz's penitent principal characters says, attempting to backpedal. Charlie Brown continues, even more desperately, in the final panel, "I'm sorry, Snoopy. . . . I spoke hastily!

Figure 3.2. *Peanuts* comic strip, October 21, 1952. PEANUTS © Peanuts Worldwide LLC. Dist. by ANDREWS MCMEEL SYNDICATION. Reprinted with permission. All rights reserved.

Figure 3.3. Opening two panels from *Peanuts* comic strip, March 10, 1962. PEANUTS © Peanuts Worldwide LLC. Dist. by ANDREWS MCMEEL SYNDICATION. Reprinted with permission. All rights reserved.

I'm sorry.... It was just an expression" (257). Snoopy, however, is unmoved by his apologies and stomps off in a huff. Of course, the humor of the strip arises from the fact that Snoopy is, in fact, a dog and thus has no right to be insulted by Charlie Brown's remark—and Charlie Brown has no reason to apologize for making it. Nonetheless, the events suggest that neither Snoopy nor Charlie Brown sees the dog as a canine.

In the years and comics that followed, Charlie Brown's pet would only expand on his feline features. Whereas dogs have a reputation for being simple creatures who live happily as well as humbly in the moment, Snoopy is known for putting on airs, for philosophizing about the future, and for having a flair for the dramatic. In the opening panels to the strip that appeared on March 10, 1962, for example, he sits atop of his doghouse and muses, "My life has become a bore! Everything I see I've seen before!" (fig. 3.3). Both the hyperbole of these comments and the existential angst that they convey are more in keeping with popular perceptions about the personalities of cats than dogs. Indeed, it is difficult to imagine even the most contemplative dog expressing such sentiments.

This strip is far from the only time that Snoopy wrestles with—or is troubled by—big philosophical issues. Defying common associations of dogs as having few worries, concerns, or even thoughts in their head beyond perhaps when they will get their next meal or treat, Snoopy is tormented by more existential anxieties in a comic that appeared just a few weeks before the end of the series (fig. 3.4). "I've been very tense lately," Snoopy reflects in a thought balloon in the first panel of the comic from January 15, 2000. "I find myself worrying about everything.... Take the Earth, for instance," he continues, his face visibly distraught. In sentiments that are far more in keeping with those that a cat might utter, he goes on to explain: "Here we all are clinging helplessly to this globe that is hurtling through space ..." The final panel is also the most morose and even nihilistic. "What if the wings

"Why Can't I Have a Normal Dog Like Everyone Else?": Snoopy as Canine—and Feline

Figure 3.4. *Peanuts* comic strip, January 15, 2000. PEANUTS © Peanuts Worldwide LLC. Dist. by ANDREWS MCMEEL SYNDICATION. Reprinted with permission. All rights reserved.

fall off?" he frets in a comment that serves as the punch line for this strip but is clearly a serious worry for Snoopy.

Together with being philosophical, Snoopy is also finicky. The *Peanuts* strip that appeared on Sunday, February 11, 1979, presents a familiar scenario: Charlie Brown hurriedly prepares Snoopy's supper dish while the impatient pooch pounds on the front door (fig. 3.5). When Charlie Brown hands Snoopy his much-anticipated bowl of food, however, he is still not satisfied. "Go ahead and eat! What's the matter?" Charlie Brown says. "Did I forget something? What did I forget?" Snoopy doesn't answer, so Schulz's principal character tries to identify what is wrong. "What do you want?" he

Figure 3.5. *Peanuts* comic strip, February 11, 1979. PEANUTS © Peanuts Worldwide LLC. Dist. by ANDREWS MCMEEL SYNDICATION. Reprinted with permission. All rights reserved.

Figure 3.6. *Peanuts* comic strip, July 30, 1967. PEANUTS © Peanuts Worldwide LLC. Dist. by ANDREWS MCMEEL SYNDICATION. Reprinted with permission. All rights reserved.

asks his pet. "Salt? Pepper? Onions? Ketchup? Parsley?" Again, no reaction from Snoopy. In the next panel, Charlie Brown rolls his eyes and lets out an exasperated "Oh . . ."; he has discovered the problem. Schulz's protagonist clasps his hands in front of him, smiles warmly, and gleefully tells Snoopy, "Bon appétit!" Snoopy's face breaks into a satisfied grin, and he responds, "Merci," via a thought balloon. The closing panel of the Sunday strip shows Snoopy walking away with his supper dish, and Charlie Brown rolling his eyes once again and saying, "Why can't I have a normal dog like everyone else?" Charlie Brown indeed does not have a typical canine. Not only might his pup want spices, toppings, or seasonings for his food before he will eat it, but he must also be told "Bon appétit!" before he will dine. If any species of pet has these requirements, it is a cat, not a dog.

Far from this being an anomalous occurrence, Snoopy has a long history in the comic of being fussy about his food: not just its quality and punctuality but its presentation and mode of delivery. In the strip that appeared on July 30, 1967, he refuses to eat his supper until Charlie Brown serves it to him on a tea cart. "I must be out of my mind," the protagonist mumbles as he heads back into the house to get the item (fig. 3.6). Likewise, a few weeks later, in the comic from August 27, 1967, Snoopy gets his owner to serve his dinner

"Why Can't I Have a Normal Dog Like Everyone Else?": Snoopy as Canine—and Feline

Figure 3.7. *Peanuts* comic strip, August 27, 1967. PEANUTS © Peanuts Worldwide LLC. Dist. by ANDREWS MCMEEL SYNDICATION. Reprinted with permission. All rights reserved.

in another specialized way: cafeteria style (fig. 3.7). "Why can't you eat your supper like a normal dog? Who do you think you are?!" Charlie Brown says, exasperated. When Charlie Brown finally acquiesces to Snoopy's request and sets out the spread, his dog doesn't respond with abundant appreciation. Instead, like a cat, he behaves in an entitled way. "Mmm! Everything looks so good," Snoopy says as he walks up to the line of dog dishes. "I'll have some of this and some of that . . ." In the strip that appeared on February 24, 1968, Snoopy's attitude and actions went one step further—and one step too far for Charlie Brown (fig. 3.8). The comic shows the protagonist happily bringing Snoopy's dinner out to his doghouse, but then grimacing and promptly

Figure 3.8. *Peanuts* comic strip, February 24, 1968. PEANUTS © Peanuts Worldwide LLC. Dist. by ANDREWS MCMEEL SYNDICATION. Reprinted with permission. All rights reserved.

turning around after seeing something out of view. "That's the last straw! If he wants his supper, he can come and get it himself!" an angry Charlie Brown says as he walks back to the house. The final panel reveals why he is so upset: Snoopy has posted a sign beside his doghouse that reads "Servants' Entrance in the Rear." Many individuals are familiar with the saying "Dogs have owners, cats have staff." Snoopy takes this viewpoint one step further. Charlie Brown's pet doesn't merely have "staff"; he has "servants."

Even when Snoopy is not being so snobby and condescending, he still routinely behaves more like a cat than a dog when it comes to his meals. On November 23, 1967, Charlie Brown brings out his pooch's supper dish. "Here you are, Snoopy . . . Happy Thanksgiving!" he says before setting it down. While most dogs would dive into a bowl that is piled high with food, Snoopy peers into it and is disappointed. The final panel reveals the source of his dissatisfaction. "No cranberries?" Snoopy laments via the thought balloon, a distraught look on his face. While this remark serves as the strip's punch line, it is not out of character for the pooch. Lest Schulz's readers (or mine, for that matter) need any more convincing, the comic that appeared on May 15, 1971, ought to suffice (fig. 3.9). The opening panel shows Charlie Brown offering Snoopy an ice cream sundae. The pooch looks down from his doghouse at the item and promptly refuses it, his nose turned up in the air. A dejected-looking Charlie Brown walks away, letting out a sigh. In the final panel, Snoopy shares the reason for his actions: "I hated to send it back, but a marshmallow sundae is not a marshmallow sundae unless it drips over the edges." As many dog owners would agree, being this particular about not simply food, but especially a treat, is something that only a cat would do. Finally, even during instances when Snoopy is satisfied with his cuisine, he is dissatisfied with another aspect of his dining experience. In the comic on September 16, 1967, for example, he happily consumes all the food in his dog dish but then laments, "No after-dinner speaker?"

Snoopy is just as particular about his beverages as he is his food. In the strip that appeared on September 13, 1988, the pet beagle brings his empty

Figure 3.9. *Peanuts* comic strip, May 15, 1971. PEANUTS © Peanuts Worldwide LLC. Dist. by ANDREWS MCMEEL SYNDICATION. Reprinted with permission. All rights reserved.

Figure 3.10. *Peanuts* comic strip, September 13, 1988. PEANUTS © Peanuts Worldwide LLC. Dist. by ANDREWS MCMEEL SYNDICATION. Reprinted with permission. All rights reserved.

water dish to Charlie Brown. After refilling it, Schulz's principal character returns it to Snoopy, who is now lounging atop his doghouse. The beagle looks into the dish and thinks, "No slice of lemon?" (fig. 3.10). The humor of this comic, of course, arises from the absurdity of a dog asking for a slice of lemon in his water, let alone lamenting the absence of one. After all, dogs commonly drink out of the toilet; they have few concerns or even standards when it comes to their drinking water. While it is unusual for a dog to expect a slice of lemon, it is far more believable for a cat.

Snoopy is more than simply eccentric; he is also egotistical. In the comic that appeared on February 26, 1959, Snoopy is perched atop his doghouse and in a ponderous mood once again (fig. 3.11). This time, however, he is wondering if there are dogs on the moon. In a sentiment whose egotism or at least bravado is once again more indicative of a feline than a canine, he is confident that if there are dogs on the moon, they are the ones in charge. The night that Snoopy gazes up at the moon is not the only time that he imagines his species being the one in power. Near the end of the *Peanuts* series, in the strip that appeared on August 11, 1993, Snoopy expresses a similar sentiment (fig. 3.12). Charlie Brown and Snoopy visit the library, and Charlie Brown asks the librarian if they have any books "where a dog takes over the whole world?" Of course, the adult librarian is out of the frame, so we do not see this figure or the speech balloon containing their answer. Nonetheless, what Charlie Brown tells the librarian next makes the response clear. Snoopy hands a sheaf of papers across the desk while Schulz's principal character quips: "Well, I think now you've got one." Once again, writing a book where the species to which they belong takes over the whole world is something that a cat is far more likely to do than a dog.

Whereas most dogs are eager to please their owners, Snoopy is different. As Schulz himself reflected, in numerous strips over the years, "I have played up the gag that he doesn't even remember his master's name, but simply

Figure 3.11. Opening two panels from *Peanuts* comic strip, February 26, 1959. PEANUTS © Peanuts Worldwide LLC. Dist. by ANDREWS MCMEEL SYNDICATION. Reprinted with permission. All rights reserved.

Figure 3.12. *Peanuts* comic strip, August 11, 1993. PEANUTS © Peanuts Worldwide LLC. Dist. by ANDREWS MCMEEL SYNDICATION. Reprinted with permission. All rights reserved.

thinks of him as 'that round-headed kid'" (Schulz, *Jubilee* 86). A series of strips that appeared in autumn 1989 take such sentiments one step further. In the comic from October 26, 1989, Charlie Brown proposes to Snoopy: "What would you say if I told you I was going to devote the rest of my life to making you happy? . . . We'll go for long walks in the woods and romp around in the yard. You'll sit in my lap and I'll scratch your ears and we'll watch TV and I'll give you cookies." While most dogs would be ecstatic at this news—seeing it as their dream come true—Snoopy's reaction is far more blasé and, thus, far more catlike. After listening to Charlie Brown's proposal, Snoopy has a question: "What kind of cookies?" he wants to know before giving his response. Although this comment forms the punch line to the strip, readers soon realize that Snoopy was not joking. In a plotline that continued through the following month, Charlie Brown carries out this plan, devoting himself to making his dog happy. Snoopy, however, is not impressed. In various comics, Snoopy is more excited about getting cookies than about seeing Charlie Brown. Additionally, in the strip from November 10, 1989, Charlie Brown worries that he is not doing a very good job of devoting his life to his dog. With a comment that once again seems more indicative of

Figure 3.13. *Peanuts* comic strip, May 21, 1971. PEANUTS © Peanuts Worldwide LLC. Dist. by ANDREWS MCMEEL SYNDICATION. Reprinted with permission. All rights reserved.

Figure 3.14. *Peanuts* comic strip, May 20, 1971. PEANUTS © Peanuts Worldwide LLC. Dist. by ANDREWS MCMEEL SYNDICATION. Reprinted with permission. All rights reserved.

the emotional indifference often associated with cats than the loving loyalty commonly attributed to dogs, Snoopy asserts that he doesn't need Charlie Brown to dedicate his life to him. He was already happy on his own.

In these and other comics, Snoopy goes further than merely behaving like a cat; he can be seen as placing Charlie Brown in the position of being the dog. Stereotypically speaking, dogs are the ones who dedicate their lives to pleasing their masters and making them happy—which is what Charlie Brown proposes to Snoopy. Moreover, dogs are also known for being loyal and loving even to owners who ignore them, take them for granted, or treat them badly—a dynamic that, once again, is reversed between Schulz's principal character and his pet pooch. Snoopy often treats Charlie Brown poorly, but Charlie Brown remains dedicated to Snoopy. The strip that appeared on May 21, 1971, gives further credence to this viewpoint (fig. 3.13). Snoopy is sitting on top of his doghouse, working on his typewriter. Linus asks him what he is writing and points out that confessional books and exposé pieces are very popular now. Snoopy recognizes the wisdom in this suggestion. The final panel reveals the title of Snoopy's new article: "How It Feels to Be Owned by an Incompetent."

This moment is not the only time that Snoopy's role as an author reveals his feline qualities. In the comic that appeared on May 20, 1971, Linus once again has some writing suggestions for Snoopy (fig. 3.14). This time, Linus encourages him to compose a biography. Snoopy demurs, saying with a scowl,

"We dogs don't like anyone." This sentiment, of course, is more commonly associated with felines than canines. Indeed, dogs are often seen as befriending everyone with whom they come in contact. By contrast, cats are often regarded as being antisocial, even with their loving owners.

FAT CAT: THE PERSONAE, POSH POSSESSIONS, AND POMPOSITY OF SNOOPY

Snoopy does more than simply make remarks and adopt attitudes that recall cats. He engages in a variety of behaviors that mirror them as well. First and foremost, Snoopy is able to imitate one of the most famous literary felines of all time. In a sequence of strips that appeared during the week of April 18, 1967, Snoopy reveals that he has a unique talent: he can mimic the Cheshire Cat from *Alice's Adventures in Wonderland* (fig. 3.15). Snoopy first demonstrates this talent to Linus, who is reading aloud from Carroll's novel. "Beginning with one end of the tail, and ending with the grin, which remained for some time after the rest of it had gone," the young boy reads. In the following panel, Linus looks beside him and is shocked to see that Snoopy has disappeared except for a big toothy grin. "I've been able to do that for years," Snoopy says nonchalantly in the final panel. In strips that appeared over the following few days, Snoopy repeats this trick, both to Linus and to other *Peanuts* characters who do not believe that he possesses this ability. The strip on April 20, 1967, depicts almost the same sequence of events as the comic two days before. However, the passage from *Alice's Adventures in Wonderland* has changed. "'Well, I've often seen a cat without a grin,' thought Alice," Linus reads aloud to Snoopy in the first panel. "'But a grin without a cat! It's the most curious thing I ever saw in my entire life!'" he continues in the second drawing. The third panel once again shows that Snoopy's body has vanished; all that remains is his big smile. Not only does Schulz's pet beagle reveal that he possesses the same talent as Carroll's cat, but he also possesses an understanding of this ability that goes beyond it being a mere coincidence. "Actually, it's a conditioned reflex," Snoopy explains to Linus in the closing panel.

Snoopy's talents are not confined to this parlor trick. Charlie Brown's dog has a myriad of other interests, hobbies, and activities. Whereas most canines enjoy simple pastimes such as catching a Frisbee, fetching a ball, or going for walks with their owner, Snoopy's activities are more lofty: he writes novels, flies fighter jets, and serves as an astronaut—to name just a few. Furthermore, in keeping with the egotism and grandiosity that is more commonly

Figure 3.15. *Peanuts* comic strip, April 18, 1967. PEANUTS © Peanuts Worldwide LLC. Dist. by ANDREWS MCMEEL SYNDICATION. Reprinted with permission. All rights reserved.

associated with cats, Snoopy does not merely partake in any of these activities but is "world famous" at them. Over the decades, Snoopy declares himself a World Famous Author, World Famous Astronaut, World Famous Hockey Player, World Famous Surgeon, World Famous Tennis Player, and World Famous Attorney. The egotism involved in declaring oneself "world famous" at anything, let alone in multiple professions, goes beyond being merely grandiose or delusional. In the words of the journalist Michael Taube, it is "a classic example of a narcissist."

Snoopy's doghouse forms another powerful locus of his feline nature. The exterior of the structure, of course, is an important prop for Snoopy's imagination. The doghouse serves as his desk when he is writing novels, transforms into the Sopwith Camel aircraft when he battles the Red Baron, and becomes his office when he is the legal beagle. The unseen interior of the doghouse, however, is even more remarkable. The space not only defies the rules of physics by being much larger than the exterior suggests (or even supports), but it also exceeds any pet's wildest imagination. As readers learn over the years, Snoopy's doghouse contains multiple floors and boasts a pool table, a library, a stained-glass window, and a Van Gogh painting (Brandt 183). Moreover, when the doghouse is destroyed by a fire on November 4, 1966, Snoopy's new abode is just as grand. In fact, the main difference between the old doghouse and the new one is that Snoopy selects a more modern painting by Andrew Wyeth to replace the former one by Van Gogh (Brandt 183).

Despite having such posh decor, Snoopy routinely sleeps on top of his doghouse instead of inside it. This choice is strange and even inexplicable for a canine. As Schulz explained about his decision, "Snoopy himself had become a character so unlike a dog that he could no longer inhabit a real dog house" (Schulz, *Jubilee* 97–98). While dogs might not be known for sleeping in unusual places, cats are notorious for forsaking the items that their owners purchase for them—or for using them in wholly unintended ways.

Not only does Snoopy live in an abode that would be spectacular for a person let alone a dog, but he also gets others to maintain it. In the comic that

Figure 3.16. *Peanuts* comic strip, June 22, 1964. PEANUTS © Peanuts Worldwide LLC. Dist. by ANDREWS MCMEEL SYNDICATION. Reprinted with permission. All rights reserved.

appeared on June 22, 1964, Charlie Brown tells Snoopy that he has a surprise for him: "Some of your friends have agreed to get together and give your house a real good cleaning" (fig. 3.16). Charlie Brown goes on to say that they will begin working tomorrow. While most individuals would be grateful and delighted by this offer, Snoopy responds in way that is snobby, entitled, and thus catlike. "Just so they don't damage my Van Gogh or tear the cloth on my pool table," he quips haughtily in the final panel. In strips that appeared for the rest of that week, Charlie Brown and Linus work diligently to clean Snoopy's doghouse: mopping, sweeping, vacuuming, and so on. The closing panel of the comic that appeared on June 23, 1964, shows Snoopy sitting atop his doghouse and thinking, "I feel like I should be doing something to help." However, in a decision that once again seems more catlike than doglike, while Snoopy supervises as well as criticizes their efforts, he never physically assists them.

This sequence is not the only time that various characters work on Snoopy's doghouse for him. Later that year, in a plotline that began on September 21, 1964, and once again spanned the full week of strips, Linus returns to Snoopy's abode. This time, however, Linus is there not to clean but to paint a mural on the ceiling. Far from fluffy white clouds and a pretty blue sky, the mural depicts nothing less than the history of civilization. Admittedly, it is not clear whether Linus selected this subject matter or Snoopy did. Regardless, Snoopy has agreed to it. Like the previous time that characters worked on his doghouse, Snoopy not only doesn't help Linus with the mural but isn't even appreciative of it. In the final comic in the sequence, Charlie Brown is having a heated argument with Snoopy. Linus has now finished painting, but Snoopy adamantly refuses to go see it. **"WHAT? You're not even going to look at it?!"** an exasperated Charlie Brown shouts in the first two panels (bold in original). Snoopy is not persuaded, however. The final panel shows him casually lounging under a tree. The thought balloon above his head provides his justification for refusing to look at Linus's mural: "For my kind, the story of civilization has always left much to be desired!" Significantly,

Snoopy says "For my kind" rather than "For dogs" in this statement. His choice of a nonspecific noun suggests that Snoopy sees himself as belonging to a group that is something other than—or at least broader than—canines. At the least, his haughty comment reveals that Snoopy is inviting readers to rethink what might be called his animal cat-egory.

Giving further credence to this viewpoint, instances where Snoopy engages in more traditional doglike behavior or "provid[es] some canine service typically result in Snoopy's resentment, or in his shirking the duties expected of him" (Brandt 181). The comics in which Frieda chastises Charlie Brown's pet pooch for not chasing rabbits offer some telling examples. In various strips during the 1960s, she tells Snoopy to go outside so that he can be with his "own kind." Furthermore, she reminds him that chasing rabbits is what beagles "naturally" do. Whereas most dogs delight in the opportunity to run, romp, and chase, Snoopy is not interested. In a feature that once again seems more feline than canine, he prefers to sleep atop his doghouse all day than engage in any physical activity. Accordingly, the pooch not only rebuffs Frieda but does so in a way that is oxymoronic. In the strip from September 15, 1967, for example, Snoopy gives the following reason why he doesn't want to play with the neighborhood canines: "I would, but I hate getting covered with a lot of dog hair." The joke, of course, is that Snoopy is already covered in dog fur—after all, he is a dog. However, the comment also suggests that Snoopy doesn't actually see himself as a canine.

Frieda is not the only character who encourages Snoopy to engage in activities commonly associated with dogs—and whose efforts are rebuffed. At various points, Sally and Rerun have the same experiences. In comics that appeared during the late 1960s, Sally is being bullied by some kids at school, so she tries to enlist Snoopy as her guard dog or even attack dog. In the strip that appeared on January 26, 1968, for example, she asks Snoopy to go bite a boy who has insulted her. Once again, whereas most dogs are fiercely loyal to the people whom they love and are eager to protect them, Snoopy's response to his owner's little sister is far different. "Bite someone . . . just to get even?" he says with dismay in the closing panels. "How gauche!" (fig. 3.17). Both the content of Snoopy's sentiments and also his aristocratic word choice are far more suggestive of the dignified demeanor attributed to cats than to dogs.

Rerun's attempt to get Snoopy to engage in some canine activities is even more disastrous—and telling. In the comic that appeared on July 5, 1995, Linus's younger brother rings Charlie Brown's doorbell and asks Schulz's protagonist if Snoopy can come out to play "chase the stick" (fig. 3.18). In the next panel, Snoopy himself has come to the door. He hands Rerun a note that reads: "Thank you for your offer to come out and play. . . . We are busy

Figure 3.17. *Peanuts* comic strip, January 26, 1968. PEANUTS © Peanuts Worldwide LLC. Dist. by ANDREWS MCMEEL SYNDICATION. Reprinted with permission. All rights reserved.

Figure 3.18. *Peanuts* comic strip, July 5, 1995. PEANUTS © Peanuts Worldwide LLC. Dist. by ANDREWS MCMEEL SYNDICATION. Reprinted with permission. All rights reserved.

at this time, however, and cannot accept your offer. . . . We hope you will be successful elsewhere." Once again, both the fact that Snoopy is declining an invitation to play and the manner in which he does so are more catlike than doglike. Although Rerun is surprised by Snoopy's note, he shouldn't be. As Schulz himself reflected about his comic strip canine, "Snoopy refuses to be caught in the trap of doing ordinary things like chasing and retrieving sticks" (Schulz, *Jubilee* 86).

Of course, *Peanuts* contains more than seventeen thousand strips. While Snoopy does not appear in all of them, his presence is sufficiently common that my discussion represents only a small sampling of his full portrayal in the series. To be fair, there are strips where Snoopy affirms and even seems to embrace his doggy identity. One of his personae during springtime, for example, is the "Easter Beagle." Additionally, on August 26 of various years, he often reminds everyone that it is National Dog Day. Finally, in a sequence of strips that appeared from February through March 1970, Snoopy is promoted to the esteemed position of "Head Beagle."

That said, even in strips where Snoopy is ostensibly embracing being a beagle, he often thinks and acts more like a stereotypical feline. The comic that appeared on April 18, 1976, provides an excellent case in point. Appearing on Easter Sunday, it showcases an episode of Snoopy as the Easter Beagle

Figure 3.19. *Peanuts* comic strip, April 18, 1976. PEANUTS © Peanuts Worldwide LLC. Dist. by ANDREWS MCMEEL SYNDICATION. Reprinted with permission. All rights reserved.

(fig. 3.19). In the opening panels, Linus attempts to rouse the pooch from atop his doghouse. Whereas most canines would leap out of bed on the day they got to be the Easter Beagle, Snoopy declares, "I'm sleeping in." In the panels that follow, Schulz's pooch shifts from resembling a lazy cat to being more like the twenty-first-century internet sensation Grumpy Cat. Saying that he is not feeling well after eating too many pizzas the night before, Snoopy has no interest in making his yearly rounds distributing colored eggs. When Linus tells him that he can't disappoint the kids, the pooch offers the following sardonic response: "Why not? It'll be good for 'em. It'll prepare 'em for adulthood." Linus eventually drags Charlie Brown's pet off the doghouse. However, Snoopy fulfills his duties as Easter Beagle not merely grudgingly but grouchily. "Stupid kids," he thinks to himself in the penultimate panel while literally chucking eggs haphazardly at a slack-jawed Sally and Lucy. Lest any doubts remain about Snoopy's sour state of mind, the thought balloon over his head also contains the words "*Grumble, Grumble, Grumble*" (italics in original).

Snoopy may act like a cat in many strips, but the full cast of *Peanuts* includes a character who is an actual feline. On May 23, 1961, Faron made his debut. As the official *Peanuts* fandom page asserts, Faron officially belongs to Frieda, but "he serves as a foil for Snoopy." At multiple points, Frieda imposes on Snoopy to watch, hold, and generally interact with her pet cat, who is always so limp and floppy that he doesn't seem to have a skeletal structure. Each time, Snoopy is perplexed by the bizarre creature, unsure what to make of him. "This is a **CAT?!!**" a bewildered Snoopy remarks upon first seeing Faron (bold in original). Even after spending some time alone with the feline, Snoopy still doesn't understand him. In the final panel of the strip on May 24, 1961, he wonders, "What do you **say** to cats?" (bold in original).

Faron's role in *Peanuts*, however, was short-lived. The cat's final appearance was in the strip from November 20, 1961, roughly six months after his debut. As Schulz commented, the reason for eliminating Faron was twofold. First and foremost, the cartoonist confessed, "I don't draw a cat well" (Schulz, "Theme" 157). While this point is debatable, Schulz offered a second, and more significant, reason. The introduction of a cat into *Peanuts*, he explained, "brought Snoopy back to being too much of a real dog" (Schulz, *Jubilee* 97). Faron turned the comic into "a traditional cat-and-dog strip, which was something I certainly wanted to avoid" ("Theme" 157). This dynamic limited Snoopy to plotlines involving little more than adversarial chases. In the words of Schulz once again, "By the time the cat had come into the strip, Snoopy was drifting further and further into his fantasy life, and it was important to that he continue in that direction" (*Jubilee* 97). For these reasons, the cartoonist returned to scenarios involving the unseen "cat next door," who first began terrorizing Snoopy back in 1958 by slashing at him and (more commonly) shredding his doghouse. As Schulz commented, "An offstage cat works better than a real one in the same way that the little red-haired girl, Linus's blanket-hating grandmother, Charlie Brown's father, the barber, and the kids' teachers all work better in the reader's imagination" (*Jubilee* 97).

Although the literal cat Faron disappeared from *Peanuts* in November 1961, the presence of a metaphorical cat remained in the form of Snoopy. In the years that followed, Charlie Brown's canine often mirrored a feline in the way that he conversed, conducted, and carried himself. From lounging around atop his doghouse and rebuffing invitations to play to being finicky about his food and having delusions of grandeur, Snoopy often behaved more like a stereotypical cat than a dog. Faron may have been eliminated by Schulz, but Snoopy routinely and even consistently exhibited an array of feline qualities.

BAD DOG: SNOOPY AND A NEW SPECIES OF FAILURE IN *PEANUTS*

Accomplishing tasks, being successful, and coming out on top are not traits with which the characters in *Peanuts* are associated. On the contrary, Schulz's figures are more commonly known for making mistakes, for having things go wrong, and even for being losers. As Tim Darling aptly noted, "Failure and rejection are both prevalent in *Peanuts*, providing the foundation for many of the strips." Many of the recurring and even most popular plotlines of the series showcase these elements. Charlie Brown is an abysmal manager of the baseball team, unable to shepherd his team to even a single victory. Likewise, he can never fly his kite without it getting caught in the same tree. Along the same lines, Charlie Brown cannot muster the courage to speak to his longtime crush, the Little Red-Haired Girl. Similarly, he never receives a valentine from any of his other classmates at school. Finally, and most famously of all, Schulz's principal character never kicks the football; furthermore, he is never even able to resist being duped into trying by Lucy. Meanwhile, Lucy, with all of her bluster and bossiness, fares little better. In spite of her efforts, she never wins the heart of her crush, Schroeder. Additionally, Lucy may have her own psychiatry booth, but she is a terrible therapist, dispensing not simply unhelpful but even insensitive advice. Lucy's younger brother Linus—who is also Charlie Brown's best friend—experiences his own disappointments. Although he patiently waits in the garden patch each Halloween, he never meets the Great Pumpkin.

Blunders, mistakes, and disappointments are so common in *Peanuts* in general and for Schulz's principal character in particular that Violet tells Charlie Brown in the comic from June 29, 1960, "You know what I see when I look at you, Charlie Brown? I see failure! I see failure written all over your face." Although her comment is harsh, it is also accurate. In strips that appeared over the next few days, Charlie Brown asks other characters whether they agree with Violet. Everyone affirms that he has what Lucy bluntly calls a "failure face." This attribute became such a core feature of Charlie Brown that it served as the basis for a song in the 1969 Academy Award–nominated animated film *A Boy Named Charlie Brown*.

For all his egotism and bravado, Snoopy is also a frequent failure. Although he touts himself as a "World Famous Author," never finds a publisher for his novel.[1] On the contrary, in numerous strips over the decades, he receives rejection notice after rejection notice, and many of them are brutal. "Dear Contributor, we are returning your stupid story," a letter from the comic that appeared on January 20, 1996, begins. "Please don't send us any more. Please,

Please, Please...." Even in the face of such harsh criticism, however, Snoopy's ego remains unscathed. Whereas many dogs would be saddened or at least unsettled after being criticized in this way, Snoopy is unfazed. The rejection notices never cause him to scale back his self-proclaimed status as a "World Famous Author" or even to doubt his talents. The comic from January 9, 1985, provides a telling snapshot of Snoopy's attitude toward criticism, especially when it comes to his writing. In the opening panel, Peppermint Patty complains to Charlie Brown about a poor grade that she received on an essay. She then proceeds to share some of the teacher's comments about her writing; needless to say, all of them are unflattering. The final panel shows Snoopy lying atop his doghouse, listening to their discussion. A thought balloon above his head relays his view on the situation. "Never listen to reviewers," he opines (fig. 3.20). Once again, cats are more commonly seen as not caring about what others think of them. Dogs, who are generally people pleasers, are usually acutely interested and even invested. It is difficult to imagine a dog not being concerned about criticism, let alone never listening to it.

Snoopy's writing is not the only arena in which he fails to achieve his goals or live up to his lofty accolades. On the contrary, disappointment and even defeat riddle nearly all the personae that he embodies.[2] In spite of identifying himself as a World Famous Attorney, for example, the legal beagle never wins a single case. Additionally, for all of Snoopy's insistence that he is a World Famous Hockey Player, he never hoists the Stanley Cup. On the contrary, he spends most of his time in the penalty box, yelling at the refs. Along the same lines, Snoopy may identify himself as a World Famous Tennis Player, but his confidence quickly crumbles once he sets foot on the court ("World Famous Tennis"). Even Snoopy's encounters with the Red Baron generally end badly: his doghouse is riddled with bullet holes, and the Flying Ace vows to get his revenge next time that the two cross paths.

The aspects of Snoopy's personality that place him in dialogue with stereotypical feline traits rather than canine qualities add a new facet to this character's failures as well as to this core theme in *Peanuts*. Together with failing at being a World War I flying ace, novelist, lawyer, and athlete, Snoopy fails at being a dog in many ways. From his disdain for playing fetch to the ambivalence that he often expresses toward his owner, Charlie Brown's pet resists and even rejects behaviors commonly associated with canines. Moreover, what could be a greater failure for a dog than to behave more like a cat? And yet many of the ways in which Snoopy does not act—as Charlie Brown often points out—like a "normal dog" are in keeping with the conduct of a "normal" or, at least, stereotypical cat. Adding another dimension to how mistakes, blunders, and shortcomings form a central theme of *Peanuts*, the

Figure 3.20. *Peanuts* comic strip, January 9, 1985. PEANUTS © Peanuts Worldwide LLC. Dist. by ANDREWS MCMEEL SYNDICATION. Reprinted with permission. All rights reserved.

ways in which Snoopy fails at being a canine constitute some of his signature traits and even hallmark qualities. From his finicky palate and penchant for sleeping atop his doghouse to his indifference to criticism and grandiose view of his artistic, intellectual, and athletic abilities, Snoopy is beloved precisely because of his traits that are more feline than canine. As with the rest of Schulz's flawed cast, these shortcomings may make Snoopy a "bad" dog, but they make him an exceedingly good character: complex, unique, and interesting. Indeed, if Snoopy behaved like a "normal dog" as Charlie Brown often wishes, he would not be as noteworthy. It is precisely because Snoopy fails at being a dog that he succeeds at being distinctive figure in the strip and a memorable personality with its audience.

This new view of Snoopy expands our understanding of this central theme in *Peanuts* while also offering a counterpoint to many of the criticisms levied against the character over the years. Many of the complaints made about Snoopy are also ones made about cats. Daniel Mendelsohn, writing for the *New York Times Book Review*, for example, accused the beagle of "smugness," "pomposity," and "rank egotism." Christopher Caldwell echoed such sentiments, asserting that Snoopy suffers from "delusional self-love." Sarah Boxer, in an essay that revisited these viewpoints, noted how critics have disliked Snoopy for decades primarily because they see him as suffering from "narcissism." She goes on to discuss how "his confidence," "his airs and fantasies," and "his total lack of concern about what other thought of him" rendered Charlie Brown's beagle "fundamentally rotten." If Snoopy's flaws as a canine character are attributed to his feline qualities, then one can hardly fault him for his egotism, pomposity, and grandiose view of himself. After all, these traits are typical of cats.

Christopher Caldwell, near the end of his essay lamenting the decline of Schulz's comic strip, wrote: "For the first half of its existence, 'Peanuts' had all the subtlety and scope of a really good novel; for the last half, it has had all the subtlety and scope of a cat calendar." Although this comment was meant to be derisive, it was also unintentionally insightful. If *Peanuts* did become more like a "cat calendar" as the years passed, it did so because its star Snoopy became more like a cat in many respects. Rather than disparage the changes that took place to this character and, by extension, to Schulz's strip, we should explore their critical, interpretive, and thematic possibilities.

Whether he is behaving like a dog, cat, or human, one detail is clear: Snoopy is a complex character. The next chapter examines the *Peanuts* figure who arguably has the most complex relationship with the already complex Snoopy: Lucy Van Pelt. Mirroring her own fickle nature, Lucy alternates between loving Charlie Brown's pet and being repulsed by him. In the strip that appeared on April 25, 1960, Lucy famously gives Snoopy a big hug and declares, "Happiness is a warm puppy." This sweet sentiment and adorable embrace formed the basis for the best-selling *Peanuts* gift book by the same name, *Happiness Is a Warm Puppy* (1962). Lucy's relationship to Snoopy, however, is not this simple or this positive. Just a few years later, in the comic that appeared on February 21, 1965, Lucy's reaction to having physical contact with Snoopy was markedly different. In lines that were antithetical to "happiness is a warm puppy" but would become just as well known, when Snoopy gives her a peck on the cheek, Lucy exclaims: "**AAUGH!** Someone get me some soap and water! I've just been kissed by a dog! Get **HOT** water! Get some disinfectant! Get some iodine!" (bold in original).[3] These two equally emphatic responses invite audiences to wonder about Lucy's true feelings toward Snoopy: does she love him, or is she repulsed by him?

The next chapter examines some additional, and long unexplored, contradictions of Lucy Van Pelt. This *Peanuts* character is widely known for being bossy, demanding, and short-tempered. Echoing her paradoxical relationship to Snoopy, however, Schulz's infamous fussbudget was not always depicted in this way. When Lucy made her debut, she had a markedly different personality and played an equally different role in the strip: she was ditzy, and she engaged in slapstick. In chapter 1, I pointed out that, contrary to popular opinion, Schulz was not able-bodied. Chapter 2 made a case that, in defiance of long-standing views, the pattern across Charlie Brown's famous shirt can be seen as something other than a zigzag. This chapter argued that Snoopy often acts more like a cat than a dog. The next chapter continues this trend. In keeping with my project of offering new perspectives on Schulz's core characters, chapter 4 calls attention to the connections between Lucy Van Pelt and another famous Lucy during the early 1950s: Lucy Ricardo. In the same way that Schulz's canine possesses an array of traits more commonly associated with felines, his character who would come to be known as "crabby" can be seen as having an initial kinship with an icon of television comedy.

CHAPTER 4

I LOVE LUCY

The Fussbudget and the First Lady of Sitcoms

If Snoopy is the most famous character from *Peanuts*, then Lucy Van Pelt is the most infamous. Making her debut on March 3, 1952, she quickly became a core member of the cast. Commonly identified by her blue party dress and saddle shoes, she was even more well known for her distinctive personality. Whereas most of the characters in *Peanuts* were gentle, quiet, and even meek, Lucy was demanding, opinionated, and loud. She tormented her younger brother Linus, stealing his beloved security blanket, mocking his belief in the Great Pumpkin, and often threatening to "knock his block off!" Linus was not the sole target of Lucy's ire; she belittled, barked orders at, and was belligerent toward other characters as well. Lucy's annual prank on Charlie Brown, for example, formed one of the strip's most well-known plotlines: every autumn, she would pull a football away from Charlie Brown when he went to kick it, even after explicitly promising that she would not. Given her grouchy, brash, and even sour personality, Lucy is often described—both by characters in the strip and by critics outside it—as "crabby" and "a fussbudget." While *Peanuts* does not have a villain, Lucy can certainly be regarded as its antagonist.

Although Lucy Van Pelt is now associated with being brash and bossy, her character did not always behave in this way. For her first few years in Schulz's strip, she was depicted as both much younger and much kinder. Lucy began as a wide-eyed toddler who was clumsy, dopey, and naive. Far from being disdainful, she was daft. Rather than acting like a bully, she acted like a baby. Instead of making sarcastic remarks, she engaged in slapstick comedy.

This chapter revisits the debut of Lucy Van Pelt, remembering and recouping her original personality. Doing so provides a far different portrait of this well-known figure from Schulz's strip, prompting us to see her in a whole new way. Even more importantly, Lucy's initial portrayal also invites us to reexamine her original sociohistorical context. In the early 1950s, when Lucy Van Pelt made her first appearance in *Peanuts*, another character named Lucy permeated American popular culture: Lucy Ricardo from the television show *I Love Lucy*. The groundbreaking sitcom, featuring the title character, her husband Ricky, and their neighbors Ethel and Fred, first aired in autumn 1951 and was an immediate success. By the time that Lucy Van Pelt appeared in *Peanuts* nearly six months later, *I Love Lucy* was not merely a runaway hit but a cultural phenomenon. The character Lucy Ricardo was a household name, and watching the show on Monday nights was a national pastime.

In a historical detail that has been long overlooked, Lucy Van Pelt was created and introduced against the backdrop of the *I Love Lucy* craze. However unexpected and even unlikely, the initial portrayal of Schulz's fussbudget shares a variety of commonalities with the figure who is commonly remembered as the First Lady of Sitcoms. Exploring the links between Lucy Van Pelt and Lucy Ricardo reveals a possible new source of influence on one of Schulz's most famous characters. The suggestive echoes between Lucy Van Pelt and Lucy Ricardo locate *Peanuts* within one of the most significant events taking place in American popular culture during the postwar years. Furthermore, they call attention to another long-overlooked area of cultural cross-pollination: the one between television sitcoms and newspaper comics.

"AMERICA SIMPLY SHUT DOWN WHEN 'I LOVE LUCY' CAME ON": REMEMBERING THE UNPRECEDENTED POSTWAR POPULARITY OF *I LOVE LUCY*

The contemporaneous success of *I Love Lucy*, along with its historical impact, is difficult to exaggerate. Although the sitcom was on the air for only six seasons, it experienced both critical acclaim and commercial popularity on a scale that had never occurred before—nor, arguably, has happened since. Lori Landay has called it "the show in which the conventions, structure, and style of the sitcom genre were codified" (Landay, "Postwar Ideology" 87). Furthermore, "It may well be the most popular situation comedy ever" (87). At the least, as Wes Gehring observed, *I Love Lucy* "forever change[d] the nature of American pop culture."

I Love Lucy enjoyed unprecedented ratings. Airing Monday nights at 9 p.m. on CBS, the show was an instant success from the broadcast of the first episode on October 15, 1951. "By February 1952, just four months after *I Love Lucy* premiered, the [sitcom] was . . . number one" (Landay, "Postwar Ideology" 92). This impressive achievement was just one of many milestones during the first season. The episode "The Marriage License," which aired on April 7, 1952, was the "first sitcom to be seen in 10 million homes—at a time when there were only about 15 million TV sets in the U.S." (Fenton 18). Soon, *I Love Lucy* would break its own record. "By May, an estimated 11,055,000 American families were inviting the Ricardos and Mertzes into their living rooms every Monday night" (Andrews 80).

In light of these figures, rather than asking who *was* watching *I Love Lucy* in the 1950s, a better question would be who *wasn't* tuning in. As Wes Gehring commented, "America simply shut down when 'I Love Lucy' came on. Across the nation, the once-popular Monday-night department store shopping hours were being switched to evenings that did not compete with the series." At Marshall Field's in downtown Chicago, "the management put up a sign in the window on State Street declaring: 'We love Lucy, too, so we're closing on Monday nights'" (Andrews x). Such comments notwithstanding, the desire of the store's staff to watch the show was a secondary issue. Arguably the real reason why Marshall Field's closed early on Monday evenings was that no customers came in: all the would-be shoppers were at home watching television.

Consumer habits were not the only area of American life affected by the sitcom. In the words of Bart Andrews, "The 'Lucy' mania was so widespread that telephone companies actually reported a 'substantial reduction' in calls during that half-hour period" (x). Similarly, taxi service also saw a dramatic drop-off during episodes of *I Love Lucy*. Not only were potential fares sitting in front of television sets rather than traveling the streets, but so were the drivers themselves. "Cabbies disappeared into bars to catch a glimpse of Lucy and Ricky and Fred and Ethel uncoiling their latest plot," Andrews writes, "and didn't turn on their ignitions again until 9:30pm" (Andrews x). Even more astounding, police departments "reported [an] ongoing drop in crime that evening in several eastern cities" during show's time slot (Gehring).

Perhaps unsurprisingly given these events, *I Love Lucy* is credited not merely with popularizing the sitcom but also with popularizing the medium of television as a whole. As Stuart Miller reported, "In 1950, there were television sets in only 10 million American households. Two years later that number had doubled. The difference? In October 1951, Lucille Ball and Desi Arnaz introduced the nation to 'I Love Lucy'" (143). Even if the show did not prompt Americans to purchase a set, it got many interested in television. Across the country, "families without TV sets crowded into neighbors' living rooms to watch their favorite redhead" (Andrews x). Indeed, many of the taxi fares in big cities before the show's airtime were individuals heading to the home of a friend, the living room of a relative, or a neighborhood bar to watch the show.

The national craze for *I Love Lucy* was so pervasive that whether someone was a fan of the program or not, it could not be avoided. Articles about Lucille Ball, Desi Arnaz, Vivian Vance, and William Frawley "hit all the major newspapers and magazines" (Landay, "Postwar Ideology" 92). Additionally, by the end of the first season, an array of consumer goods that were either branded with the *I Love Lucy* logo or modeled after items featured in the Ricardo apartment appeared in stores. Fans of the show could purchase collectibles, toys, home decor, paper dolls, kitchenware, clothing, stationary, and jewelry (Landay, "Lucy Mystique" 29). At one point, a bedroom set that was an exact replica of the one on the sitcom was available. "Live Like Lucy (You'll Love It!)," the ads for the multipiece furniture suite announced (Johnson-Carper Furniture Company 38).

Far from being a fleeting fad, *I Love Lucy* remained exceedingly popular throughout its time on the air. The show was number one in the Nielsen ratings for four out of its six seasons (Nussbaum 2). Moreover, viewership for some episodes remains unparalleled. An episode from season 2, "Lucy Goes to the Hospital," which aired on January 19, 1953, and featured the birth of Little Ricky Ricardo, attracted 44 million viewers, or an astounding "92% of all people watching television that night" (Miller 143). Furthermore, the audience for that episode "actually beat President Dwight Eisenhower's inauguration in the ratings when broadcast in January 1953" (Pitman 56). Whereas many television shows experience a gradual decline the longer they are on the air—as the characters grow stale, the plots less innovative, the writing not as sharp—*I Love Lucy* continued to deliver. As Chay Lemoine has noted, episodes that have come to be considered classics are spread out over the seasons. "Lucy Does a TV Commercial," where she gets drunk from the health tonic Vitameatavegamin, for example, aired in season 1. "Job Switching," where Lucy and Ethel stuff themselves with chocolate when they can't keep up with the conveyer belt at the candy factory, aired in season 2. "L.A. at Last," where Lucy dons a fake nose made out of putty to hide her appearance from the movie star William Holden, aired in season 4. Finally, "Lucy's Italian Movie," where she takes a job stomping grapes at a vineyard to practice for a movie role, aired in season 5.

I Love Lucy was as lauded by critics as it was loved by audiences. The show was nominated for no fewer than twenty-three Emmy Awards, winning five times: for Best Situation Comedy in 1953 and 1954; for Best Comedienne and Best Actress for Lucille Ball in 1953 and 1956, respectively; and for Best Supporting Actress for Vivian Vance in 1954. These accolades, however, do not fully capture the show's impact on the entertainment industry. In comments that have been echoed by many other critics over the years, Emily Todd VanDerWerff observed, "The series is legitimately the most influential in TV history, pioneering so many innovations and normalizing so many others." Examples include the show's use of three different camera positions, the decision to perform in front of a studio audience, and the fact that the show was recorded on film rather than broadcast live (Bianculli 264–68). As Chris Morgan has written, all these features, which were either pioneered by *I Love Lucy* or popularized by the series, "would become a staple of the sitcom." Given the important role that *I Love Lucy* played in the development of this entertainment genre, it is only fitting that the sitcom "was the first show inducted into the Television Hall of Fame" (Morgan).

By any metric, *I Love Lucy* exerted a tremendous influence on postwar American life. The 1950s are commonly identified as inaugurating "the Golden Age of Television." As figures like David Bianculli and Saul Austerlitz have written, the decade gave rise to a multitude of programs—from *The Adventures of Ozzie and Harriet* (1952–66), *Father Knows Best* (1954–60), and *The Honeymooners* (1955–56) to *Perry Mason* (1957–66), *The Twilight Zone* (1959–64), and *Gunsmoke* (1955–75)—that would become classics, serving as touchstones for decades to come. Given the key role that *I Love Lucy* played both in popularizing television and in establishing its conventions, this era might need to be renamed. Instead of the fifties being termed the Golden Age of Television, the centrality of the CBS sitcom and especially the appeal of its redheaded star suggest that a more accurate description might be the Auburn, Scarlet, or Ginger Age.

LUCY GOOSEY: LUCY RICARDO AND LUCY VAN PELT

When Charles M. Schulz created Lucy Van Pelt, he modeled her after a real-life person. As the cartoonist often commented—and critics and biographers have just as frequently repeated—the new *Peanuts* character was based on the cartoonist's stepdaughter, Meredith.[1] "'[Lucy] didn't do much at first,' recalled Schulz. 'She came in as a cute little girl and at first she was patterned after our own first daughter,' rambling through the house in her Dr. Denton sleepers, speaking of herself in the third person, falling out of her crib, fussing" (Michaelis 248). Although the cartoonist insisted throughout his career that he did not base his comic strip on his life, "Lucy's ploys—waiting until *after* her father had tucked her in and returned to his easy chair and newspaper before demanding a glass of water—were Meredith's" (248–49). So too was the character's now-famous nickname. "Schulz would remember calling Meredith 'a fussbudget' when she was very small, 'and from this I applied the term to Lucy'" (249).²

While Lucy Van Pelt undeniably had her roots in Schulz's stepdaughter, this real-life individual may not have been the only source of influence. As Michael McClay has commented, "Few people have a monopoly over a name, and Lucille Ball was one of them. Anywhere in the world where *I Love Lucy* is seen—and that's just about everywhere—the name 'Lucy' can only mean one person" (McClay 3). This observation was arguably even more true in the early 1950s, when the popularity of the sitcom consumed the nation. Both while Schulz was crafting his new *Peanuts* character, and especially when she made her debut on March 3, 1952, the name "Lucy" was strongly associated with one individual: Lucy Ricardo. Perhaps unsurprisingly, given the original cultural context for *Peanuts*, Lucy Van Pelt shares an array of physical, behavioral, and personal traits with Lucy Ricardo. Whether these areas of overlap were conscious or unconscious, intentional or unintentional, deliberate or coincidental, they shed new light on Lucy Van Pelt's original personality, visual presentation, and comedic role in the strip. Remembering and recouping the popularity of *I Love Lucy* restores an important but long-overlooked backdrop to the debut of Lucy Van Pelt while also connecting Schulz's comic with one of the most significant events in postwar popular culture—along with American entertainment history.

While the basic premise, individual plots, and sharp writing for *I Love Lucy* were all key factors in the sitcom's success, none of these details would have been the same without Lucille Ball. The actress's performance in each episode made *I Love Lucy* so funny, so popular, and so memorable to this day. Akin to other comedians, many of the laughs that Ball generated came from the way that she used her physical body. More specifically, as Chay Lemoine has noted, "Ball played to the audience with her over-the-top facial expressions" (7). From the hilarious looks that she gives Ethel as they fall hopelessly behind when wrapping chocolates at the candy factory to the faces that she makes while getting increasingly drunk on Vitameatavegamin, much of Ball's humor was rooted in her face. One of her signature visages, in fact, was the "saucer-sized eyes when she was caught in a lie" (Gehring). Nearly every episode includes a moment when Ball looks into the camera with her eyes opened wide in amazement, confusion, or surprise (figs. 4.1–4.3). Indeed, this expression is such a common feature of her performances that it is routinely featured in still images of the show. Similarly, it is also the one chosen to adorn the cover of many *I Love Lucy* books, video sets, and collectibles (figs. 4.4–4.6).

I Love Lucy: The Fussbudget and the First Lady of Sitcoms

Figure 4.1. Still image from *I Love Lucy*. Season 1, ep. 27, "The Kleptomaniac." First aired on April 14, 1952. CBS.

Figure 4.2. Still image from *I Love Lucy*. Season 2, ep. 1, "Job Switching." First aired on September 15, 1952. CBS.

Figure 4.3. Still image from *I Love Lucy*. Season 3, ep. 18, "Ricky Loses His Temper." First aired on February 22, 1954. CBS.

Figure 4.4. Front cover of *Ball of Fire: The Tumultuous Life and Comic Art of Lucille Ball*, by Stefan Kanfer (Knopf, 2003).

Figure 4.5. Front cover of *The Best of "I Love Lucy" Collection*, set 1. Paramount, 2003. VHS.

Figure 4.6. *I Love Lucy* magnet. Lucy-Desi Museum Official Shop.

Figure 4.7. *Peanuts* comic strip, March 3, 1952. PEANUTS © Peanuts Worldwide LLC. Dist. by ANDREWS MCMEEL SYNDICATION. Reprinted with permission. All rights reserved.

Figure 4.8. Side-by-side comparison of Lucy Van Pelt and Lucy Ricardo. Image constructed using the final panel from the *Peanuts* comic strip of March 7, 1952, in which Lucy makes her debut, and an *I Love Lucy* collectible magnet.

While Lucy Van Pelt is now commonly associated with her black hair, blue party dress, and saddle shoes, she possessed another signature physical trait when she appeared in 1952: her eyes. To distinguish the new character from existing members of the *Peanuts* cast, Schulz added round circles around the black dots of Lucy's eyes (fig. 4.7). The effect succeeded in making the new figure distinctive, but not in the way that the cartoonist had hoped. The circles around her eyes caused her to look stunned and even hypnotized. Regardless of the emotion that the character was feeling—happiness, sadness, boredom, contentment, joy, anger—the circles gave her face a dazed and even psychedelic look. The circles also caused Lucy Van Pelt to look remarkably like Lucy Ricardo. The wide-eyed expression gave her countenance a sense of surprise, dismay, and even vapidity that was surprisingly similar to Lucy Ricardo's signature comedic visage (fig. 4.8). Especially for Schulz's original readership, who were immersed in the popularity of *I Love Lucy* and surrounded by images of Lucille Ball displaying this signature facial expression, the way that the young comics character resembled the adult television character may have been even more apparent—and more striking.

The age of Schulz's new character forms another, unexpected area of overlap between her and Lucy Ricardo. Like many new members of the *Peanuts* cast, when Lucy Van Pelt debuted in the newspaper strip, she was still a toddler who slept in a crib. The humor in a variety of these early strips, in fact, showcases behavior that is typical for kids her age: Lucy delays bedtime by asking for another glass of water (March 17, 1952), deliberately throws a toy out of her crib and then calls for her father to pick it up (March 24, 1952), and makes a huge mess in her high chair during mealtime (May 22, 1952).

Lucy Ricardo, of course, is a grown woman. Not only is she married, but—in a groundbreaking moment from season 2—she becomes a parent herself. Although Lucy is a full-grown adult from the start of the sitcom, she often does not act like one. On the contrary, in nearly every episode, she sulks, pouts, cries, lies, whines, and schemes in ways that are more in keeping with the conduct of a young child. This trait did not go unnoticed by critics, past or present. Elizabeth Edwards, for example, remarked how often Lucy Ricardo "acts like a pre-schooler" (*Fifty Years* 43). Saul Austerlitz went one step further, writing, "She is an overgrown infant playing housewife" (16). In subsequent comments, Austerlitz expanded on these sentiments: "She can no more hide her emotions than a young child can," he observed; "her two most prominent—petulance and sadness—arc over the full emotional palette of the toddler" (16). Even critics who were less harsh in their assessment of Lucy Ricardo agreed that her behavior was uncharacteristic of a grown woman. Over the years, a common adjective used to describe her is "childlike" (Lemoine 6; Jordan 16; Edwards, *Fifty Years* 9).

Together with pouting, whining, and crying, another trait fueling Lucy Ricardo's childlike nature is her foolishness. Despite her character's penchant for concocting schemes and finding loopholes, she is not presented as being particularly sharp. On the contrary, "Lucy is addle-headed" (Austerlitz 16). Her plans are never fully thought out—or thought through. They usually overlook a key detail—such as the alcohol content on the bottle of Vitameatavegamin—or minimize an essential component, like the fact that she and Ethel have no experience working in a candy factory. As a result, Lucy's schemes always backfire in hilarious ways. The end result, as Emily Todd VanDerWerff notes, is that Lucy is "generally running around acting like an idiot." Indeed, in the same way that Lucy is often described as "childlike," she is also routinely characterized as "ditzy" (Keogh 37) and a "dingbat" (VanDerWerff).

The same descriptors could be applied to the original portrayal of Lucy Van Pelt. Although this character would eventually become quick-witted—especially when it came to insulting Charlie Brown or harassing her young brother Linus—she was initially presented as dim, dense, and even dumb. Moreover, such traits could not be attributed simply to the fact that she was a young child. While toddler-age kids might be unaware, uninformed, and even naive, Schulz presented Lucy as obtuse, idiotic, and even vapid. The comic in which Lucy Van Pelt made her debut provides a snapshot of her nature—as well as of her initial portrayal in the strip (fig. 4.7). The first panel shows Charlie Brown sitting in the grass and hearing someone out of the frame say "One, one, one" repeatedly (Schulz 158). The image that follows shifts the perspective to reveal the individual uttering this number over and over again: it is Lucy, who is jumping rope. In an effort to help the younger girl out, Charlie Brown shouts "TWO, LUCY! TWO!" The final panel provides the punch line while also offering a commentary about Lucy's intelligence. The character continues to jump rope, only now she is counting "Two, two, two" with each revolution.

The scenario depicted in this strip was not atypical. A variety of subsequent early comics present Lucy in a similar way. In the strip from July 17, 1952, for example, she shouts, "Hello? Hello?! HELLO?!!" at a ringing telephone without picking up the receiver, then walks away dumbfounded after no one responds (Schulz 222). Likewise, in the comic that appeared a few weeks later, on August 2, 1952, Lucy continues to call for her father to get her out of the crib after she has already climbed out on her own and run down the hallway looking for him to help her (222). Once again, these scenarios go beyond merely depicting the impish behavior of a young child. The humor of these scenes arises from Lucy's inanity. To quote the name of another well-known television show, kids say (and do) the darnedest things. But Schulz's portrayal of Lucy goes beyond simply capturing the amusing blunders of a typical toddler. The cartoonist presents Lucy as a particularly dim-witted toddler whose blunders are therefore exceptionally amusing.

Lucille Ball's talent as a comedienne went far beyond her knack for making funny facial expressions; she also had a gift for physical comedy. Much of the humor in *I Love Lucy* arises from slapstick, usually involving the title character. Whether she is getting squirted in the face with a seltzer bottle in "The Quiz Show" in season 1 or taking repeated falls in a grape-stomping vat in "Lucy's Italian Movie" in season 5, Lucille Ball is "the virtuoso of physical comedy" (Pittman 183). Slapstick forms such a central element of each episode that, as Emily Todd VanDerWerff notes, "the show isn't a series of stories so much as it is a series of excuses for comedic sketches." From attempting to become a ballerina (season 1, ep. 19, "The Ballet") to slapping a pair of handcuffs on Ricky as a practical joke and then predictably not being able to find the key (season 2, ep. 4, "The Handcuffs"), the premise of each show was a vehicle for "showcasing Ball's considerable talents as a clown" (Hulse 38).

Charles M. Schulz's *Peanuts* is not commonly associated with slapstick humor. Aside from Charlie Brown's annual back flop after attempting to kick the football, physical humor is not a core or even recurring feature of the strip. On the contrary, as Jared Gardner, Ian Gordon, and M. Thomas Inge have all discussed, the humor in Schulz's strip is more subtle and cerebral. It largely arises from characters making astute, morose, or ironic philosophical observations, not from taking pratfalls. That said, slapstick humor formed a frequent component of the strips involving Lucy Van Pelt when she first appeared in *Peanuts*. The number of times during those first few months that the toddler-age character fell down, fell over, or fell on her head is staggering. For example, the strips from March 12, April 16, April 27, and May 25 all include such moments (figs. 4.9–4.11). Moreover, in many instances,

Figure 4.9. *Peanuts* comic strip, March 12, 1952. PEANUTS © Peanuts Worldwide LLC. Dist. by ANDREWS MCMEEL SYNDICATION. Reprinted with permission. All rights reserved.

Figure 4.10. *Peanuts* comic strip, April 27, 1952. PEANUTS © Peanuts Worldwide LLC. Dist. by ANDREWS MCMEEL SYNDICATION. Reprinted with permission. All rights reserved.

Figure 4.11. Opening panels from *Peanuts* comic strip, May 25, 1952. PEANUTS © Peanuts Worldwide LLC. Dist. by ANDREWS MCMEEL SYNDICATION. Reprinted with permission. All rights reserved.

Lucy's pratfall occurs in the closing panel, forming the strip's primary source of humor—akin to *I Love Lucy*. Once again, although taking a tumble is a common part of childhood in general and toddlerhood in particular, the frequency and consistency with which Lucy engages in slapstick humor raise the possibility that something more is at play.

JUMPING ON THE BANDWAGON: MUSICIANS AND MIXED FEMINIST MESSAGES IN *I LOVE LUCY* AND *PEANUTS*

Identifying a possible kinship between Lucy Van Pelt and Lucy Ricardo does more than simply add a new perspective to the material and comedic origins of Schulz's character; it also causes us to see other core aspects of her personality in new ways. Both Lucy Ricardo and Lucy Van Pelt, for example, are in love with musicians. Lucy Ricardo's husband, Ricky, is a successful bandleader and multitalented musician: he plays the conga (or tumbadora) as well as the guitar, and he also sings. Far from nominally mentioning his profession in the show, many episodes of *I Love Lucy* include scenes from the Tropicana Club, where Ricky works. His band rehearses, and Ricky also performs, singing and playing various instruments. Indeed, some of the most famous moments from *I Love Lucy* involve Ricky making music. In "The Audition" from season 1, for example, he plays "Babalu" for the first time. The Afro-Cuban song was popularized by Arnaz—who both sings and plays the conga drum on it—before he appeared on television. Performances of "Babalu" would become a recurring feature of *I Love Lucy*. Another memorable musical moment comes when Ricky sings "We're Having a Baby" in the episode "Lucy Is Enciente" from season 2. Ricky initially thinks he is serenading a couple in the audience who are expecting, but in a now-iconic moment, he realizes midway through the song that his wife is the one who is pregnant.

Even episodes that do not feature Ricky with his band at the club often revolve around his work as a performer. In one of the most common recurring plotlines of the series, Lucy longs to be an entertainer and is constantly scheming to get herself into her husband's act. As she complains in an episode from season 1, "Being a housewife is a big bore . . . cook the meals, do the dishes, make the beds, dust the house, cook the meals" (qtd. in Landay, *Love* 99). Anticipating arguments made by Betty Friedan more than a decade later, Lucy feels unfulfilled by the traditional gender roles expected of white, middle-class, heterosexual women. She longs to have a career beyond merely a wife and—after the arrival of Little Ricky—a mother. The plots of numerous episodes showcase Lucy's attempt to become a performer at Ricky's Tropicana Club—as a singer, dancer, comedienne, musician, clown, and so on—or to break into show business in general. In fact, of the thirty episodes that make up the sitcom's first season, a full twelve focus on this issue.[3] From auditioning as a backup dancer at the Tropicana in "The Diet" (ep. 3) and taking over an act as a vaudeville clown in "The Audition" (ep. 6) to becoming a dramatist in "Lucy Writes a Play" (ep. 17) and doing a commercial for Vitameatavegamin (ep. 30), Lucy keeps trying to fulfill her dream of being an entertainer.

Of course, Lucy's schemes always fail in some hilarious way. Although initially disappointed by this turn of events, she ends up being relieved by them. In a detail that undercuts viewing Lucy Ricardo as a vehicle for second-wave feminism, "Lucy's a woman who dares leave her station, only to realize she was wrong to ever wish for better things" (VanDerWerff). By the end of each episode, the central character is usually embarrassed by, and even apologetic about, her attempt to break into show business. Lucy happily and even gratefully returns to the domestic sphere, recognizing that it is both appropriate and even wise for Ricky to be the professional performer and family breadwinner (VanDerWerff).

Forming another commonality between the two characters, Lucy Van Pelt's love interest is also a musician: the classical pianist Schroeder. Akin to the number of *I Love Lucy* scenes involving Ricky and his band, Schroeder's music forms an important role in Lucy's interactions with him. Lucy first encounters Schroeder sitting at his toy piano in the strip from January 27, 1953. Exemplifying her ditzy nature early in the series, she asks him what song he is playing, and he tells her, "This is 'Waltz of the Flowers' . . . from the 'Nutcracker Suite'" (Schulz 12). The final panel shows Lucy walking away, elated. "'Sweet'! He called me 'sweet'!! I've never been so happy in all my life!" she says in another example of her initial portrayal as dim-witted. From this point onward, Lucy has a crush on Schroeder. Moreover, strips featuring the pair commonly show Lucy visiting Schroeder while he is practicing. In what would soon become an iconic portrayal of the pair, she leans on his piano, chatting with him, much to his annoyance. Like Ricky, Schroeder doesn't want Lucy to disturb him while he is playing. Mirroring Lucy Ricardo, Lucy Van Pelt finds every excuse imaginable to do so. Indeed, there is no topic too banal or idea too vapid for her to talk about with Schroeder when he is playing the piano.

The motivation behind Lucy Van Pelt's incessant intrusion on Schroeder's music, however, is far different from that of Lucy Ricardo. Whereas the protagonist of *I Love Lucy* is constantly vying to get out of her domestic role as a housewife and into the professional realm of show business, Lucy Van Pelt seeks to do the opposite: she is trying to get Schroeder to make his music less of a priority so that he can focus on domestic life with her. Many of her (one-sided) conversations with Schroeder center on their future life as husband and wife: Will he make enough money playing his music to properly provide for her? Will he love her as much as he does Beethoven? Will he like her cooking?

In the same way that it is a mistake to see Lucy Ricardo as a purely feminist icon, it would also be a mischaracterization to say that Lucy Van Pelt's main aspiration in life is simply to be a wife and mother. On the contrary, David Michaelis points out, "Lucy is the most ambitious figure in *Peanuts*" (309). She is the only character in the comic to start her own business: the psychiatrist booth. The wooden sidewalk stand debuted on March 27, 1959, and remained a recurring feature of the strip over the next four decades. In many ways, the psychiatrist booth could have been a gag on *I Love Lucy*. One can image Lucy Ricardo coming up with the idea to open her own business offering guidance and information, then quickly realizing she is in way over her head and giving hilariously terrible advice, akin to Lucy Van Pelt.

Even when Lucy Van Pelt isn't sitting in her psychiatrist's booth, a surprising number of things she says—not just in the early strips already mentioned but throughout her appearance in the series—could conceivably have come out of Lucy Ricardo's mouth. For example, in the comic that appeared on September 24, 1987, an exasperated Charlie Brown asks her how she could miss catching such an easy pop fly during their baseball game. With an excuse that one could imagine Lucy Ricardo giving Ricky, Schulz's Lucy replies: "Fall got in my eyes." Similarly, in the comic from April 14, 1975, Linus asks his older sister, "What do you do when you want to talk to someone, and they don't answer the phone?" Lucy's response could just as conceivably have been uttered by Lucy Ricardo to Ethel in the middle of one of their harebrained schemes: "Dial louder!" she says.[4]

While *I Love Lucy* is known for introducing an array of innovations to the medium of television, one of its most influential was also accidental. In spring 1952, producers learned that Lucille Ball was expecting. After making the groundbreaking decision to incorporate her pregnancy into the sitcom rather than cancel the series—which at the time was the standard response when the lead actress became pregnant—they needed to figure out a way to record enough episodes before the arrival of Ball's baby. As the head producer Jess Oppenheimer quickly realized, even working over the summer, "he couldn't possibly film enough episodes before Ball became unavailable for the cameras" ("When 'I Love Lucy' Invented"). The solution to this predicament marked another groundbreaking moment in the history of television: the network would air some of the shows from the first season to help fill out the second. On October 20, 1952, CBS rebroadcast the first-season episode "The Quiz Show," making it "TV's first-ever rerun" ("When 'I Love Lucy' Invented"). Over the coming weeks, "nine more episodes were also rerun during the second season of *I Love Lucy*—each employing a flashback from the show's current storylines leading into the repeat" ("When 'I Love Lucy' Invented"). Although originally intended as fillers to hold audiences over until Ball returned from maternity leave, something unexpected happened: "those repeats proved just as popular as new episodes" (VanDerWerff). Viewers who had missed earlier installments of *I Love Lucy* were thrilled by the second opportunity to see them. Meanwhile, avid fans were equally delighted to witness some of Lucy's hilarious hijinks again.

The success of rerunning episodes during Ball's maternity leave prompted the network to do it again. In the fall of 1955, as the series began what would become its penultimate season, "CBS began showing *I Love Lucy* reruns on Saturday night. To their astonishment, the reruns landed in the Top 10, getting higher ratings than some first-run shows (including *The Honeymooners*)" (Gaar 51). This phenomenon solidified reruns as a legitimate new programming option.

On May 23, 1972, the Van Pelt family in *Peanuts* welcomed their third child. Lucy was annoyed not only by the arrival of a new sibling but also by the fact the new baby was a boy. After all, she already had a younger brother, Linus, and she certainly didn't need—or even want—another one. "At first, I wanted to be an only child," Lucy says to Linus in the comic that appeared on May 31, 1972. As she continues in the next panel, "**You** spoiled that!" (bold in original). She then proceeds to discuss the current situation, and the word she uses to describe her new baby brother is noteworthy: "I thought it would be nice to have a sister. So what happens? I get another brother ... *a rerun!*"

(my emphasis). While Lucy's comment is apt in many ways—not only is her new sibling a boy, but he also looks strikingly similar to Linus—it is also telling. Of all the terms that Lucy could have used to describe her new baby brother—a copycat, a clone, a duplicate, a twin, and so on—she chose a term from television and, more specifically, one that pointed back to *I Love Lucy*. Instead of being offended by his sister's crass characterization of their new baby brother, Linus is excited by it. "THAT'S IT!" he shouts in the third panel, knocking Lucy completely off her feet. The closing exchange settles the issue. "We'll call him 'Rerun!'" Linus happily announces. Lying on the ground, Lucy mutters, "'Rerun' Van Pelt . . . Good Grief!" Although intended as merely a nickname, "Rerun" is the only appellation by which the youngest Van Pelt child is known throughout *Peanuts*. Readers never learn the boy's actual name. Moreover, the strip that appeared on September 11, 1996, indicates that he doesn't know it either. When he arrives at school for his first day of kindergarten, the teacher asks him his name. "My name is 'Rerun,'" he replies. "I don't know . . . that's what they call me."

Despite all the physical, behavioral, and personal ways that Lucy Van Pelt echoes Lucy Ricardo, *Peanuts* never directly mentions *I Love Lucy*. Over its fifty-year run, the newspaper comic included many strips in which characters watch television. Based on speech balloons that emanate from the set, figures like Charlie Brown, Linus, and Lucy tune in to quiz shows, movies, dramas, cartoons, news broadcasts, and, of course, comedies. Additionally, some strips over the years mention shows by name. The comic from August 30, 1955, for example, refers to "Miss Frances," who was the host of a popular program for young children at the time, *Ding Dong School*. However, the groundbreaking sitcom *I Love Lucy*—either when it originally aired in the 1950s or when it was rerun in the decades that followed—never directly appears in *Peanuts*.

Charles M. Schulz likewise never explicitly mentioned being a fan of *I Love Lucy*, but he did enjoy watching television. As the biographer David Michaelis notes, throughout Schulz's adult life, he routinely relaxed by tuning in to a sitcom, movie, game show, or drama. That said, no extant interviews, personal essays, or biographical portraits pinpoint the precise date when Schulz first acquired a TV set. That said, a television first appears in the strip in June 1952, and—as Benjamin Clark, the curator at the Charles M. Schulz Museum and Research Center, notes—the medium makes "regular appearances throughout *Peanuts* after that, picking up steam in the Fall of 1952" (Clark, "FW: Research question"). So this period or one close to it is a good guess. Whatever the precise date when Schulz bought his first television, it seems unlikely that he could have avoided knowing about *I Love Lucy*. As I have discussed, the show dominated American popular culture during the 1950s. Articles about the show, images of its stars, merchandise based on it, and discussions of its popularity were so ubiquitous in newspapers, magazines, stores, and radio that being unaware of it seems not simply improbable but impossible. Even if Schulz himself did not watch *I Love Lucy*, he would surely have encountered media coverage about it.

While it is unclear whether Schulz was a fan of Lucy Ricardo, he did have a well-documented place in his heart for redheads—or, at least, for one redhead. In what has become an oft-cited biographical detail about the cartoonist, Donna Johnson, the woman whom Schulz had been dating just before *Peanuts* debuted, turned down his marriage proposal in summer 1950, opting to wed a different suitor instead. The cartoonist was devastated. "'You never get over your first love,' he would remark when he was seventy-five" (Michaelis 215). Johnson became the basis for Charlie Brown's unrequited love interest, the Little Red-Haired Girl. In both the newspaper comics and the animated television specials, the *Peanuts* protagonist pined for the ginger-haired figure.

While Charlie Brown was the one who yearned for the Little Red-Haired Girl, another equally well-known character from the strip might also have been influenced by a redhead. The initial portrayal of Lucy Van Pelt, along with the role she played in the strip, suggests an overlooked kinship with Lucy Ricardo. In later years, Schulz's fussbudget would become infamous for dispensing psychiatric advice. The time is long overdue to turn the analytic process around on Lucy and probe the possible pop culture origins of her character.

'TOONING IN: THE UNEXPLORED FEEDBACK LOOP BETWEEN POSTWAR NEWSPAPER COMICS AND TELEVISION SITCOMS

The areas of overlap between Lucy Van Pelt and Lucy Ricardo have implications that extend beyond simply *Peanuts* and *I Love Lucy*. They also call attention to the overlooked interaction between postwar newspaper comics and television sitcoms as a whole. Putting these markedly different and often even adversarial entertainment modes in dialogue with each other reveals an array of previously neglected creative, cultural, and critical connections.

Previous discussions about postwar comics have largely framed them as having an antagonistic relationship with the new medium of television. As David Hajdu, Bradford W. Wright, and Paul Lopes have all discussed, television competed for the time, attention, and resources of audiences for sequential art. For decades, comic books had been the most popular form of leisure-time entertainment, especially for young people. In statistics that are astounding, "*Publishers Weekly* reported that the American public in 1953 spent over $1 billion on comic books. Surveys suggested that over 90 percent of boys and girls under 18 read them" (Wright 155). Comics also enjoyed a strong readership among adults. Most individuals who read a daily newspaper—which was the vast majority of the adult population in the mid-twentieth century—perused the comics section. Additionally, a subset of this audience enjoyed comics so much that when they visited the newsstand, they purchased a comic book or two. As Wright has documented, comic books were one of the most popular forms of reading material for soldiers during World War II and "remained the literature of choice for American G.I.s" in the postwar era (155). Given this situation, Wright refers to the United States from the late 1930s through the early 1950s as "Comic Book Nation."

The advent of television challenged and ultimately contributed to changing this situation.[5] Although sets were expensive to purchase, once a household acquired one, it provided hours of free entertainment for adults and children alike. From sitcoms and dramas to game shows and children's programs, television had something for everyone—and, with multiple channels, nearly all the time. As TV sets appeared in increasing numbers of American homes during the early 1950s, comics "publishers engaged in intensifying competition," but in nearly every instance, the new medium of television "overwhelmed their efforts" (Wright 225). Rather than purchasing comic books to satisfy their desire for storytelling, Americans were watching TV shows on the sets that were already in their homes. In a telling index of the way in which television encroached on the world of comics, a variety of popular characters and titles—including Superman, Batman, and Dick Tracy—were adapted as programs during the late 1950s and early 1960s. As the cinematic adaptation of novels has repeatedly demonstrated, far more individuals watch the visual production than read the printed book, including when the source text is a comic book. So while TV shows based on Batman or Superman augmented the popularity of the comic book series for some fans, they supplanted it for many others. After all, why spend the money from your paper route, babysitting job, or allowance on monthly installments about these characters at the comic book stand when you could watch weekly episodes about them on television at home for free. By the end of the 1950s, television had eclipsed comic books as the most popular form of entertainment among young people (Wright xvi).

Of course, comic strips like *Peanuts* appeared in daily newspapers rather than monthly comic books. Nevertheless, the medium did not regard the rise of television in a neutral or disinterested way. Newspapers were also affected by the new technology. After all, television broadcasts throughout the day relayed the news, lessening the need for individuals to purchase a paper. If you missed reading the newspaper, you could always learn about the day's events on television later. Moreover, after the news ended, you might be able to catch the latest episode about a favorite comic strip character like Dick Tracy, making up for not seeing the funny pages. For many, this situation—at least on some days—may have prompted them to forgo purchasing a paper. As the Pew Research Center reveals, newspaper circulation had grown steadily throughout the 1940s. Between 1940 and 1945, for example, weekday readership of newspapers increased by 7.2 million; from 1945 to 1950, it rose by another 6.5 million. By contrast, the same five-year span a decade later, from 1950 to 1955, only saw an increase of 2.3 million (Pew Research Center). Of course, many factors played a role in this phenomenon, not just the proliferation of television. Nevertheless, the end result was the same: television was surging during the 1950s, while newspapers were slowing.

The possible kinship between Lucy Van Pelt and Lucy Ricardo adds a new dimension to the interaction between comics and television in the early 1950s. Rather than existing solely in opposition to each other as competing modes of leisure-time entertainment, comics and television may have been more interactive. Comic strips released during the postwar era may have consciously or unconsciously been influenced by the mass popularity of the sitcom. Likewise, this new television format may itself owe a debt to newspaper strips.

Although newspaper comics and television sitcoms exist in different media for different audiences, they share an array of commonalties. First and foremost, they are both serial productions consisting of regular installments that focus on a recurring cast of core characters. From Richard Outcault's *Hogan's Alley* (debut 1895), Winsor McCay's *Little Nemo in Slumberland* (1905–27), and Milton Caniff's *Terry and the Pirates* (1934–73) to Mort Walker's *Beetle Bailey* (1950–2018), Morrie Turner's *Wee Pals* (1965–2004), and Bill Watterson's *Calvin and Hobbes* (1985–95), newspaper strips developed a fan base because readers developed a connection to the characters and wanted to see what happened to them. The same observation, of course, applies to television sitcoms. From *Gilligan's Island* (1964–67) and *All in the Family* (1971–79) to *Seinfeld* (1989–98) and *Grace and Frankie* (2015–22), the appeal of the characters forms the basis for the appeal of the show.

While both the general premise and specific plotlines featured in newspaper strips and television sitcoms varied widely, they were united by a common goal: to make their audiences laugh. Comics got their name because they were comical in nature. To this day, in fact, the section of the newspaper where the comics appear is known as "the funny pages." Even strips that are geared toward political commentary or social satire, such as *Doonesbury* (1970–present) and *The Boondocks* (1996–2006), strive to generate a sardonic smile or mordant chuckle. Television sitcoms likewise revolve around humor. The word "sitcom," of course, is a portmanteau for "situation comedy." The genre distinguishes itself from other television formats—drama, variety show, soap opera, and so on—with its focus on humor.

Another key area of overlap between newspaper comics and television sitcoms is their formulaic nature. Although each of these entertainment modes gave rise to an array of technical, aesthetic, and storytelling innovations, they were successful largely because they adhered to specific generic conventions. As Saul Austerlitz has written, "Sitcoms exemplified the phenomenon of eternal return, promising endless variation without ever fundamentally altering the world that contained them" (2). Indeed, once you've seen a few episodes of any given show—be it *I Love Lucy*, *Leave It to Beaver* (1957–63), *The Brady Bunch* (1969–74), *Three's Company* (1977–84), *Friends* (1994–2004), or *Parks and Recreation* (2009–15)—you've pretty much seen them all. In the words of Austerlitz once again about sitcom plotlines, "There were the scrapes—an infinite series of easily resolved predicaments and indiscretions that plagued sitcom families, demanding their immediate attention without ever lingering or affecting the unchanging dynamic of families themselves" (2). This observation certainly applies to *I Love Lucy*. If Lucy Ricardo wasn't getting into a hilarious predicament at a candy factory, she was doing so at a wine-making facility or while making a commercial for a new health tonic. Not to worry, however, because no matter how sticky (literally) a situation the title character found herself in, everything would be worked out and cleaned up by the end of the episode.

Newspaper comics also follow their own set of narrative conventions. Like sitcoms, they tell strikingly similar stories over and over. Numerous installments of George Herriman's *Krazy Kat* (1913–44) feature the title character feuding with Ignatz Mouse and getting hit on the head by a brick. Similarly, a multitude of strips from Jim Davis's *Garfield* (1978–present) depict the title character complaining about Mondays, scarfing down lasagna, or taking naps. Of course, *Peanuts* has its own recurring plotlines with the equally predictable outcomes: Charlie Brown and the baseball team, Snoopy and the Red Baron, Peppermint Patty and schoolwork.

The repetitive nature of both newspaper strips and television sitcoms did not deter fans; it delighted them. Both of these forms became hugely popular modes of mass entertainment in the United States. However, in a detail that embodies yet another area of overlap, neither was taken seriously by critics. In the words of Saul Austerlitz once again, sitcoms were "obsessively watched and critically ignored all at once" (1). For generations, television was dismissed as "the idiot box" or "boob tube." Although the shows were enjoyed by millions, they were analyzed by almost no one. The serious, sustained, and systematic critique of television did not occur in the United States until the 1970s (Boddy). It was during this era that television studies emerged as a distinct academic discipline. Given the lag time between the emergence of television and its recognition as an important mode of storytelling, Austerlitz argues that "for much of its history, [television embodied] the most critically ignored form of American culture" (5).

Comics share this trait. Commercial strips first appeared in newspapers during the 1890s and were an immediate success. The "Sunday supplement," as the weekly comics section was initially called, delighted readers, attracted fans, and (as it was intended to) boosted circulation, so much so that the strips became a daily rather than merely weekly feature. Far from a passing fad, newspaper comics continued to be massively popular as the nineteenth century turned into the twentieth. Titles like Winsor McCay's *Little Nemo in Slumberland* (1905–27), Harold Gray's *Little Orphan Annie* (1924–2010), and Ernie Bushmiller's *Nancy* (1938–present) attracted large fan bases and became pop culture phenomena. Then, in the early 1930s, a new physical format for the genre made its debut: the comic book. The public pervasiveness and thus cultural power of comic books is difficult to overestimate. As Bradford W. Wright points out, "Before television became a fixture in the American home, comic books were the foremost medium of youth entertainment" (xvi).

Like every new entertainment mode, the television sitcom did not emerge from a cultural vacuum. On the contrary, the genre had its roots in existing entertainment forms. As Elizabeth Edwards has discussed, sitcoms drew on elements from vaudeville, radio, and theater to create this new performance mode (*Celebration* 2–22). All these elements are powerfully present in *I Love Lucy*: the show was based on CBS's successful radio drama *My Favorite Husband*, which starred Ball. Additionally, to convince the network that audiences would not only accept her pairing with a Cuban bandleader but delight in it, Ball and Arnaz did a touring vaudeville act that formed the basis for the *I Love Lucy* episode "The Audition." Finally, when *I Love Lucy* began production, each episode was filmed from the start of its plot to its closing scene in front of a live studio audience, akin to a stage play. Bart Andrews has discussed how Lucille Ball's form of physical comedy worked best in front of a flesh-and-blood audience, where she could respond to their reactions and especially to their laughter (75–77). Soon the assertion that a television program had been filmed "in front of a live studio audience" was so common that it became a cliché.

While the role that radio, vaudeville, and theater played in the development of the sitcom is undeniable, the suggestive echoes between sitcoms and newspaper strips raise the possibility that comics may also have had a direct or indirect influence. In details ranging from their episodic nature and use of a recurring cast of characters to their reliance on plot conventions and focus on humor, television sitcoms and newspaper strips share a number of compelling points of correspondence. Forming a common feature of television broadcasts during the 1950s, announcers, hosts, and advertisers encouraged audiences to "tune in" to the next episode of a show. That said, in a potentially overlooked feature in the history of television and the development of the sitcom, some of these programs—when it came to their conventions—may have been "tooning in" to comics. Many of the narrative elements that made newspaper strips successful and popular were also facets of this new storytelling mode.

Furthermore, this influence may have been reciprocal. Although newspaper strips predate the advent of television sitcoms by more than fifty years, comics released during the postwar era may have been shaped by television. Cartoonists and the strips that they produced were not unaware of, or unaffected by, the rapid growth of this new entertainment format. Indeed, as TV became more popular, it not only competed with comics but also began to infiltrate them. During the postwar years, for example, popular television shows began being released as comic books. Both *The Lone Ranger* (1949–57) and *The Honeymooners* (1955–56) appeared as a ten-cent floppies.[6] So too did *I Love Lucy*. In 1954, at the apex of the show's popularity, Dell released a comic book version of the popular sitcom (figs. 4.12, 4.13). The publication ran longer than the sitcom was on the air; the last issue of the *I Love Lucy* comic book appeared in 1962, five years after the show's finale ("*I Love Lucy* Comics").

Together with encroaching on the realm of comic books, television also began appearing in newspaper strips. *Peanuts* and television arrived in American popular culture at roughly the same time. Perhaps not surprisingly, references to the new entertainment mode appear during the first year of Schulz's strip. In the comic that appeared on November 19, 1950, Charlie Brown is walking with Patty. "Everybody's buying television sets these days," the protagonist remarks as they stroll down the sidewalk. Patty, however, is not convinced by his statement. "Everybody?" she asks skeptically. The third panel both answers Patty's question and provides the strip's punch line. As Charlie Brown and Patty pass Snoopy's doghouse, we see that the peak of its roof has been outfitted with a television antenna. The image stops the two characters in their tracks; they both stand at the picket fence, staring in silence. In the fourth and final panel, Charlie Brown and Patty have resumed

Figure 4.12. *I Love Lucy* comic book, no. 10 (Dell Publications, May 1956).

Figure 4.13. Page from *I Love Lucy* comic book, no. 10 (Dell Publications, May 1956).

their walk once again. As Patty looks back to catch just one more glimpse of Snoopy's doghouse, Charlie Brown reaffirms his previous comment about who is buying television sets these days: "Uh huh . . . Everybody!"

Snoopy may have been the first *Peanuts* character to acquire a television set, but he would not be the only one. Far from a one-off gag or isolated subject, the growing presence of television in US culture became a growing feature of Schulz's comic. Both Charlie Brown's house and the Van Pelt home soon contained sets. Instead of an item featured solely in the background, the TV becomes the main focus of the strip. In the comic that appeared on December 11, 1952, for example, Lucy insists that her baby brother Linus sit closer to the set so that he can see the screen better; the final panel shows him looking out at the reader with his eyes all scrambled. In the opening few panels of the strip that appeared on June 3, 1952, Charlie Brown diligently dons all his baseball catcher's gear. He does not go outside to play, however; the final image shows him sitting in front of the television set to watch a game. Finally, during a ten-day span in September 1952, television served as the focus of a *Peanuts* strip on three separate occasions.

In the decades to come, television would continue to play an increasing role in *Peanuts*. One of the standard settings for a strip was a character sitting in a beanbag chair in front of the set. Furthermore, the experience of watching TV was often the focus of the comic: what program was on, what the actors were saying, how the *Peanuts* characters reacted to this content, and so on. Then, beginning on December 9, 1965, with the broadcast of *A Charlie Brown Christmas*, Schulz's comic strip would have its own direct relationship to television. Forming yet another area of overlap—or, at least, striking coincidence—with *I Love Lucy*, the Emmy Award–winning animated special aired on the same station as the groundbreaking sitcom, CBS. Given both the number and the popularity of *Peanuts* animated specials over the years—including classics like *It's the Great Pumpkin, Charlie Brown* (1966) and *A Charlie Brown Thanksgiving* (1973)—Schulz's characters are at least as well known as television characters as they are as figures from a comic strip, perhaps more so.

The physical, personal, and behavioral links between Lucy Van Pelt and Lucy Ricardo suggest that *Peanuts* may have had a connection with television long before any members of its cast acquired a set—and certainly well before the strip appeared as an animated TV special. The groundbreaking and phenomenally popular show *I Love Lucy* may have consciously or consciously shaped the creation of Lucy Van Pelt and, with it, *Peanuts* as a whole.

For decades, the interpretive touchstone for sequential art has been film. As Scott McCloud, Thierry Groensteen, and Bart Beaty have all written, film studies has long served as a model for comics studies. The theoretical lenses as well as critical language used to examine and interpret works of sequential art have been based on, or at least have borrowed heavily from, those used to analyze cinema. Employing concepts like montage, mise-en-scène, and focalization, comics are seen as having a strong critical, cultural, and creative kinship with film. Indeed, Beaty, in the introduction to a 2011 special issue of *Cinema Studies* devoted to comics, noted that "the current state of the scholarly study of comics is strikingly akin to that of film in the 1960s" (106).[7] The two fields share an array of similar tactics, terms, and approaches.

While the critical examination of comics has benefited greatly from being placed in dialogue with film, this genre is not the only mode of visual entertainment with which comics can be seen to share a kinship—or to which comics owe a possible debt. As the connections between Lucy Van Pelt and Lucy Ricardo suggest, in the same way that sitcoms may have been " 'tooning in" to comics for inspiration, ingredients, and influence, postwar strips like *Peanuts* may have been "channeling" television, not just figuratively but also literally.

Thomas Wagner, in an essay discussing the legacy of *I Love Lucy* in general and its redheaded star in particular, asserted: "From any perspective, show-business history or cultural phenomenon, Ball's contributions to the American zeitgeist remain unmatched" (60). Few would argue with this statement. From Ball's unparalleled talent for physical comedy to her influence on the sitcom genre as a whole, her mark on American popular culture is indisputable. To the already impressive list of phenomena that were shaped by *I Love Lucy*, *Peanuts* might be added. After the arrival of Rerun, Lucy Van Pelt laments never getting the younger sister that she always wanted. In what could be seen as a long-overlooked source of influence on *Peanuts*, however, Schulz's fussbudget may have had an older sister, Lucy Ricardo.

The next chapter likewise reconsiders the cultural touchstone for another classic *Peanuts* character: Franklin Armstrong. That said, it does so in a way that is both similar to, and dissimilar from, this analysis. Whereas my discussion of Lucy Van Pelt rethinks her origins by placing her in the context of an event that was taking place during the era when she debuted—namely, the popularity of the television sitcom *I Love Lucy*—my discussion of Franklin does so by placing him in the context of a historical phenomenon: namely, the long-standing racist association in US popular culture of blackness with dirt. The surname that Schulz chose for his new Black character was an homage to the legendary musician Louis Armstrong. As my discussion in the next chapter suggests, however, the shading technique that Schulz used to indicate Franklin's race gave him an unexpected and deeply problematic kinship with an existing character from *Peanuts*: Pig-Pen.

CHAPTER 5

FRANKLIN AND PIG-PEN

The Aesthetics of Blackness and Dirt

July 31, 1968, is commonly seen as a landmark date both in the history of the newspaper strip *Peanuts* and in the history of US comics as a whole. On this day, a new character made his debut in Charles M. Schulz's popular strip: Franklin. An African American boy who is roughly the same age as the rest of the *Peanuts* gang, Franklin meets Charlie Brown on a sunny beach one day. The pair strike up a conversation. In strips that appeared over the following few days, the two talk about building sandcastles, about their fathers, and about baseball. In the closing panel of the final comic, Charlie Brown has had such an enjoyable time with Franklin that he invites him to his house. "Ask your mother if you can come over and spend the night!" he shouts after Franklin has been called back to his family. "We'll play baseball and build another sand castle!" (Schulz, *1967–1968* 249).

Christopher P. Lehman has made the following observation about both this specific sequence in *Peanuts* and the larger sociopolitical backdrop against which it takes place: "The sunny public beach was the setting for the hope of integration when Charlie Brown and Franklin met" (145). During a time when desegregation was receiving widespread national attention—along with intense regional resistance—Schulz made a bold statement about inclusion. Franklin was "a cartoon black face in a sea of cartoon white faces, in a strip drawn by a white cartoonist" (Wong, par. 29). As a result, for nearly fifty years, Franklin has been viewed in an overwhelmingly laudatory way. As Kevin Wong has written, "The addition of a black character to the *Peanuts* cast was a positive, forward-thinking act" (par. 27). Then, as well as now, Franklin has been hailed as nothing short of groundbreaking (Halliday; Ha; Page).

This chapter continues my interest in revisiting core characters from Schulz's cast and examining them in new, different, and alternative ways by taking another look at the comics life and cultural legacy of Franklin. While the appearance of this figure marks an important moment in US comics, it was also not without complications and even problems. In a heretofore overlooked aspect of *Peanuts*, the shading technique that Schulz used to signify the race of his new Black character possess an uncanny and uncomfortable kinship to the one he used to shade another long-established figure from the strip: Pig-Pen. As his name implies, Pig-Pen is known for being filthy: his face is dirty, his clothes are soiled, and his body is surrounded by an ever-present cloud of dust. Schulz uses a similar hatching method to indicate that Pig-Pen's skin is dirty as he does to indicate that Franklin's is black. In so doing, *Peanuts* connects itself with the long history in American popular culture of likening blackness with dirt. The visual links or aesthetic connections that occur between Franklin and Pig-Pen complicate celebratory views of Franklin as a progressive character in *Peanuts*. At the same time, they add a new facet to one of the core themes of *Blockheads, Beagles, and Sweet Babboos*: the importance of paying attention to Schulz's line.

"SUGGEST RACIAL AMITY IN A CASUAL DAY-TO-DAY SENSE": THE HISTORICAL ORIGINS AND SOCIOCULTURAL AIMS OF FRANKLIN

Ironically, given all the praise that Charles M. Schulz has received over the decades for including a Black character in *Peanuts*, it was not his idea. The suggestion came from Harriet Glickman, a white schoolteacher from Los Angeles. On April 15, 1968, at the height of the civil rights movement, Glickman wrote a letter to the cartoonist imploring him to add an African American character to his comic (Johnson, par. 2). As she explained, doing so would help to combat "the vast sea of misunderstanding, fear, hate, and violence" (qtd. in Ha, par. 6). By showing a Black character engaging in the strip's everyday scenes of playing baseball and flying kites with white peers, *Peanuts* would offer an important "first step toward a future climate of 'open friendship, trust and mobility' between the races" (Halliday, par. 6).

Schulz responded quickly to Glickman. In a letter dated April 26, 1968, the cartoonist expressed his support for the idea, but also his concern that "it would look ... patronizing [to] our Negro friends" (qtd. in Ha, par. 9). The cartoonist rightly realized that he knew very little about the daily lives of nonwhite children, and thus his depiction of them would be riddled with inaccuracies (Kamp, par. 15). "I'm not an expert on race," Schulz remarked in an interview years later with Michael Barrier. "I don't know what it's like to grow up as a little black boy, and I don't think you should draw things unless you really understand them" (Schulz, "Charles M. Schulz: An Interview"). As a result, he felt that any portrayal would seem forced and even condescending, especially to Black readers of his strip—which would contradict his goal for adding a Black character to *Peanuts* in the first place.[1] Given this situation, the cartoonist was at a loss for what to do. "I don't know what the solution is," he lamented in the closing line of his reply to Glickman (qtd. in Ha, par. 9).

Glickman was not willing to let the matter drop, however. She asked Schulz if she could share his letter with some Black friends who were both parents and fans of *Peanuts* (Erickson, par. 7). As she explained, "Their response may prove useful to you in your thinking on this subject" (qtd. in Erickson, par. 8). One of the individuals that Glickman approached was Kenneth C. Kelly, "a space engineer who worked on the *Surveyor* lunar vehicle, and would later become a housing discrimination rights activist" (par. 7). Kelly was also the father to two young boys. His letter to Schulz was as candid as it was impassioned. "An accusation of being patronizing would be a small price to pay for the positive results that would accrue!" he told the cartoonist (qtd. in Kamp, par. 9). Kelly went on to suggest that Schulz begin with a secondary character, who "would quietly and unobtrusively set the stage for a principal character at a later date" (qtd. in Kamp, par. 9). This approach, Kelly explained, "would serve the dual purpose of not burdening Mr. Schulz and 'Peanuts' with the duty of making a Major Social Statement" and would also present "friendship between black and white children as utterly normal" (Kamp, par. 9). Schulz needed no further persuasion. Within a few weeks of receiving Kelly's letter, the cartoonist sent Glickman a note asking her to check the strip during the week of July 29. "I have drawn an episode which I think will please you," he told her (qtd. in Ha, par. 12).

The sequence pleased not just Glickman but many others. As Adrian Florido has discussed, Schulz "drew praise from across the country" for Franklin's debut (par. 11). Readers and critics alike viewed the new Black character as a positive step toward breaking down racial barriers, promoting greater racial understanding, and ultimately helping to achieve sociopolitical equality. For instance, Barbara Brandon-Croft, who was the first Black woman to have a newspaper strip become nationally syndicated, found Franklin's debut "downright exhilarating" (qtd. in Kamp, par. 12). "I remember feeling affirmed by seeing Franklin in 'Peanuts,'" she reflected in an interview. "There's a little black kid! Thank goodness! We *do* matter" (qtd. in Kamp, par. 12). Franklin gave much-needed visibility to young Black children, whose lives, experiences, and even very existence were routinely ignored by mainstream American popular culture.

Of course, not everyone was happy about the addition of Franklin to the *Peanuts* gang. Among some readers in the South, "his presence sparked outrage" (Halliday, par. 13). These individuals objected to the mere inclusion of a Black cast member in the comic. Furthermore, they were even more incensed a few months later when Franklin appeared in a classroom alongside other members of the *Peanuts* gang. Racial integration was one thing, but school desegregation was another matter entirely. Editors from newspapers in the South wrote to United Feature Syndicate—the company that handled the national licensing and distribution of *Peanuts*—to stop sending strips that featured Franklin in classrooms with white children because they would not run them (Cavna, par. 17). Fearing the cancellation of subscriptions, United Feature Syndicate contacted Schulz about these concerns. When the syndicate asked the cartoonist if he would consider eliminating classroom scenes or drawing a separate strip for newspapers in the South, Schulz became angry. In a rare break from his usually calm, controlled, and polite midwestern demeanor, he told his editor: "Either you run it the way I drew it, or I quit" (qtd. in Cavna, par. 14).

Readers in the South were not the only ones who raised concerns about Franklin. While some objected to the fact that *Peanuts* had a new Black character, others called attention to the problem with the series having only one. As John H. McWhorter explains, "Schulz meant well. But Franklin was a classic 'token black'" (par. 2). He was the sole nonwhite figure to appear in Schulz's strip, and he was never developed into a significant protagonist. "Franklin did not carry a single daily episode alone," Christopher P. Lehman pointed out, "and he was not even in an individual panel by himself until his fourth year in the strip" (137). Instead, Schulz more commonly showed Franklin simply being in the company of one of the strip's more well-known characters (137). As a result, while Franklin did appear in the comic, he was not given an important or even meaningful role. Instead, he remained a minor character who visually symbolized the strip's diversity without actually saying or doing anything to substantively contribute to it.

Together with not having a robust presence in *Peanuts*, Franklin also did not have a robust personality. In a strip that was known for characters who possessed strong and distinctive identities, Franklin was dull. Unlike the rest of the *Peanuts* gang, he had no quirks, no foibles, no flaws, no eccentricities, no obsessions, no hang-ups—in sum, no individuality. Regardless of the events unfolding in the strip or the sociopolitical circumstances occurring outside it, Franklin was unfailingly pleasant, kind, and positive. In many ways, in fact, he was "an 'ideal' boy: sweet, empathetic, athletic, smart, family-centered, and God-fearing" (Wong, par. 33). This situation was not accidental. As Kevin Wong has written, "Schulz knew that every racist, anti-integration editor in the country would be searching for a reason to reject the character out of hand" (par. 29). As a result, "Franklin's one-dimensionality was understandable, if not necessary. Schulz needed to make Franklin unimpeachable, so that editors could only reject him on explicitly racial grounds" (par. 29).

Ironically, Franklin's universally positive nature was a negative trait. Although Schulz's presentation of his new Black character as unwaveringly good was intended to humanize him, make him "likable," and thereby engender empathy among white readers, it paradoxically dehumanized him: it denied Franklin the ability to be a fully developed character who possessed both strengths and weaknesses in the same way that his white peers did. As Rebecca Wanzo has said about Franklin and characters like him in US comics, they are "denied the individuality of their white counterparts" (13). The desire to avoid giving the Black character any personality traits that could be viewed as negative—and thus might be seen as affirming a racial stereotype—comes at the expense of presenting the character in a three-dimensional way (Wanzo 13). McWhorter has discussed this situation in *Peanuts* even more candidly: "Charlie Brown was a loser, Lucy was bossy, Snoopy was insane," he writes, "but Franklin was, well, 'black'"—and Black is not a personality type (par. 1). This portrayal limited not only the narrative possibilities for Franklin but also his connection and appeal to Black audiences. As Clarence Page remarked, "The humor in 'Peanuts' is derived precisely from those qualities Franklin did not have. Anxieties, longings, hang-ups and obsessions gave other characters a wholeness of life and an ability to engage and surprise us." For this reason, while Page viewed Franklin with pride—pointing out how the character "discussed philosophy with Linus, talked about his grandfather and played terrific center field on Charlie Brown's losing baseball team"—he also confessed that throughout the run of Schulz's strip, "I have been waiting for Franklin to develop some character flaws" (Page).

Just as problematically, Franklin's bland, blasé, and agreeable nature had a deleterious impact on white readers. His personality traits made him a wholly nonthreatening figure for white people. Christopher P. Lehman has pointed out that "Schulz conceived of Franklin as a conservative African American. His curly hair more closely resembled a short, traditional cut instead of an Afro. He wore pants and shirts of mainstream [white] America—not dashikis or bell-bottoms" (133–34). Furthermore, even though Franklin appears during the height of the civil rights movement, he never discusses his experiences with racism, never calls attention to social injustice, and never challenges the worldview of his white peers. Consequently, Franklin embodies what

Robert M. Entman and Andrew Rojecki famously termed "the black image in the white mind." Franklin is a white conception of who Black people are—or even should be—rather than a realistic depiction of them.

COLOR/LINES: FRANKLIN, PIG-PEN, AND THE VISUAL LINKING OF RACE AND DIRT

Previous criticisms about Franklin have focused largely on his personality. Both during the 1960s and in the present day, these analyses call attention to the fact that he is a token Black character, and he is portrayed in a milquetoast way, or both. Regardless of the specific focus of these discussions, they have concentrated on Franklin's demeanor.

While these critiques have all raised valid and important points, an additional aspect about Franklin is equally problematic but has been overlooked: how he is artistically drawn and aesthetically rendered. As Ayun Halliday has remarked, Franklin's "skin tone [is] indicated by closely set diagonal lines" (par. 12). In some strips, these lines are very neat, controlled, and orderly; they consist of precise parallel strokes that are spaced almost the same distance apart (fig. 5.1). Meanwhile, in other strips, the shading is more loose, scribbly, and free-form; the lines are irregular, sketchy, and the hatching even becomes cross-hatching (fig. 5.2). Because Schulz drew and inked all the *Peanuts* comics himself by hand, Franklin's appearance is not uniform.

The shading technique that Schulz used to indicate that Franklin was Black echoes the method that he used for another member of the *Peanuts* gang: Pig-Pen. Like Franklin, Pig-Pen was not part of the original cast when

Figure 5.1. Panel from *Peanuts* comic strip, December 6, 1970. PEANUTS © Peanuts Worldwide LLC. Dist. by ANDREWS MCMEEL SYNDICATION. Reprinted with permission. All rights reserved.

Figure 5.2. Panel from *Peanuts* comic strip, October 20, 1968. PEANUTS © Peanuts Worldwide LLC. Dist. by ANDREWS MCMEEL SYNDICATION. Reprinted with permission. All rights reserved.

the strip began on October 2, 1950. However, he made his debut just a few years later, on July 13, 1954. Consequently, by July 1968, when Franklin introduced himself to Charlie Brown on the beach, Pig-Pen was a readily recognizable member of the ensemble; he had been appearing in strips for fourteen years.

The premise for Pig-Pen's character is announced via his name. As the official character profile explains, "Being constantly dirty is a trait that 'Pig-Pen' is best known for" (par. 3). Not only is this character's face always filthy, but his clothes are soiled, and "he is best known as the character with a cloud of dirt that constantly follows him" (par. 1). Indeed, the profile notes, "In spite of his best efforts, it appears that [Pig-Pen] cannot stay clean. He can get dirty even by walking in a rainstorm" (par. 3). As Charlie Brown learns in the comic that first appeared on July 17, 1954, Pig-Pen is not averse to soap and water. "Oh, no . . . I like to take baths," he tells a surprised Charlie Brown (Schulz, *1953 to 1954* 241). However, every time Pig-Pen cleans up, he immediately becomes filthy again. As he rightly observes in the comic that appeared on November 25, 1959, "You know what I am? I'm a dust magnet!" The rare moments in isolated strips when Pig-Pen is actually clean, he is unrecognizable to the rest of the *Peanuts* gang. Without his coating of dirt, cloud of dust, and attire of soiled clothes, the other characters do not realize who he is. Pig-Pen appeared in Schulz's comic strip for nearly fifty years. Throughout that entire time, his actual name is never mentioned. He is known simply by the descriptive nickname "Pig-Pen."

The shading method that Schulz uses to signal that Pig-Pen's skin is dirty is remarkably similar to the manner in which he indicates that Franklin's is black. While the line hatching tends to be more scribbly with Pig-Pen and

Figure 5.3. Side-by-side comparison of Franklin and Pig-Pen. The panel on the left, featuring Franklin, is from a *Peanuts* comic strip published on November 2, 1969. The one on the right, depicting Pig-Pen, is from August 15, 1967. PEANUTS © Peanuts Worldwide LLC. Dist. by ANDREWS MCMEEL SYNDICATION. Reprinted with permission. All rights reserved.

more controlled and orderly with Franklin, the technique remains the same. Indeed, there are many instances throughout the strip in which Pig-Pen and Franklin look remarkably similar (fig. 5.3).[2] Moreover, that Franklin is still depicted with line hatching even in the Sunday comics when his skin is shaded brown only furthers this association. If the hatching on Franklin's arms and especially his face was used to indicate his race, then why didn't Schulz omit this feature from the Sunday strips when this character is clearly depicted as being nonwhite? Because the line hatching is not needed in these full-color comics to indicate that Franklin is Black but still appears on his skin, it can be seen as indicating that he is dirty like Pig-Pen—an association that carries over to the daily black-and-white strips. Indeed, in numerous strips throughout *Peanuts*, these two characters possess a visual kinship. Given the analogous shading method that is used to signal their identities, being Black is aesthetically likened to being dirty. Finally, the fact that Franklin's face is generally fully covered in line hatching, while Pig-Pen's clothes are heavily hatched but his face is often more sparingly so, can also be seen as augmenting this connection. While it is possible to see this distinction as indicating that the line hatching serves a different purpose for each character, it is equally possible to read the difference as signaling that Franklin's face is even dirtier than that of the notoriously filthy Pig-Pen.

This situation is far from an anomaly that is unique to *Peanuts*. As Frantz Fanon, Robin Bernstein, and Traci C. West have all documented, there is a long history of "racial cultural imagery that equates blackness with dirtiness" (West 30). For centuries in both Europe and the United States, "Blackness [has been] commonly considered the opposite of that which is pure, clean, and innocent" (30). As a result, "When this symbolic meaning of blackness is

Figure 5.4. Advertisement for Vinolia Soap, 1895. Available via Google Images.

wedded with the stereotype of black people being unkempt, unwashed, and comfortable in a squalid environment, a disparaging racial link to dirtiness is unmistakable" (30).

While this phenomenon can be located within an array of sites and sources, it is perhaps most vividly apparent in advertisements for soap during the nineteenth century. Soap companies were not simply acutely aware of the racialized association of blackness and dirt; they explicitly drew on it in their marketing campaigns. An advertisement for the Vinolia company from 1895 forms a poignant example (fig. 5.4). The left side of the promotion depicts a cherubic white girl at the seashore. She is offering a bar of soap to a Black child standing opposite her. "You Dirty Boy!" the ad announces in large script above the two figures and presumably spoken by the white one. Meanwhile, below the children's feet is a second line of text: "Why don't you wash yourself with Vinolia Soap?" This question, of course, implies that the Black playmate would not be Black if he were clean. If the Black child's mother just washed him with a good soap, he would become white as well. Blackness is akin to dirt; it can be scrubbed away.

The Pears Soap Company took the associations of blackness with dirtiness even further. In what has become an infamous print advertisement from 1884, the company presented a stunning demonstration of not simply figurative but literal "racial cleansing" (fig. 5.5). In the scene that appears on the left side, a white boy in an apron offers a large bar of soap to a Black peer who is sitting in a metal washtub. In the scene on the right, the Black child has now gotten out of the tub, presumably after completing his bath. From the neck down, his skin is now Caucasian white. The white child in the apron holds

Figure 5.5. Advertisement for Pears's Soap, 1884. Available via Google Images.

up a mirror to show the bather these results. His face bears a large smile; he is clearly delighted by this development. Lest any doubts remain about the highly racialized nature of this advertisement, it was based on Aesop's fable "Washing the Blackamoor White." The implication, both of the original tale and especially of the advertisement, is clear: Pears's soap "cleans so well" that it can turn Black children into white ones.[3]

Images of this kind also appeared in newspaper comics in the early twentieth century. As Lara Saguisag has written, a 1902 strip from Rudolph Dirks's popular *The Katzenjammer Kids* and a 1906 comic from Richard Outcault's equally successful *Buster Brown* series featured the title characters playing a prank on their families: they swap their clothing with a Black peer and then have him enter their home to see what happens. The reaction of both Buster Brown's mother and Mamma Katzenjammer when they see a Black child who they believe is their white one is the same: they are shocked by how "dirty" their youngster has become and immediately place him in a bathtub to scrub his skin "clean"—meaning white—again. Maternal consternation ensues when no amount of washing is effective. Mirroring both the overt and covert messages of Victorian soap ads, these sequences affirm, as Lara Saguisag has commented, "the notion that black skin 'connoted filth and ugliness'" (66).

Although this phenomenon is seemingly unrelated to the world of *Peanuts*, the strip can be connected with it. Schulz's use of a similar shading technique to indicate that Pig-Pen's skin is dirty and Franklin's skin is black places the comic in dialogue with long-standing racialized associations of blackness with dirt. Some *Peanuts* strips, in fact, recall both the imagery and the messages of Victorian soap ads in ways that are uncanny. The comic that

Figure 5.6. Panel from *Peanuts* comic strip, August 6, 1954. PEANUTS © Peanuts Worldwide LLC. Dist. by ANDREWS MCMEEL SYNDICATION. Reprinted with permission. All rights reserved.

appeared on August 6, 1954, offers a powerful example. The sequence opens with an image of Patty carrying a metal bucket that has a soapy sponge sticking out of the top. "I'm going to find 'Pig-Pen' and personally give him a **good** scrubbing!" she declares in the speech bubble (264; bold in original). When Patty arrives at the playground and sees Pig-Pen in the sandbox, she is astounded: he is impeccably clean. His clothes are unsoiled, his skin is free of even the smallest speck of dirt, and there is no trace of the dust cloud that usually surrounds him. After declaring, "I guess there's **some** hope for him, after all," she walks away with her supplies, presumably heading back home (264; bold in original). This closing speech balloon, however, does not tell the whole story of this strip—or reveal the source of its humor. As readers see in the final panel, Pig-Pen is only half-clean, literally (fig. 5.6). The angle from which he is presented has shifted. Instead of seeing him from only his right side—as Patty first did when she entered the playground—we now see the character from the front. This change in perspective reveals a striking contrast about his state of cleanliness: while the right side of Pig-Pen's body is sparkling, the left side is as filthy as ever. This gag forms another example of this character's perpetual connection to dirt, but it also recalls the racist soap ads in which "a good scrubbing" washes away the "dirtiness" of race. Indeed, in this strip and many others, Pig-Pen's dirtiness is assigned a clear value judgment: cleanliness is good and desirable; dirtiness is bad and undesirable.

Viewing Pig-Pen in this context opens up the character to other racialized readings. Together with being physically dirty, Pig-Pen is also disheveled. More specifically, his hair is unkempt. Especially by the mid-1960s, when Franklin made his debut, Pig-Pen's locks were almost always sticking up in a variety of directions from his head (fig. 5.7). This feature places him in dialogue with another highly racialized phenomenon in the United States:

Franklin and Pig-Pen: The Aesthetics of Blackness and Dirt   117

Figure 5.7. Panel from *Peanuts* comic strip, August 15, 1967. PEANUTS © Peanuts Worldwide LLC. Dist. by ANDREWS MCMEEL SYNDICATION. Reprinted with permission. All rights reserved.

blackface minstrelsy. A mode of popular entertainment in which white performers blackened their face with burned cork and imitated the music, speech patterns, and mannerisms of African Americans to mock them for the amusement of white audiences, blackface minstrelsy first emerged in urban theaters in the United States in the 1830s and 1840s. By the Civil War, its visual style and comedic methods permeated nearly all areas of American society. However unexpected and even seemingly unlikely, Pig-Pig contains a visual connection to this phenomenon. His wild hair recalls the woolly wigs worn by minstrel performers as well as the highly minstrelized way that young Black children were rendered in advertisements (figs. 5.8, 5.9).

Figure 5.8. Still image of Judy Garland in *Everybody Sing* (MGM, 1938).

Figure 5.9. Reproduction of a tin sign for Picaninny Freeze frozen treats, circa 1920s.

Figure 5.10. Panel from *Peanuts* comic strip, November 2, 1969. PEANUTS © Peanuts Worldwide LLC. Dist. by ANDREWS MCMEEL SYNDICATION. Reprinted with permission. All rights reserved.

Finally, the ways in which dirt and race overlap and interlock in *Peanuts* do not emanate solely from the representation of Pig-Pen. They can also be found in the depiction of Franklin. As mentioned earlier, Schulz drew all the comics by hand. As a result, his shading technique is not uniform: in some strips, the cartoonist drew thicker and more densely packed line hatching for Franklin, whereas in others the shading is more minimal. The result of this variation is that Franklin's skin tone changes from strip to strip. There are comics where he is presented as being lighter skinned, and others where his skin tone is considerably darker (figs. 5.1, 5.2, 5.10). These inconsistencies further the kinship between Franklin and Pig-Pen and, by extension, between blackness and dirt. The extent to which Pig-Pen is soiled varies, and so does the extent to which Franklin is shaded as black. If Franklin's skin tone can vary, then it is not something fixed but something variable. In this way, it further equates his blackness with dirtiness. A parallel arises between the variations to Franklin's skin tone and the variations to Pig-Pen's level of cleanliness. Moreover, given the way in which Pig-Pen's dirtiness is repeatedly denigrated, the same value judgment can easily be extended or extrapolated to Franklin's blackness.

BOTH GROUNDBREAKING AND ENTRENCHED: THE DIRECT AND INDIRECT MESSAGES OF FRANKLIN

The visual kinship that Franklin possesses with Pig-Peg complicates and even undercuts his reputation as a progressive character. The shared shading technique for these two figures connects them in ways that seriously compromise and even wholly contradict Schulz's intended activism. The cartoonist introduced a Black character to his comic strip with the intention of fostering compassion, encouraging empathy, and generating understanding. The visual elements that link Franklin to Pig-Pen have the opposite effect. Instead of helping to break down racial enmity, they work to maintain it. Even if only on an unconscious level, presenting Franklin in this manner reaffirms long-standing ways in which blackness has been stigmatized and Black people have been denigrated. In so doing, Schulz's inclusion of Franklin ironically reinforces some of the same harmful attitudes about race that he was created to combat.

To be clear, no evidence suggests that Charles M. Schulz presented Franklin's blackness in this manner to deliberately deride it or symbolically denigrate it. Again, the cartoonist was trying to engage in activism that would be progressive and would advance the cause of racial justice, equity, and civil rights. In fact, Schulz may have employed the line-hatching technique to indicate that Franklin is African American because he was following the example of another Black cartoonist. From the origins of American cartoon art in the nineteenth century, nonwhite characters had been presented, both in the plots to comics and in their visual depiction on the page, in highly stereotypical ways. As Frances Gateward and John Jennings have discussed, "The first images of Black people in comics were loosely based on the stereotypes generated in blackface minstrelsy" (5). Beginning with the Black youngsters who appeared in the background of Richard F. Outcault's the Yellow Kid during the 1890s, continuing with named characters such as Ebony White from Will Eisner's popular newspaper strip *The Spirit* during the 1940s, and extending through secondary sidekicks such as Jackson in *Dennis the Menace* in 1970, African American figures were depicted as comedic buffoons who more closely resembled simians than humans. Whether male or female, adult or child, these characters had dark black skin, big white eyes, and thick red lips. They were merely stock racist caricatures, not realistic individuals. Given this situation, Rebecca Wanzo has noted, "Racist caricature was thus not a side note to US cartooning's emergence. It was central to it" (7).

Morrie Turner, in his landmark newspaper strip *Wee Pals*, sought to change this trend. Making its debut on February 15, 1965, the comic was the first to feature a racially and ethnically diverse cast of young characters (Howard 16). Just as significantly, it also presented these individuals in ways that did not traffic in long-standing aesthetic stereotypes (16). Turner, for example, used line hatching, rather than dark shading, to indicate that Nipper was African American.

Charles M. Schulz was not only familiar with *Wee Pals*; he knew Morrie Turner professionally. As Martha Ross reported, the Black cartoonist "admired Schulz's 'Peanuts' and mulled creating a black Charlie Brown" (par. 13). Schulz encouraged him to do so. "He ran with that," recalled David Bellard, a family friend; *Wee Pals* was the end product of that process (par. 13).

When Schulz introduced an African American character to *Peanuts* in 1968, he may have employed line hatching to signal Franklin's race because of Turner's *Wee Pals*. The white cartoonist might have been following the lead of his Black colleague for how to depict African American characters in a more appropriate, nonbiased, and nonracist way. However, the fact that Schulz had already long employed the same aesthetic feature in *Peanuts* to signal dirt complicated and even nullified that objective.

This situation offers a powerful illustration of the gap that can occur between people's intentions and their actual impact. While Schulz's intentions were to combat racist stereotypes, his actions actually had the opposite effect: they perpetuated them, however unwittingly. Moreover, the ramifications of his actions extend far beyond this one individual. The way in which Schulz unconsciously, unintentionally, or accidently drew his new Black character in a manner that mirrored his dirty white character also exemplifies the insidiousness of racism. Disparaging attitudes about race become ingrained; by becoming ingrained, they become normalized; and by becoming normalized, they are perpetuated. Schulz did not notice that he used the same shading technique for Franklin's blackness as he did for Pig-Pen's dirtiness—or the often uncannily similar way that the two figures looked as a result. These features likewise cause readers of the strip—especially white ones—to associate Franklin's blackness with Pig-Pen's dirtiness, however unconsciously. When Harriet Glickman first contacted Schulz about adding a Black character to *Peanuts*, she was acutely aware of the power that this media wielded. As she explained in her initial letter, newspaper comics "are of tremendous importance in shaping the unconscious attitudes of our kids" (qtd. in Ha, par. 6). The messages that popular strips like *Peanuts* send, both directly and indirectly, explicitly or implicitly, influence adult and especially child readers in ways of which they might not be entirely aware.

The widespread public recognition of Franklin further underscores the gravity of this situation. As Christopher P. Lehman has written, "By 1973, Charles M. Schulz had developed one of the most durable and widely seen African American comic strip characters in the history of the industry" (133). Of course, Franklin was not the only Black character to appear in American newspaper comics during this era. The late 1960s and early 1970s saw the release of several new strips that not only featured Black child characters but were penned by Black cartoonists. As mentioned earlier, in 1965, Morrie Turner's *Wee Pals* made its debut. Showcasing a group of kids known as the "Rainbow Gang," the strip featured male and female youngsters who hailed from a diverse array of racial and ethnic backgrounds: Black, white, Chicano, Native American, Asian, and Jewish. Three years later, in 1968—the same year that Schulz added Franklin to *Peanuts*—another comic featuring young Black protagonists appeared: *Luther*. Created and drawn by Brumsic Brandon Jr., the strip ran until 1986 and presented some of the most pointed sociopolitical commentary in the history of American comics. Finally, but far from insignificantly, in 1970, Ted Shearer's strip *Quincy* began its sixteen-year run.[4] The comic chronicled the experiences of the title character, a young Black boy about nine years old who is being raised by his grandmother in Harlem. Although the strip had a clear protagonist, it featured a diverse array of characters: classmates whom Quincy meets at school, children who live in his neighborhood, and friends of his grandmother.

Given these titles, newspaper readers in the United States had a choice of several strips featuring nonwhite characters. However, none matched the popularity of *Peanuts* and thus the visibility of Franklin. From the mid-1960s through the early 1970s, Schulz's newspaper strip reached the apex of its success. Indeed, it is difficult to overestimate the commercial popularity as well as the cultural power of *Peanuts* during this period. As Chip Kidd has reported, "The comic strip ran in over 2,600 newspapers, with a readership of 355 million in seventy-five countries, translated into twenty-one languages" (n.p.). As a result, Franklin was seen by far more Americans, especially white Americans, than Luther, Quincy, or the characters from *Wee Pals*. Not only did Franklin appear in a strip that was exceedingly popular, but he was also one of the few Black characters on the comics page. In 1988, "*The Detroit Free Press* counted the number of characters in its comic pages in a given month, and came up with 5,250 Whites and 31 Blacks (0.6 percent)" (Howard 16–17). The statistics in 2004—four years after Schulz's death and the official end of *Peanuts*—were not much better. In the opening years of the twenty-first century, "96 percent of [comics] characters were White and only 2.5 percent were Black" (Tyree 45). Given this context, the messages that Schulz's character conveyed about race—both directly and indirectly, consciously and unconsciously, intentionally and inadvertently—wielded tremendous sociopolitical power. Franklin helped to shape popular attitudes about Black people in ways that audiences may not have been fully realized.

In the introduction to *The Blacker the Ink: Constructions of Black Identity in Comics and Sequential Art* (2015), Frances Gateward and John Jennings remarked: "There simply are not enough images of Black people in the mainstream not to be critical of the way they are constructed and portrayed" (7). The same observation applies to Franklin in *Peanuts*. This character has been too socially prominent, and his legacy too culturally powerful, for us not to examine and—in the words of Gateward and Jennings—be critical of the way in which he is constructed. Rebecca Wanzo has discussed the "expansive visual grammar" that makes up cartoon art (4). From speech balloons and emanata to panel frames and gutters, comics use these elements in ways that are both deliberate and also infused with symbolic meaning. Charles M. Schulz's *Peanuts* also had its own distinctive visual grammar. For over a decade, the line hatching that appeared on Pig-Pen's face and body was used to denote dirt. When a strikingly similar method of shading appeared on the new Black character Franklin, it is difficult to see this element as signaling a wholly new and entirely different feature. The time is long overdue not simply to read the lines that are used to indicate Franklin's race, but to read between them.

DRAWING LESSONS: THE AESTHETICS OF RACE AND THE RACIALIZATION OF AESTHETICS IN *PEANUTS*

The areas of visual overlap between Franklin and Pig-Peg complicate laudatory views about Schulz's groundbreaking Black character while also calling added attention to the importance of the line in both *Peanuts* and sequential art as a whole. As Jared Gardner has written on this subject, this feature is "arguably the most undertheorized element in comics scholarship" (53). While analyses of the medium from a narratological perspective have flourished in recent decades, these discussions have focused largely on the use of time, the role of focalization, and the question of genre (53–54). As Gardner observes, "Very little attention has been spent addressing the one feature of comics that marks them as profoundly different—and perhaps even irreducibly so—from both novel and film: the trace of the hand, the graphic enunciation that is the drawn line" (54). The drawn line is not only a signature feature of sequential art but also a rich source of aesthetic, literary, and semiotic meaning. The type of line that a cartoonist uses—its shape, size, thickness, appearance, and so on—is anything but an incidental or unimportant detail. On the contrary, this feature plays a crucial, though commonly overlooked, role in telling the story. The cartoonist's style of line—be it scribbly or controlled, thick or thin, and so on—also has a profound impact on the way that readers approach, view, and understand a comic. Different lines make different visual impressions, possess different cultural associations, and convey different moods. Consequently, our engagement with comics "is inseparable from our sense of the quality of [the artist's] line" (Gardner 59).

Figure 5.11. *Peanuts* comic strip, May 23, 1988. PEANUTS © Peanuts Worldwide LLC. Dist. by ANDREWS MCMEEL SYNDICATION. Reprinted with permission. All rights reserved.

Be it a serial comic strip or a single-issue graphic novel, "no reader could imagine that the narrative would mean the same way were it drawn with a *different* line" (58–59).

Both the narrative message and the sociocultural meaning that can be conveyed through the choice of line are vividly evident in Schulz's depiction of Franklin. The specific type, style, and shape of line that the cartoonist chose for rendering the race of his new Black character were far from unimportant or inconsequential. On the contrary, this feature is imbued with aesthetic, literary, and cultural significance. Paying attention to the significance of Schulz's line for shading Franklin alters our view of this character and, by extension, the commentary that the comic strip is making about race.

Schulz himself may have recognized this issue. Nearly twenty years after introducing Franklin, he changed the shading technique that he used for this character. In the strip that appeared on May 23, 1988, Franklin's skin is shaded using a method known as screentone (fig. 5.11). Screentone is not a hand-drawn shading technique; rather, it is a preprinted sheet with an adhesive back that is affixed to the page. Screentone comes in a variety of patterns: dots, lines, checks, gray scale, and so on. The sheets allow cartoonists to introduce different effects into their work. Moreover, because screentone is machine printed, it provides a consistency and uniformity that is not possible with hand drawing.

Beginning with the comic that was published on May 23, 1988, and in every strip that appeared thereafter until the cessation of *Peanuts* with Schulz's death in 2000, Franklin's skin is shaded via screentone. It is important to note that this shading option was available to Schulz when he first created Franklin. Printed images that used patterned plates and halftone screens were in wide circulation in the United States by 1900 (Benson 222–30). These elements were also a recurring feature of comics and comic books. Indeed, the dot pattern was a common method for coloring both figures and backgrounds. During the 1930s, Zip-A-Tone was one of the most popular manufacturers for cartoonists (Gurney). Screentone sheets were standard supplies for many cartoonists, as commonplace and even as necessary as pencils and ink. As a result, when Schulz first created Franklin, line hatching was not the only option available to him for shading. Screentone also had a long history of being used for this purpose.

In addition to the fact that screentone predated the creation of Franklin, it is equally important to note that this method was more costly, time-consuming, and laborious than hand-drawn shading. Instead of simply drawing a series of lines to shade Franklin's skin, Schulz had to engage in multiple steps. First he had to purchase the screentone sheets, which are expensive. Then he needed to peel off the adhesive back and affix the sheet to his drawing. The sheets are extremely thin, and applying them without leaving any air bubbles, crinkles, or creases can be difficult. Next Schulz needed to use a precision knife to cut away the portions of the screentone that he did not want to appear in the drawing: that is, any areas that were not Franklin's face, arms, legs, and so on. Once again, doing so is tricky; the sheets can tear if the cut misses even a small segment. Conversely, if the cuts are too deep, the cartoonist can gouge the drawing beneath, damaging it. Finally, Schulz needed to firmly press and carefully smooth down the screentone areas that remained, lest they peel off in transit to his syndicate. Consequently, Schulz's switch from line hatching to screentone for rendering this character was also a decision that made his work as a cartoonist harder, not easier.

Given the multiple steps as well as the potential hazards that accompany working with screentone, Schulz's decision to shift to this shading technique was certainly deliberate. This method was one that he clearly felt was worth the extra time, effort, and expense. Unfortunately, the cartoonist never commented on the reason for this change. None of his professional correspondence, personal conversations, or creative notes indicate whether he made this change because he was dissatisfied—or recognized any problems—with how he had been presenting Franklin's race.[5]

The aesthetic rendering of Black characters in major American newspaper strips between the debut of Franklin in 1968 and his redesign two decades later, however, offers some possible insight into Schulz's decision. Over this period, groundbreaking comics such as *Dateline: Danger!*, *Luther*, and *Quincy* were created by Black cartoonists and featured protagonists who were African American. None of these titles, however, used line hatching to indicate race. In *Dateline: Danger!*, the artist Al McWilliams employed chiaroscuro techniques, sometimes referred to as modeling. Both Brumsic Brandon Jr. in *Luther* and Ted Shearer in *Quincy* used screentone. The same observation also applies to Black characters who appeared in strips that were drawn by white cartoonists. For example, Mort Walker eschewed line hatching when he introduced Lieutenant Jackson Flap to his popular military-themed comic *Beetle Bailey* on October 5, 1970. Rather than shading the character in any way, the cartoonist indicated race through alternative visual cues, such as Jackson's Afro. The character's skin tone, however, looks exactly like that of his white peers: it is not marked, literally or figuratively, in any manner. One exception to this trend was also one that faced criticism. Garry Trudeau employed line hatching to identify the race of a new cast member in *Doonesbury*, Rufus "Thor" Jackson. Making his debut on April 5, 1971, Rufus's face and arms were covered with even more closely packed parallel lines than those used for Franklin. That said, Trudeau did not include hatching around the character's mouth, a detail that suggested the prominence of his lips.[6] Trudeau's aesthetic choices drew criticism and undercut the sociopolitical messages that the cartoonist was trying to make via the addition of a recurring Black figure (Hébert).

Admittedly, the physical appearance of every character in *Peanuts* changed over the strip's long run. Snoopy, for instance, stands up and begins walking on two legs instead of four. Additionally, Charlie Brown acquires his signature shirt with the black zigzag around the bottom. Finally, the proportions of all the characters shift: their heads transform from oblong ovals to round circles, their bodies grow taller, and their facial features are aged up. Charlie Brown, for example, is identified as "roughly four years old" in November 3, 1950. He is later identified as "six years old" in the comic that appeared on November 17, 1957. Finally, in a strip published on July 11, 1979, he is identified as being "eight and a half years old" ("Charlie Brown").

Nonetheless, the change to Franklin's appearance seems particularly significant. Together with the aforementioned extra effort, cost, and hassle involved with using screentone rather than line hatching to represent the character's race, this shift also occurred during a time when the appearance of Schulz's characters had largely stabilized. During the first decade or so of *Peanuts*, both the aesthetic style of the comic and the physical depiction of the figures underwent significant modification. Strips that initially appeared during the 1950s look markedly different; they are immediately recognizable as earlier strips from the series. By 1988, however, Schulz had found his style, and *Peanuts* settled into the aesthetic look that it would possess for the remainder of its run. To be sure, comics that were published during this period are virtually indistinguishable from ones that were released in the final few years of the series.

Accordingly, Schulz's decision to change Franklin's appearance takes on added artistic import as well as sociocultural significance. As Jared Gardner has observed, "*How* something is said is often explicitly more important than *what* is said" (57–58). This maxim has long been recognized in the realm of text-only narratives. Gardner's work demonstrates that it also applies to comics when we notice the importance of the line. Perhaps Schulz had the exact same realization about Franklin. The "what" of his Black character was positive: he is kind, smart, and considerate. However, the "how" for this figure—that is, the way that his race was being visually represented—was not. Clearly, Schulz decided that he could do better with Franklin by literally trying harder. That this change also severed any visual similarities between the *Peanuts* character who was Black and one who was dirty seems too strong to be merely coincidental.

FROM BREAKING THE COLOR LINE TO BECOMING COLOR-BLIND: THE PROBLEM WITH NOT SEEING RACE BOTH INSIDE AND OUTSIDE OF COMICS

Harriet Glickman was moved to write Charles Schulz about introducing a Black character to the cast of *Peanuts* by a specific event: the assassination of Dr. Martin Luther King Jr. On April 4, 1968, the civil rights leader was shot and killed in Memphis, Tennessee. News of King's death weighed heavily on the white schoolteacher from Los Angeles. "Since the death of Martin Luther King, Jr.," Glickman told Schulz in the opening sentence of her letter, dated just eleven days after the murder, "I've been asking myself what I can do to help change those conditions in our society which led to the assassination" (qtd. in Ha).

Of the many poignant letters, essays, and sermons that Martin Luther King Jr. wrote during his all-too-brief career, his "I Have a Dream" speech is among the most famous. Delivered on August 28, 1963, at the March on Washington, the speech contains the now-famous line "I have a dream that my four little children will one day live in a nation where they will not be judged by the color of their skin, but by the content of their character" (5). King's remarks, of course, offered a commentary on the long-standing practice of racial segregation. For more than a century, African Americans, especially in the South, were not permitted attend to certain schools, not allowed to patronize various business, and not able to exercise their constitutional right to vote simply because they were Black. King's statement about the hope that he had for his children indicted this unjust racist practice. It called for an end to discrimination based on race.

In so doing, the "I Have a Dream" speech is commonly seen as inaugurating what has come to be known as an ethos of "color blindness" with regard to race. In marked contrast to the long-standing practice of segregation, in which the color of an individual's skin was paramount, color blindness—as its name implied—purported not to see race. Given that discrimination in the United States had long been based on race, not seeing race was an obvious way to end this practice. By not paying attention to skin color, individuals would no longer be subjected to bias or prejudice.

This approach sounds like an appropriate, logical, and even fail-safe means to end discrimination and create racial equality. Mychal Denzel Smith has written, "Certainly, a world where we all loved one another would be ideal, where each person is seen as equal, where 'the dream' of children of all different racial backgrounds holding hands with one another without prejudice is a reality" (par. 3). That said, as Smith goes on to explain, the way that color-blind attitudes about race have operated in the United States has been markedly different. In the years since King's speech, color-blind policies have been predicated on a "misunderstanding [of] the message of Martin Luther King, Jr." (par. 3). The problem arises from a lack of awareness among white people about the difference between individual and structural forms of racism. In the words of Smith once again: "The lessons [white] Baby Boomers and Gen-Xers gleaned from the Civil Rights era is that racism is a matter of personal bigotry—racists hate people because of the color of their skin, or because they believe stereotypes about groups of people they've never met—not one of institutional discrimination and exploitation" (par. 3). As a result, white "Baby Boomers and Gen-Xers generally decided to ignore King's diagnosis of the problem—white supremacy—and opted to make him a poster-child for a colorblind society, in which we simply ignore [the] construct of race altogether and pray that it will disappear on its own" (par. 3). Of course, systemic societal change does not happen in this way. These shifts occur because individuals, groups, and sociopolitical institutions make deliberate, consistent, and usually ardent efforts to enact them.

This oversight leads to a situation whereby individuals can be "fluent in colorblindness and diversity, while remaining illiterate in the language of anti-racism" (Smith, par. 2). An inability to see race also becomes an inability to recognize continuing forms of structural racism: police profiling, redlining, the school-to-prison pipeline, and so on. In the words of Nicole Akoukou, "While the colorblind generation's ambitions are charming, removing race without addressing practices and policies based on race or racism is futile" (par. 8). As she explains, "Conversations about fairness, equality, privilege and discrimination with a special emphasis on race must take place, not be neglected, otherwise there will be no progress" (par. 8). Furthermore, the ethos of color blindness has led many white people to believe that merely talking about race or calling attention to it in any way is discriminatory. Instead they must remain "color-blind" at all times. Thus many white people lack the verbal terminology, the critical skills, and the sociopolitical awareness to even discuss race and racism. They simply have no practice or experience doing so.

King's death moved Harriet Glickman to urge Charles M. Schulz to add a Black character to his newspaper strip, and Franklin's debut broke the color line in mainstream American newspaper comics. That said, it would be a mistake to view the character through a lens of color blindness. Not only did the fact that a Black character joined the cast of *Peanuts* matter a great deal, but how his race was visually presented was equally important. Contrary to the famous line from King's "I Have a Dream" speech, in the case of Franklin, we must pay attention both to the content of his character and to the color of his skin. Ignoring how his blackness was represented for nearly twenty years in *Peanuts* is not being racially progressive; it is ignoring and thereby perpetuating another facet of systemic racism. We must see the color of Franklin's skin to see the commonalities it shares with the depiction of Pig-Pen. If we do not see Franklin's race, then we cannot see the way in which his blackness has a visual affinity with dirtiness.

Jared Gardner has written: "Comics is a medium that calls attention with every line to its own boundaries, frames, and limitations—and to the labor involved in both accommodating and challenging those limitations" (65). Franklin is a powerful example of this phenomenon. He exemplifies the way in which comics can break barriers while also reinforcing them. Paying attention to the aesthetics of race with Franklin makes this character's legacy far more politically problematic, but also more socioculturally precise. Schulz's intention in adding a Black character to the *Peanuts* gang was to increase racial visibility, promote greater understanding, and ultimately combat racism. Critics have long focused on the ways in which Franklin achieved these goals. However, recognizing, unpacking, and discussing the ways in which Schulz's efforts paradoxically contradicted such goals is just as important—and arguably even more so.

The next chapter makes a radical departure from this one. First, it examines a nonhuman character: the bird Woodstock. Additionally, it places him in the context of contemporaneous events rather than historical ones: namely, the Woodstock music festival after which the avian figure was named. Finally, it eschews an interest in the aesthetics or appearance of Schulz's bird, focusing instead on his actions, behaviors, and personality traits. In so doing, chapter 6 differs not only from this one but also from previous discussions in *Blockheads, Beagles, and Sweet Babboos*. Such details notwithstanding, my consideration of Woodstock shares the same ultimate goal: to present a familiar *Peanuts* character in an unexpected way. Woodstock's namesake has long been widely known. However, as with other equally prominent but underexplored elements of *Peanuts*—Charlie Brown's zigzag shirt, Snoopy's feline tendencies, Franklin's line shading, and so on—its cultural meaning and symbolic significance have never been fully explored. The 1969 Woodstock music festival was marketed as "an Aquarian Exposition." The next chapter asserts that, in Schulz's strip, the event became an avian one as well.

CHAPTER 6

CHIRPING 'BOUT MY GENERATION

Woodstock, Youth Culture, and Innocence

Franklin Armstrong was not the only new character to be introduced to *Peanuts* in the 1960s. So too was another figure: Woodstock. Although a bird rather than a human, Woodstock quickly became a beloved member of the *Peanuts* cast as Snoopy's comedic sidekick and good buddy. Indeed, of the comic's many famous pairings—Peppermint Patty and Marcie, Lucy and Schroeder, Linus and his security blanket—Snoopy and Woodstock rank among them. For many fans, in fact, the image of Snoopy sitting atop his red doghouse is not complete without the presence of the little yellow bird.

As one might imagine given the distinctive nature of Woodstock's appellation, Schulz's character was named after the legendary music festival that took place in upstate New York in August 1969. The cartoonist explained in an interview from 1973: "At one point I began to draw the bird a little better. I needed a name for him, and with the Woodstock festival being so prominent in the news, I said, 'Why not?'" (Schulz, *Conversations* 74). Little birds had flown into and out of *Peanuts* since the early 1960s. Most of the time, they appeared in small groups and interacted with Snoopy, stopping at his doghouse as they migrated south for the winter or—in one well-known strip from April 29, 1967—scouting for a place to play dominoes. In March 1966, the feathered creature who would eventually be dubbed Woodstock was introduced to the strip: a mother bird lands on Snoopy's stomach while he is sleeping atop his doghouse, builds a nest, and lays her eggs. Woodstock is one of the hatchlings. The little bird returns again the following spring, becoming a recurring character. That said, it was not until the comic that appeared on June 22, 1970, when the character was given a name.

In the fifty years since Schulz unveiled the name of his yellow bird, critics, biographers, and fans have been puzzled by the choice. Benjamin Clark, the curator of the Charles M. Schulz Museum and Research Center, notes that the cartoonist was "kind of cryptic" about this decision (qtd. in Cavna C01). Although Schulz discussed the creation of Woodstock at various points during his career, he never explained his specific rationale for naming the character after the festival. Comments that Schulz made during a 1987 interview typify his remarks on the subject. "I had been reading the *Life* magazine article about the Woodstock Festival and I had the little bird in the strip," he reflected. "It was a she and she was Snoopy's secretary and I was doing secretary jokes quite often so then I thought Woodstock would be a good name for this bird and also, it will get the attention of these people that liked that kind of thing. Suddenly she was not a secretary; she became Woodstock, the boy. It just happened. But that's what's good about a comic strip—you can just do it" (qtd. in Combemale). As these remarks indicate, Schulz had no clear creative reason or compelling narrative purpose for selecting the name. Instead, as the cartoonist would reiterate in a variety of other articles and interviews, "Woodstock" just seemed to fit the avian character. Given this situation, Benjamin Clark went on to speculate, "I can see him saying: 'That sounds like a bird species name'" (qtd. in Cavna C01).

Adding to the mystery, of course, is the fact that Woodstock doesn't possess any of the traits commonly associated with the legendary concert: he is not a musician, he does not wear tie-dye, and he does not flash the peace sign. Because of the lack of obvious links, historians have speculated that perhaps Schulz was inspired by the now-iconic logo for the Woodstock festival—which shows a bird sitting on the neck of a guitar. The image appeared in media coverage about the festival, including the cover of a special issue of *Life* magazine that the cartoonist saw. However, Schulz's bird character looks nothing like the one in the logo. Snoopy's feathered friend is canary-like, with a thin body, large head, short legs, and spiky plumage encircling his head. By contrast, the bird on the poster for the Woodstock music festival is a catbird, a dovelike species that has a tiny head, plump body, long legs, and no head plumage. Given that the two creatures have no obvious kinship beyond both being birds, the common critical consensus for the past five decades has been that no direct relationship exists between the comic strip character and iconic rock concert. As Clark commented about the cartoonist's creative decisions, "He may reference things in the strip, but sometimes it was only because it was popular or just felt apt that day, like naming Woodstock. He didn't have any connection, had no real affinity, [Schulz] just felt the name fit" (Clark, "Research").

This chapter continues my overarching project of revisiting, reexamining, and rethinking the core cast members of Schulz's comic by taking a second look at Woodstock. Although the bird is a key figure in *Peanuts* for the second half of its run, he has yet to be the focus of sustained critical analysis. The pages that follow offer a corrective to this trend by revisiting one of Woodstock's most stubbornly elusive features: his name. While previous critics have concluded that there is no link between the appellation that Schulz chose for his yellow bird and the historic musical festival, I make a case that the moniker is highly resonant. By naming the avian figure after the well-known event, Schulz invites his readers to see the character as a metaphor or even metonym for it. At the same time, and perhaps even more importantly, the cartoonist is also encouraging readers to see Woodstock as an embodiment of the era's young people, the Woodstock Generation.

Reexamining Schulz's Woodstock through this lens changes our perception of him along with his role in the comic. The yellow bird has long been seen as Snoopy's best friend and comedic sidekick. This new viewpoint reveals that he is also a conduit for an array of sociopolitical issues that evoke some of the core topics and foundational themes of Schulz's work. When *Peanuts* debuted on October 2, 1950, the comic strip offered a pointed commentary on US children and childhood. Twenty years later, in June 1970, with the decision to name a character Woodstock, Schulz can be seen as revisiting this interest for a new generation of young people. The little bird, through both his semantics and his plotlines, takes up questions of youth and youth culture once again. Echoing a well-known lyric from a song that the British rock band The Who performed at Woodstock, Schulz's avian character is not simply named after this famous music festival; he can be seen as chirping 'bout his generation.

"A CROWD OF WILD, USELESS KIDS": HATRED FOR HIPPIES AND WOODSTOCK'S WONDROUS WEEKEND

The importance of the Woodstock music festival—or, as it was officially known, the Woodstock Music and Art Fair (WMAF)[1]—is difficult to overstate. The event took place from August 15 to 18, 1969,[2] in Bethel, New York, and, in the words of John Anthony Moretta, is "one of the most mythologized events in the history of the 1960s counterculture" (285). Roughly four hundred thousand people attended the free outdoor concert on Max Yasgur's dairy farm.[3] Over the course of the four days, more than thirty acts performed. Many of these musicians were at the height of their popularity then and remain legends today: Joan Baez, Janis Joplin, Creedence Clearwater Revival, Jimi Hendrix, the Grateful Dead, Santana, The Who, Joe Cocker, and Crosby, Stills, Nash & Young.

The size of the crowd and the caliber of the performers, however, are not the only elements that make the WMAF so historic. As Andy Bennett has written, the event "remains, in the popular imagination, the point at which the creative and political energies of the 1960's counter-cultural movement briefly united" (xiv). The WMAF was not merely successful; it was utopian. The closing years of the 1960s were marked by social unrest, political upheaval, and even civic violence. However, as *Life* magazine reported about the WMAF, "there wasn't so much as a fist fight" all weekend (n.p.).[4] In this way, the WMAF demonstrated that "people from all realms of the human condition could come together, share peace, love and music, celebrate the death of hatred, bigotry and senseless war, social injustice, and ecologically disastrous materialism" (Evans i). For this reason, both during the 1960s and today, more than fifty years later, "'the happening' at Woodstock created a generational legend that shows no sign of fading" (Moretta 285).

While today the WMAF is widely lauded as a defining moment of the 1960s, the positive press that it received at the time was the exception, not the rule. For much of the decade, the ideals, the events, and especially the individuals who constituted the youth counterculture movement known as the hippies were vilified. Whereas most generations rebel against the one that preceded them, a segment of primarily white, middle-class, heterosexual young people in the 1960s took this phenomenon one step further. These individuals challenged more than merely their parents' values through standard outlets like their taste in music or choice of clothes; on the contrary, they challenged the foundations of American society as a whole. Hippies saw white, middle-class, mainstream American life as spiritually empty, emotionally unfulfilling, and economically corrupt—as well as corrupting (Miller xiv–xv). For them, the postwar American dream—a white-collar job, monogamous marriage, house in the suburbs, and so on—was a nightmare. Far from bringing happiness or even contentment, that life yielded little more than suffocating social conformity, shallow consumerism, and prudish sexual mores. As a result, the white, middle-class, heterosexual young men and women who overwhelmingly were the hippies rejected this life trajectory altogether (xiv–xv). Heeding the advice of Timothy Leary, they decided to "tune in" to alternative modes of communal living, "turn on" to mind-expanding drugs like LSD, and "drop out" of the capitalistic system altogether.

Unsurprisingly, given these views, the hippies were not held in high esteem by mainstream American society. John Anthony Moretta has written that the popular press "cast all such youth as spoiled, selfish, lazy, and hedonistic cowards and sissies . . . or worse, outright losers, drop-outs disguising themselves as members of a 'love generation' that preached peace and brotherhood while living the life of a privileged slacker" (341). Either way, the end result was the same: hippies were scorned, derided, and condemned. *Time* magazine's cover story about hippies on July 7, 1967, painted a representative portrait. "Once unleashed, most hippies first become insatiable hedonists," the article that appeared during the Summer of Love asserted, "smoking and eating whatever can turn them on in a hurry; making love, however and with whomever they can find (including 'group grope')" ("The Hippies"). This kind of coverage was far from unusual; the *Saturday Evening Post* dedicated a full issue to the growing counterculture movement a few months later. The headline that adorned the cover from September 1967 provided a clear indication of the magazine's view on the phenomenon: "The Hippie Cult: Who They Are, What They Want, Why They Act That Way." Such attitudes persisted over the coming years. Boston municipal court chief justice Elijah Adlow, in an article that appeared in the *Boston Globe* on October 21, 1968, saw nothing positive in the countercultural movement: "These youth know nothing of their responsibilities and have a distorted concept of their rights" (qtd. in Lewis 54). Adlow went on to denounce the entire hippie generation, calling them "a crowd of wild, useless kids" (qtd. in Lewis 54).[5]

The widespread public antipathy to hippies, in fact, is the reason that the WMAF ended up in Bethel, New York. The event was originally scheduled to take place in the town of Wallkill—about fifty miles west—but the organizers were forced to move less than a month before opening day when the locals passed an ordinance that forbade public events of more than five thousand people. The new law was specifically designed to expel the WMAF. Long before the legislation was proposed, the townspeople had expressed their disapproval in ways that were far harsher than the language of the new ordinance. Lee Blumer, who worked for the festival, "remembered hearing locals [in Wallkill] declare 'They were going to shoot the first hippie that walked into town'" (Moretta 287).

The WMAF's reception in Bethel was only marginally better. Although the town did not pass any last-minute ordinances to prevent the festival from taking place, many (if not most) residents were not pleased that it was happening there. Max Yasgur, the local dairy farmer—and conservative Republican—on whose land the event was held, was quickly vilified. Makeshift signs went up around town calling for the boycott of his milk and milk products. "Stop Max's Hippie Music Festival. No 150,000 hippies here. Buy No Milk," a representative placard read (Warner 59). Harm to his business was not the only consequence that Yasgur faced; he was also threatened with physical violence. Organizers recounted "seeing people approach Yasgur on the street 'with red faces and tempers flaring . . . threatening to blow up his house'" (Moretta 288). While Yasgur was the primary target for the town's ire, anyone who supported the WMAF or was working with it was subject to verbal abuse and even physical threats. As John Anthony Moretta has written, "Another one of the festival's town supporters, White Lake resort owner Elliot Tiber, also received menacing phone calls and threats. 'They'd say that it'll never happen, that we will break your legs. There was terrible name-calling. It was anti-Semitic and anti-hippie. It was dirty and filthy'" (Moretta 288).

Widespread dislike for hippies also shaped early media coverage of the WMAF. In everything from the musical groups who played to the young people who attended, the event was regarded "as the quintessential hippie gathering" (Moretta 286). As a result, both while the festival was taking place and then in its immediate aftermath, the WMAF was denounced. The *New York Times* was the closest national newspaper to the event and had coverage about it each day. On August 16, 1969, Barnard L. Collier called the festival "a squalid freakout, a monstrous Dionysian revel, where a mob of crazies gathered to drop acid and groove to hours of amplified cacophony" (A1). The paper reiterated this view over the next few days. On August 18, the closing day of the WMAF, the *New York Times* called the event "Nightmare in the Catskills" (34). An editorial that appeared two days later, on August 20, went even further. Written by the crime reporter Alfonso Narvaez, it focused on the reaction of the local community to the WMAF. Bearing the headline "Bethel Farmers Call Fair a Plot to Avoid the Law," the article discussed the pervasive drug use, widespread trespassing on private property, and extensive damage to local farmland that had been caused by the sheer size of the crowd and the muddy conditions.

In the weeks after the WMAF, the tone of mainstream coverage would shift. On August 25, 1969, the *New York Times* ran a lengthy article revisiting and reconsidering the WMAF. Interviewing a group of young people who had attended, the article's overarching view was "the sense that something of considerable significance had taken place" ("Morning After" 42). The mythologizing of the WMAF had begun. This trend would accelerate in the months and years that followed. Before long, the WMAF would be immortalized as "one of the most significant political and sociological events of the age" (Moretta 291). For this reason, as Mike Greenblatt reflected on the fiftieth anniversary of the WMAF, "that beautiful, bizarre and implausible scene would define a generation" (11).[6]

"NOW, I'VE SEEN EVERYTHING . . . A BIRD HIPPIE!": SNOOPY'S FEATHERED FRIEND AS COUNTERCULTURE CREATURE

Charles M. Schulz was anything but a hippie. First and foremost, he was a full generation older than the young people who formed the counterculture movement in the 1960s. When the WMAF took place, the cartoonist was forty-six, well beyond the cutoff of the hippie credo "don't trust anyone over thirty." Several of Schulz's children, who were born between 1950 and 1958, were in the age range for attending the WMAF, but none of them did, nor did any of their friends, classmates, or acquaintances (Clark, "Exhibit"). The cartoonist's musical tastes were also far afield from the performers who played at the festival. As Michael Cavna has written, "Schulz was not particularly a fan of rock music—his record collection leaned toward classical and country western" (C01). The curator of the Charles M. Schulz Museum and Research Center noted that the cartoonist "owned no records of anyone that performed at Woodstock" (Clark, "Exhibit"). Finally, while Schulz did engage in some forms of progressive politics—such as adding the Black character Franklin to his strip's cast in July 1968—his attitudes, opinions, and actions were far more conservative. The cartoonist identified as an "Eisenhower Republican" in the 1960s (Clark, "Another").[7] Schulz supported Nixon, not Kennedy, in the 1960 presidential election (Lind 159).[8] Moreover, in 1967, Schulz not only met but befriended Ronald Reagan, who was the governor of California at the time. "The Reagans invited Schulz and his first wife Joyce for lunch at the Governor's Mansion in Sacramento," a meeting that would mark the beginning of a long association and friendly correspondence (Huntsinger). As Stephen J. Lind reports, "Nancy Reagan even once instructed her limousine driver to make a detour by the studio just to visit Sparky" (113). Moreover, when her husband was running for president in 1980, he sent Schulz a letter asking if Snoopy could be dissuaded from entering the race if he promised him a cabinet position (Reagan 683).

Schulz lived roughly an hour north of San Francisco throughout the 1960s, first in Sebastopol and then in Santa Rosa. Not only did San Francisco's Haight-Ashbury area serve as a geographic hub for hippies, but Golden Gate Park was the setting for the much-publicized Summer of Love in 1967. Although Schulz was in close proximity to these events, he rarely included them in his comics. As Cavna notes, "The tumultuous decade was mostly reflected only glancingly in the strip, through the mostly warm and fuzzy filter of situational humor" (C01). For example, Peppermint Patty, who makes her debut in 1966, reflects changing fashion trends in general and the hippie style in particular by wearing sandals. Additionally, in July 1968, Snoopy uses the word "groovy" to describe himself and his nascent presidential campaign.

Of all the characters in *Peanuts*, in fact, Snoopy is most commonly regarded as the one who engages with issues and events of the Vietnam era. Jessica K. Brandt has observed that both the beagle's outward actions and especially his rich inner life can be viewed as a "vibrant, if sometimes misguided . . . function of Cold War fantasy" (179). Not only does Snoopy enter the tumultuous 1968 presidential race, but—in the same year—he also serves as a mascot for NASA's Apollo space program. Additionally, during a decade of growing unrest at colleges and universities, Snoopy increasingly appears in his "Big Man on Campus" persona. Even more pointedly, in a series of comics during the first week of July 1970, Snoopy is invited to give the commencement speech at the Daisy Hill Puppy Farm. Just as he takes the stage, however, tear gas is fired at demonstrators who are protesting dogs being sent to Vietnam; the chemical cloud compels the beagle to flee the podium. Finally, and perhaps most powerfully of all, are Snoopy's World War I Flying Ace episodes. First appearing on October 10, 1965, most offer a war-is-hell message that makes them difficult not to see as commentary on Vietnam. Indeed, Schulz scaled back these sequences as the war escalated, feeling that they were both too evocative of scenes on the nightly news and, given that they featured a dog on a doghouse, too flippant (Michaelis 394–95). A war veteran himself, Schulz knew the horrors of combat all too well, and he did not want to be seen as trivializing, minimizing, or making light of them in any way.

Although Snoopy has long been identified as the *Peanuts* character who has the most direct, sustained, and multifaceted engagement with events from the 1960s, his avian best friend offers an important—and long-overlooked—locus of commentary. Years before Woodstock was given his symbolic name, the character was associated with signature elements from the decade. In September 1964—after a summer that saw both widespread racial unrest in cities like New York and Philadelphia and the passage of the landmark Civil Rights Act—the little yellow bird and his feathered friends engage in a series of demonstrations. In keeping both with the inscrutability of the birds' verbal communication and with Schulz's tendency to avoid taking a direct stance on political issues, the protest signs that the birds hold are nonspecific: they contain either punctuation marks or symbols such as the G clef, pi, and so on—details that contribute to their humor. The bird protest sequence occupies two full weeks of weekday strips, concluding on September 12, when Snoopy declares that he always supports the "underbird." Schulz reprised this sequence four years later, in July 1968. During a tumultuous summer

Figure 6.1. *Peanuts* comic strip, July 12, 1967. PEANUTS © Peanuts Worldwide LLC. Dist. by ANDREWS MCMEEL SYNDICATION. Reprinted with permission. All rights reserved.

that began with the assassination of Robert F. Kennedy in early June and ended with the brutal assault on protesters at the Democratic National Convention in late August, the diminutive bird and his feathered friends begin frequenting Snoopy's doghouse while holding a series of signs. Once again, the placards contain no words, only images, ranging from punctuation marks to symbols like "R" and "π." In some strips, the birds seem to be picketing Snoopy's doghouse with their signs; in others, the birds are cast as delegates at a political convention, and their signs reveal the candidate whom they are supporting. Regardless, the sequence extends for two full weeks in July 1968. At one point, Snoopy joins the birds with his own placard: an image of a dog's footprint, which, as Linus explains to Sally in the comic from July 8, 1968, stands for "Paw Power."

It should perhaps come as no surprise that the small bird and his pals are the ones who stage demonstrations. The character who would ultimately be dubbed Woodstock is associated with another core aspect of the 1960s: hippies. In the strip that appeared on July 12, 1967, Snoopy is roused from sleeping atop his doghouse by a puzzling sight out of the frame (fig. 6.1). "Now, I've seen everything . . . ," he says, sitting up. The final image reveals the source of Snoopy's amazement: it shows a Woodstock-like bird joining the beagle on his doghouse. The feathers on the back of the bird's head hang down very long, akin to shaggy hair. Lest readers see the plumage as merely the appearance of this particular species, Snoopy explains why this sight is

Figure 6.2. *Peanuts* comic strip, July 13, 1967. PEANUTS © Peanuts Worldwide LLC. Dist. by ANDREWS MCMEEL SYNDICATION. Reprinted with permission. All rights reserved.

Figure 6.3. *Peanuts* comic strip, November 1, 1967. PEANUTS © Peanuts Worldwide LLC. Dist. by ANDREWS MCMEEL SYNDICATION. Reprinted with permission. All rights reserved.

so unusual and thus noteworthy. With his eyes opened wide in a look that is part amazement, part disbelief, Snoopy exclaims in the thought balloon above his head: "A bird hippie!"

The long-haired bird joins Snoopy again in the comic on the following day (fig. 6.2). The first two panels show the bird talking passionately to Snoopy about an unknown subject. After the creature flies away, Snoopy offers his opinion about the bird's complaints. "I don't see why he gets so upset," the beagle reflects as he lies down atop the doghouse. "No one understands **my** generation, either!" (bold in original).

Lest the little bird is not firmly associated with the 1960s counterculture by this point, Schulz reiterates the association a few months later, by repeating one of his previous gags. On Halloween, Snoopy joins Linus for his annual vigil waiting for the Great Pumpkin. Forming a cliff-hanger to the strip that appeared on October 31, 1967, the pair are startled by the sound of rustling across the pumpkin patch. The comic that appears the next day ends the suspense (fig. 6.3). Taking place the following morning, it depicts Linus relaying his profound disappointment that the rustling was not caused by the Great Pumpkin. "And who does it turn out to be?" Snoopy says in dismay via thought balloons that occupy the closing two panels. "A bird-hippie!" In the drawing that accompanies his comment, the long-haired bird strolls nonchalantly through the patch.

AS FREE AS A BIRD: SCHULZ'S WOODSTOCK AND THE WOODSTOCK GENERATION

Schulz's bird was dubbed "Woodstock" on June 22, 1970, a full ten months after the music festival itself and nine months after the cartoonist saw the special issue of *Life* magazine. By this point, much of the positive press that the WMAF received had been overshadowed and even undercut. Two other events, both of which took place in Schulz's home state of California and were associated with the youth counterculture, had tarnished the public image of hippies once again: the first was the Tate-LaBianca murders, and the second was the Rolling Stones' concert at Altamont Speedway.

Less than a week before the WMAF began, Los Angeles was shocked by back-to-back nights of gruesome slayings. Just after midnight on August 9, 1969, the actress Sharon Tate, three friends, and a young salesman who had just pulled down the driveway were brutally murdered at the home that Tate and her husband, the director Roman Polanski, were renting. The actress was eight and a half months pregnant at the time. The details from the crime scene were horrific: Tate was stabbed 16 times; Abigail Folger, 28 times; and Wojciech Frykowski, who fled the house only to be tackled on the front lawn, was stabbed 51 times, shot twice, and struck in the head by the butt of a gun an additional 13 times (Kneeland, "Coroner" 27). Making this already grisly crime even more macabre, some of Tate's blood was used to write the word "PIG" on the front door.

On the following night, the murder spree continued when Leno and Rosemary LaBianca were killed in their home in the Los Feliz neighborhood of Los Angeles. Once again, the crimes were exceedingly violent. Leno LaBianca was stabbed a dozen times, and the word "WAR" was carved into his abdomen. Rosemary was stabbed forty-one times (Kneeland, "Manson" 22). Finally, blood was used to write the words "Rise," "Death to Pigs," and "Healter Skelter" in various places around the house.

The Tate-LaBianca murders stunned the nation. Adding to the shock and horror, the ghastly crimes stumped investigators. For nearly six months, they had few leads and made no arrests. However, in December 1969, members of a hippie commune founded and led by Charles Manson were charged in the killings. This development caused irrevocable damage to the youth counterculture movement. Prosecutor Vincent Bugliosi noted, "No one associated hippies with violence and murder, just drugs, peace, free love, etc. Then the Manson Family came along, looking like hippies, but what they were all about was murder. That was their religion, their credo" (qtd. in Sachs). The positive press that the counterculture movement had received in the wake of the WMAF was immediately and even irrevocably eradicated. When news broke about the Manson Family being responsible for the crimes, "hippies almost overnight became sex-crazed, blood-thirsty beings living in spaced-out communes" (Moretta 308). Although hippies vociferously denounced the killings, "the mainstream media predictably had a field day with the Manson murders, bombarding the public with sensationalized, shocking portraits of the hippie community as one that no longer promoted peace, love, and gentleness but rather one that was full of rage, perversion, and outright savagery" (308). Meanwhile, others maintained that the hippie credo had always been a ruse; from the beginning, the true goals were mayhem and murder.

The same month that Manson and members of his hippie commune were arrested for the Tate-LaBianca murders, another calamity took place in the youth counterculture movement. On December 6, 1969, the Rolling Stones organized their own free outdoor music festival in Northern California: "Woodstock West," as it quickly came to be known. The event was held on the grounds of the Altamont Speedway, just outside San Francisco, and featured many of the same bands that had played at the WMAF: the Grateful Dead, Santana, Jefferson Airplane, and Crosby, Stills, Nash & Young. The shared musical lineup, however, is where the similarities ceased. Whereas the WMAF was a utopian dream, Altamont was a dystopian nightmare. The Rolling Stones approached the Hells[9] Angels biker group to handle their security "in exchange for $500 worth of beer" (Yusko). The Angels took a heavy-handed approach to their crowd control duties: they shoved, punched, and struck people with cutoff pool cues. The violence escalated as the concert progressed, eventually turning lethal. Alan Passaro, a white member of the Hells Angels, stabbed Meredith Hunter, an eighteen-year-old Black man,[10] to death during a melee that took pace right in front of the stage while the Rolling Stones were playing. A documentary film crew captured the horrifying event on camera. As the music critic Ralph Gleason wrote in the *San Francisco Chronicle*, "If the name 'Woodstock' had come to denote the flowering of one phase of youth culture, 'Altamont' has come to mean the end of it" (qtd. in Moretta 319). What happened at the WMAF was quickly regarded as an anomaly. The weekend in upstate New York was so special because—as both the Manson Family and Altamont revealed—it was so atypical.

This societal opinion was supported by scientific research. Dr. Lewis Yablonsky, a sociologist who had conducted a multiyear study of hippie communities, published his findings in the academic tome *The Hippie Trip* (1968). On December 12, 1969, after the violence at Altamont and the arrests of members of the Manson Family for the Tate-LaBianca murders, *Time* magazine ran an article titled "Hippies and Violence." Yablonsky was quoted extensively throughout the piece. "Many hippies are socially almost dead inside," the sociologist concluded from talking with, living among, and even smoking marijuana with hippies from the East Village in New York to Haight-Ashbury in San Francisco ("Hippies and Violence" 25). Contrary to their espousal of freedom, love, understanding, "they can be totally devoid of true compassion. That is the reason why they can kill so matter-of-factly,"

Figure 6.4. *Peanuts* comic strip, June 22, 1970. PEANUTS © Peanuts Worldwide LLC. Dist. by ANDREWS MCMEEL SYNDICATION. Reprinted with permission. All rights reserved.

Yablonsky went on to assert (25). In viewpoints that typified his remarks in other media venues, Yablonsky declared that hippiedom was little more than "a magnet for severely emotionally disturbed people" (25).

Jury selection for the Tate-LaBianca murder trial began a week before Schulz unveiled the name of his avian character. The voir dire process lasted a full month and put the murderous machinations of hippies like the Manson Family firmly back in the media spotlight—and on the public's mind. As Moretta has written about the cultural impact of these events, "When an individual such as Manson emerged, wrapping himself in the hippie mantle and mouthing the hippie mantra, and then ordering the brutal slaying of eventually nine people . . . that was the end of any patience, understanding or empathy mainstream Americans might have had for the hippie movement" (311).

Given the negative societal view of hippies before, during, and then again shortly after the WMAF, it is difficult not to see Schulz's decision to name his bird Woodstock as a commentary on this issue. The comic where Schulz unveils the bird's name encourages such speculation (fig. 6.4). "I finally found out what the stupid bird's name is," Snoopy says via a thought balloon in the second panel of the comic on June 22, 1970. "You'll never believe it," he cautions, looking directly at the reader. "Woodstock!" he announces in the final image, giving readers the side-eye.

From that strip onward, Schulz challenges his audience to believe it by considering how the bird's personality, behavior, and qualities connect with the WMAF. Of all the characters in *Peanuts*, Woodstock is arguably the kindest, sweetest, and most unassuming. Indeed, many strips present Woodstock in a childlike way: as playful, cute, and innocent. The comic that appeared the day after Snoopy reveals the name of his feathered friend establishes this quality (fig. 6.5). The opening panel to the strip on June 23, 1970, shows the beagle and his feathered buddy happily strolling together. "Woodstock and I enjoy going on little picnics," Snoopy reveals in the thought balloon, a smile on his face and his supper dish atop his head. In the next two panels, Snoopy offers more details about Woodstock's methods for getting to their picnics:

Figure 6.5. *Peanuts* comic strip, June 23, 1970. PEANUTS © Peanuts Worldwide LLC. Dist. by ANDREWS MCMEEL SYNDICATION. Reprinted with permission. All rights reserved.

"Sometimes he walks . . . sometimes he flies." Regardless of how Woodstock arrives at the picnic, he leaves the same way. In a detail that mirrors the actions of many young children after a fun day outside, Snoopy says in the final panel: "But then he sleeps all the way home!" The beagle is now walking in the opposite direction, holding the supper dish in his mouth. The little bird is lying in the dish with his eyes closed; a speech balloon with a large "Z" appears just above his head.

Many of the other comics featuring Woodstock have a similar theme. They present the bird in a childlike way. In the strip that appeared on June 27, 1970, for example, Woodstock practices his landings in a tree that is out of the frame (fig. 6.6). As tufts of leaves fly and the word "BONK!" appears, the small bird clearly needs more practice. The next comic that features Woodstock shows him engaging in another playful activity: diving into Snoopy's water dish (fig. 6.7). "That was a good swan for a non-swan," Snoopy tells him in the final panel to the strip from July 28, 1970.

Figure 6.6. *Peanuts* comic strip, June 27, 1970. PEANUTS © Peanuts Worldwide LLC. Dist. by ANDREWS MCMEEL SYNDICATION. Reprinted with permission. All rights reserved.

Figure 6.7. Peanuts comic strip, July 28, 1970. PEANUTS © Peanuts Worldwide LLC. Dist. by ANDREWS MCMEEL SYNDICATION. Reprinted with permission. All rights reserved.

Figure 6.8. *Peanuts* comic strip, May 12, 1970. PEANUTS © Peanuts Worldwide LLC. Dist. by ANDREWS MCMEEL SYNDICATION. Reprinted with permission. All rights reserved.

Figure 6.9. Peanuts comic strip, February 5, 1970. PEANUTS © Peanuts Worldwide LLC. Dist. by ANDREWS MCMEEL SYNDICATION. Reprinted with permission. All rights reserved.

Woodstock appears in roughly one thousand comics over the course of *Peanuts*.[11] While a fair number of these strips show the bird in his recurring role as Snoopy's secretary or as a mechanic for his Sopwith Camel, a considerable portion depict him enjoying simple pleasures that are commonly associated with children and childhood. In the strip that appeared on May 12, 1970, for example, Woodstock is sitting atop Snoopy's doghouse, holding a small, thin book and—as the musical notes that appear in speech balloons above his head indicate—whistling a pleasant tune (fig. 6.8). "It doesn't take much to make him happy," Snoopy explains. "I let him put in all the blue skies in my coloring book."[12] The *Peanuts* comic that appeared on February 5, 1970, can be viewed in a similar way (fig. 6.9). The wordless strip shows Woodstock flying past Snoopy's doghouse, only to return quickly once snow begins falling. The final panel shows the little bird sitting between Snoopy's legs, both to take shelter from the flakes and to stay warm.

In many strips, Snoopy is more than merely protective of his avian buddy; he behaves in a way that can more accurately be described as parental. Akin to the interactions between a father and son, Snoopy teaches Woodstock how to play sports like football, baseball, and hockey; he tries to help him improve his flying; and he even serves as the leader for Woodstock's scout troop. Additionally, whenever Woodstock is ill or needs help, Snoopy responds like a concerned parent rather than simply a caring friend. When the small bird

Chirping 'bout My Generation: Woodstock, Youth Culture, and Innocence   145

Figure 6.10. *Peanuts* comic strip, January 30, 1982. PEANUTS © Peanuts Worldwide LLC. Dist. by ANDREWS MCMEEL SYNDICATION. Reprinted with permission. All rights reserved.

Figure 6.11. Peanuts comic strip, April 4, 1976. PEANUTS © Peanuts Worldwide LLC. Dist. by ANDREWS MCMEEL SYNDICATION. Reprinted with permission. All rights reserved.

complains that he has a headache in the strip on January 30, 1982, Snoopy lovingly carries him—nest and all—to the vet (fig. 6.10). Likewise, in the strip that appeared on April 4, 1976, Snoopy is sleeping atop his doghouse when big raindrops start falling (fig. 6.11). The beagle gets up, goes over to the tree that Woodstock calls home, and—much to the bird's surprise—flips his nest upside down so that his feathered friend stays dry.

In these and other comics, Woodstock emerges not simply as a comedic sidekick in *Peanuts* but as a type of proxy child. His diminutive size, clumsy nature, and cute appearance render him more like a young human than an adult bird. When these traits are reconsidered through the context of the bird's namesake, they assume a sociopolitical significance. In marked contrast to the criticisms levied against members of the Woodstock Generation, Schulz's Woodstock is not a spoiled, lazy, entitled brat. On the contrary, he is unpretentious, unassuming, and guileless. Additionally, in direct opposition to pronouncements about the youth counterculture after Altamont and the Manson Family, Schulz's avian figure is neither violent nor emotionally disturbed. In many ways, in fact, Woodstock ranks among the least neurotic figures in *Peanuts*. He doesn't have self-esteem issues like Charlie Brown, he doesn't have delusions of grandeur like Snoopy, and he doesn't have a sadistic streak like Lucy.

When members of the Woodstock Generation weren't being accused of acting like spoiled brats or being deranged murderers, they were accused of being immature. In an article about the Summer of Love, for example, *Time* magazine said about the young men and women who attended this counterculture event: "They find an almost childish fascination in beads, blossoms and bells" ("The Hippies"). Many other journalists, sociologists, and cultural commentators agreed. The historian Theodore Roszak, in an essay titled "The Misunderstood Movement," noted how the actions, ideals, and efforts of the hippies were dismissed for much of the 1960s as "little more than an adolescent outburst" (A23). Rather than seeing the hippie decision to "tune in, turn on, and drop out" as a powerful rejection of social, political, and economic norms that left many Americans feeling dissatisfied and even disillusioned, many people viewed it as a desire to simply "extend adolescence" (Moretta 340). As the headline to an article that appeared in the *Chicago Tribune* on March 5, 1969, declared authoritatively: "Doctor Says Hippies Fear Role of Adult" (A5). Citing the work of Dr. Stuart Finch, a professor of psychiatry at the University of Michigan, the article asserted that "most hippies are against society because they are fearful of growing up and assuming the adult role" ("Doctor Says" A5). Many mainstream Americans regarded the hippie movement as the by-product of "infantile attitudes, implicitly affirming the virtues of immaturity, instant gratification, self-centeredness, impulsivity, entitlement and flights of fancy" at best (Fischer 315).[13] Meanwhile, at worst, they decreed that it was "the children of the favored classes turning political tantrums into terrorism" (Burner 6).

Schulz's Woodstock is named after one of the most famous hippie festivals, and he can be seen as offering a pointed critique of this view. The little bird is presented as innocently childlike, not immaturely childish. Both in his relationship with Snoopy and in his interactions with other characters, Woodstock is good, kind, gentle, sweet, and caring.[14] In an editorial that appeared amid the changing media coverage about the WMAF, the *New York Times* remarked, "In spite of the prevalence of drugs . . . it was essentially a phenomenon of innocence" (qtd. in Warner 64). The music festival was marked by goodness, kindness, and love. In this way, it embodied all the best qualities that the hippie movement had to offer.

Schulz's Woodstock can likewise be viewed as "a phenomenon of innocence." The diminutive bird is known for his goodness, kindness, and friendship. He thus embodies many of the best traits that individuals—whether human or avian—have to offer. By naming his character Woodstock, Schulz did more than merely pay homage to the landmark music festival. He also memorialized the manifestation of hippie counterculture that typified the WMAF, rather than the forms associated with the Manson Family or Altamont. Max Yasgur, in a commentary that appeared in the special issue of *Life* magazine that Schulz read about the WMAF, remarked: "I think these kids have made a lot of us feel guilty because we haven't really been fair to them" (Yasgur). The larger article in which Yasgur's comments appeared bore the telling title: "These Kids Were Wonderful." In naming his bird character after the WMAF, Schulz can be seen as making the same point.

Reexamining Woodstock's connection to the youth counterculture movement of the 1960s also offers a new perspective on one of his most well-known traits: the manner in which he communicates. As anyone familiar with the strip knows, the bird's "speech is rendered almost entirely in 'chicken scratch' marks, with Snoopy either directly translating or allowing the reader to deduce Woodstock's meaning in the context of Snoopy's replies" ("Woodstock" Wiki). A common lament by adults during the 1960s was that they did not understand the younger generation. As Paula S. Fass and Michael Grossberg—among other historians—have discussed, both the nature and the depth of this iteration of US intergenerational conflict were different. White, middle-class Baby Boomers had come of age amid a time of postwar plenty. To the dismay of their parents, whose childhoods had taken place during the Great Depression and whose adulthoods had begun amid the shortages and rationing of World War II, though, these young people condemned materialism, consumerism, and upward mobility as a whole. Even more baffling, they also harbored contempt for what their elders regarded as sacred national institutions: the military, the police, the president. While generational gaps between parents and children are common, the situation in the 1960s was unique. The postwar years, as Fass and Grossberg discuss in their preface to *Reinventing Childhood after World War II*, "introduced major elements of change that have fundamentally altered both the lives of children and how we understand them through our conception of childhood" (x).

More than simply "not getting" the clothes, music, and slang of the era's young people, adults were baffled by their entire worldview. White, middle-class parents had worked hard to ensure that their children had the educational, economic, and social opportunities to achieve a better life. Their sons and daughters, however, were not merely passively disinterested in this goal; they actively rejected it. As a result, countless mainstream Americans remarked that they didn't understand today's young people; it was as if today's kids were "speaking another language."

In a detail that can be connected to his hippie namesake, no one understands Schulz's Woodstock, either. Communicating via what the cartoonist called "chicken scratches," Woodstock's speech is inscrutable. The one exception to this situation, of course, is Snoopy. That the beagle is the only member of the *Peanuts* cast who understands what Woodstock is saying should come as no surprise. As mentioned earlier, during the 1960s, Snoopy self-identifies as "groovy."[15]

Simon Warner points out that the name of the WMAF "is a misnomer" (71). After all, he explains, "none of the festival took place within 60 miles of that location" (Warner 71). The event was so dubbed because it was originally intended to publicize the opening of a new recording studio in Woodstock, New York. Before long, however, the organizers realized that the three-day concert was more exciting, more important, and—from a business standpoint—more lucrative (*Woodstock: Three Days*). Although the music festival separated itself both geographically and creatively from Woodstock, New York, the name remained.

For more than fifty years, the appellation of Schulz's bird character has also largely been regarded as a misnomer. The cartoonist's decision to name his little bird after the WMAF may seem incongruous and even misleading. However, the personality of the character reveals that when it comes to embodying the WMAF's legacy of goodness, love, and friendship, birds of a feather flock together.

FROM DOUR CHILDREN TO FLOWER CHILDREN: CHANGING VIEWS ABOUT YOUTH AND YOUTH CULTURE IN *PEANUTS*

Reconsidering Woodstock in light of the WMAF has a significance that extends beyond merely identifying previously unforeseen links between this well-known character and his namesake. The connections also have implications for a larger and more long-standing theme of *Peanuts*: its portrayal of youth and commentary on youth culture. As Sharon Begley has written, one of the reasons why *Peanuts* was so groundbreaking when it debuted on October 2, 1950, was because the comic "upended the belief that childhood is a time of innocence and happiness." The very first comic, with its narrative arc of "Here comes good ol' Charlie Brown . . . How I hate him!" offered a powerful demonstration that, far from being angelic and adorable, children can be unkind and even cruel. Lest this inaugural strip be seen as atypical, the second one reinforced it. Patty strolls down the sidewalk, happily reciting the nursery rhyme "Little girls are made of sugar and spice and everything nice." She then pauses to punch a boy in the eye—spontaneously, unexpectedly, and, of course, incongruously—before continuing on her merry way. Given these messages, Umberto Eco observed about Schulz's characters in an essay from the mid-1980s: "The poetry of these children arises from the fact that we find in them all the problems, all the sufferings, of the adult" (72). In marked contrast to beliefs that childhood is a happy time, Charlie Brown's days are filled with despair. Moreover, he is not alone in this experience. The protagonist's best friend Linus is beset by theological worries and philosophical conundrums. Meanwhile, Linus's older sister Lucy has outbursts of anger caused by her contempt for people and even disgust for humanity. Steven Mintz, Paula S. Fass, and Stephen Lassonde have all discussed how the postwar years are commonly seen as a halcyon time for white, middle-class, heterosexual, cisgender young people. In the words of Lassonde: "The two decades after World War II are popularly remembered as the golden age of family life and childhood in the United States" (52). The 1950s and early 1960s are widely regarded as a time of physical freedom and personal fun, when white, middle-class kids spent their days outdoors, playing games, riding their bicycles, and having adventures around the neighborhood with their friends until the streetlights came on (Fass 6; Mintz 41). For this reason, "a Cold War childhood remains the yardstick against which Americans assess contemporary childhood" (Mintz 41). *Peanuts* stood in marked contrast to such views. Whereas Norman Rockwell offered idyllic scenes of white, middle-class American family life in his cover illustrations for the *Saturday Evening Post* during the postwar years, Schulz depicted US childhood as riddled with disappointment, failure, and loneliness via his comics in the daily newspaper.

Schulz's invocation of the WMAF signals both continuity and change with this long-standing theme. The cartoonist's decision to name one of his characters after the landmark music event carries on the strip's engagement with youth and youth culture. The WMAF took place nineteen years after *Peanuts* debuted, making the young people who attended the festival the next generation of American children. Although Charlie Brown, Linus, and Lucy had aged very little over the decades, they were boys and girls of a previous era. When Schulz names his bird Woodstock, he invites readers to think about the current cohort of young people, the Woodstock Generation.

Schulz's yellow bird signals kids of a different generation, and the strip's commentary about them is likewise different. Whereas Charlie Brown and his peers formed what might be called the "dour children"—challenging 1950s views about white, middle-class childhood as an idyllic time of innocence—Woodstock and the Woodstock Generation are part of the "flower children." In keeping with the strip's iconoclastic views about youth and youth culture, *Peanuts* challenges mainstream beliefs about the young people who constituted the decade's counterculture. Through the combination of Woodstock's namesake and his personality traits, the strip can be seen as making a case that—contrary to their portrayal as selfish, immature, unstable, and even violent—hippies are good, kind, loving, and even innocent. In sum, Woodstock does more than merely invite readers to *think* about 1960s youth; he urges the strip's mainstream audience to *rethink* them.

Timothy Miller, in his book *The Hippies and American Values*, called attention to a powerful paradox. "Although the four or five years that comprised the heyday of the counterculture passed into history several decades ago," Miller wrote, "the cultural legacy of hippies remains surprisingly strong" (xii). In areas ranging from fashion and politics to slang and especially music, there is scarcely a facet of American society that was not changed by the hippie movement. This situation prompted John Anthony Moretta to assert: "Few Americans would deny that there was an America before the 1960s hippies and a very different America afterwards" (365).

A similar observation could be made about *Peanuts* and Woodstock. The comic offered one viewpoint about youth and youth culture before the symbolically named avian character was introduced—and a different message afterward. In 1950, it was radical for *Peanuts* to suggest that young people were not cute and innocent. A generation later, in 1970, it was just as radical for the comic to suggest that they were. In the same way that the hippie movement was short-lived but enjoyed a long legacy, Schulz's bird was physically small but had a big thematic impact. Woodstock did more than simply change the character of Snoopy by becoming his comedic sidekick; he changed one of the core messages in *Peanuts*.

Previous chapters in *Blockheads, Beagles, and Sweet Babboos* have spotlighted a different core personality from Schulz's comic strip cast: Charlie Brown, Snoopy, Lucy, Franklin, Pig-Pen, and Woodstock. The epilogue both builds on and breaks from this approach. On the one hand, it brings to the forefront another of Schulz's beloved figures: Linus Van Pelt. As Charlie Brown's best friend, Linus plays a prominent role in the strip. On the other hand, the critical end point for this character study is far different. Whereas my previous chapters have been directed inward—examining the meaning and significance of the profiled character in Schulz's strip—this final discussion is directed outward: it considers the meaning and significance that Linus exerted on other cartoonists and comics creations. The notion that *Peanuts* in general and Linus Van Pelt in particular influenced other works of sequential art is far from radical or even revelatory. However, in keeping with the against-the-grain readings offered in the previous chapters, the epilogue traces the presence of Linus in what might be regarded as an unexpected arena: Alison Bechdel's landmark LGBTQ comic series *Dykes to Watch Out For*.

EPILOGUE

PEANUTS TO WATCH OUT FOR

Linus Van Pelt, Alison Bechdel, and the Legacy of Charles M. Schulz

When *Peanuts* made its debut on October 2, 1950, no one could have predicted how successful it would become. As Jared Gardner and Ian Gordon observed, "There is in the history of American comics no strip more beloved or more familiar" (3). By the time of Schulz's death on February 12, 2000, he was "America's favorite and most highly respected cartoonist" (Inge, "Introduction" ix). Over the past seventy years, *Peanuts* has become woven into the fabric of American society. Characters like Charlie Brown, Snoopy, and Lucy are more than merely household names. In the words of Fred Hunt, they have become "universal icons," recognized even by individuals who had never read Schulz's newspaper comic. In 2021, a special issue of *Life* magazine dedicated to the comic strip went even further. "We love the *Peanuts* gang," it asserted, "because we recognize them for who they are: members of our family" (Back Cover).

The individuals who wrote the forewords to volumes of *The Complete Peanuts* (2004–16) provide a telling snapshot of the scope of Schulz's influence. The short essays were authored by writers like Garrison Keillor and Jonathan Franzen, journalists such as Walter Cronkite and Al Roker, cartoonists like Matt Groening and Lynn Johnston, musicians such as Bill Melendez and Diana Krall, actors like Whoopi Goldberg and Alec Baldwin, and legendary athletes like the tennis pro Billie Jean King. Moreover, the introduction to the final volume of *The Complete Peanuts* was written by none other than President Barack Obama. As the forty-fourth commander-in-chief aptly noted, "In his final strip, Charles Schulz wondered how he could ever forget the *Peanuts* gang" (x). Like the cartoonist himself, Obama notes that "the rest of us never will" (x). In the former president's words once again, "Like millions of Americans, I grew up with *Peanuts*. But I never outgrew it" (x). Schulz's characters and comic strip shaped who we are and how we see the world.

Although each of the preceding chapters has focused on a different figure from *Peanuts*, they have shared the same goal: to present Schulz's exceedingly familiar characters in decidedly unfamiliar ways. From the suggestion that the zigzag pattern on Charlie Brown's shirt might be a triangle wave to the connections between Lucy Van Pelt and Lucy Ricardo, these discussions have offered new perspectives on a cast of comic strip characters whom many readers consider old friends.

This epilogue is no different. In the same way that all the previous discussions offer alternative and even unexpected analyses about Schulz's characters, this final segment engages in the same process with the issue of the cartoonist's legacy. To the already impressive array of individuals whose lives have been affected by Charles M. Schulz's work, this closing discussion adds another, less obvious, and even seemingly incongruous cartoonist to the list: Alison Bechdel and her series *Dykes to Watch Out For*. Bechdel's strip began in 1983 as a single-panel comic that offered clever, sardonic, and amusing observations about LGBTQ life and experiences. Appearing in feminist magazines, queer print media, and alternative newspapers, *Dykes to Watch Out For* soon shifted to become what one commentator would later call "the greatest lesbian soap opera" ("*The Essential*" 32). The weekly strip chronicled the experiences of a group of queer friends who lived in an unnamed midwestern city. Centered on protagonist Mo Testa, the comics depicted these characters working at their jobs, living with their roommates and partners, hanging out with their friends, and, of course, navigating their love relationships.

Dykes to Watch Out For (*DTWOF*) quickly became a "countercultural institution" among queer women (Queer Comics Database). Providing much-needed visibility during an era where representation was rare and often negative, the series was "as important to new generations of lesbians as landmark novels like Rita Mae Brown's *Rubyfruit Jungle* (1973) and Lisa Alther's *Kinflicks* (1976) were to an earlier one" (Garner). Bechdel's strip featured a large cast of diverse characters: white, Black, and Latina as well as lesbian, bi, and trans. Additionally, it tackled a wide array of social, cultural, sexual, and political issues, from polyamory, environmentalism, and partisan politics to homonormativity, the US military-industrial complex, and vegetarianism. *DTWOF* ran for more than twenty years.[1] Moreover, the strips were collected and published in no fewer than a dozen books over this period. By the dawn of the new millennium, Bechdel's series had established itself as not only the longest-running lesbian comic in US history but also the most successful one (Garner).

On the surface, *DTWOF* seems to have little in common with *Peanuts*. After all, Bechdel's "strip features a cast of recurring characters in a lesbian community in an unnamed mid-sized American city, and it often comments explicitly on current events" (Bernstein 127). Indeed, Bechdel has called *DTWOF* "half op-ed column and half endless, serialized Victorian novel" (qtd. in Bernstein 129). Over the course of its run from 1983 to 2008, the comic engaged with a myriad of social, political, and economic issues that are far different from *Peanuts*: from attacks on women's reproductive rights and the inequities of laissez-faire capitalism to the brutality of the nation's military-industrial complex and the growing social consciousness concerning gender fluidity and trans identities. These features of *DTWOF* ostensibly place it far outside the realm of Schulz's comic about a group of largely white, elementary-age, suburban, and seemingly all heterosexual children. Nevertheless, a variety of thematic, aesthetic, and narratological traits connect *DTWOF* and *Peanuts*. Both strips, for example, possess similar emotional registers, focusing on anxiety, disappointment, and neuroticism. Additionally, the two comics also feature a central character who wears a striped shirt and has a penchant for philosophizing. Finally, but far from insignificantly, *Peanuts* and *DTWOF* possess a strong interest in psychology as well as recurring story lines about psychoanalysis or, at least, talk-based therapy.

Identifying various elements of *Peanuts* in *DTWOF* does more than simply bring together two hugely important cartoonists and their equally iconic strips; it also reveals fresh critical insights about them both. First and foremost, these connections call attention to a new creative influence on Alison Bechdel. Although *DTWOF* was a queer comic that operated outside mainstream culture, it had a kinship to one of the most well-known comics in the history of American newspaper strips. Just as importantly, the suggestive echoes between *DTWOF* and *Peanuts* also shed new light on the relationship that Bechdel's strip has to history, popular culture, and life writing. That Bechdel may have consciously or unconsciously incorporated facets of Schulz's comic adds a new dimension to how we understand the ways in which her life informed her work. Much has been written about how the plotlines in *DTWOF* were influenced by contemporaneous events that were taking place during Bechdel's adulthood as she composed the strips: the AIDS crisis, the war on terror, the fight for marriage equality, and so on. The presence of *Peanuts* suggests that *DTWOF* may just as significantly have been shaped by cultural experiences from Bechdel's childhood. Finally, and just as importantly, our understanding of Charles M. Schulz is equally enriched by these connections. The ways in which Bechdel's series can be viewed as "*Peanuts* to Watch Out For" reveals the ongoing and even unexpected life of Schulz's cartooning. In keeping with my overarching aim to offer fresh perspectives on *Peanuts*, its influence on Bechdel's strip adds a new facet to the range, reach, and resonance of Schulz's legacy.

THE AGE OF AQUARIUS AS THE ERA OF THE BEAGLE: *PEANUTS* AND THE 1960S

Alison Bechdel was born in 1960, the year that Christopher Caldwell identifies as inaugurating the Golden Age of *Peanuts*. Throughout the 1960s and into the 1970s, Schulz's comic and characters permeated American print, popular, and material culture. Alison Bechdel's childhood took place amid this phenomenon; the future cartoonist grew up in a world saturated with *Peanuts*. Given the ubiquity of Schulz's strip during her childhood, it seems certain that she was not merely exposed to, but would have been familiar with, *Peanuts*. In many respects, it is difficult to imagine how she would have been able to avoid it.

First and foremost, Schulz's comic strip enjoyed tremendous circulation levels throughout the period when Bechdel was growing up. By 1975, *Peanuts* appeared "in approximately 1,480 US and 175 foreign newspapers with 90,000,000 readers" ("Timeline of Charles M. Schulz"). *The Express*, the local newspaper in Lock Haven, Pennsylvania, where Bechdel was born, featured *Peanuts* comics at least since 1971, when she was eleven years old (Liberator). That said, the comics section of the newspaper was not the only place where individuals could encounter Schulz's work. Paperback reprints of the strip, which began appearing in 1952, increased in both number and popularity during the 1960s. As David Michaelis has documented, by 1966, twenty different titles had been released. Collectively, these books sold "four and a half million copies—or one [book] every thirty seconds" (Michaelis 339).

The popularity of Schulz's original strip also inspired new material. In 1962 he released *Happiness Is a Warm Puppy*. The short gift book was inspired by the *Peanuts* comic from April 25, 1960, and featured a series of sweet variations on the titular theme: "Happiness is finding someone you like at the front door," "Happiness is a thumb and a blanket," "Happiness is a bread and butter sandwich folded over," and so on. By 1967, *Happiness Is a Warm Puppy* had sold "1,350,000 copies in three languages" (Michaelis 339). Furthermore, in the coming years, Schulz would release multiple sequel texts, each with "hefty seven-figure sales, and unprecedented stints on the bestseller lists" (Kidd, n.p.).

The mid-1960s also saw the publication of Robert L. Short's *The Gospel according to Peanuts* (1964). As the title implied, the book examined both how Schulz's strip had become a type of national religion and the comic's Judeo-Christian influences and overtones. *The Gospel according to Peanuts* became a "national best seller in hardback, snapped up at the rate of four thousand copies a week, with more than ten million of its paperback edition eventually scattered throughout the world" (Michaelis 352).

Schulz's comic and characters also migrated to new cultural platforms. On December 9, 1965, the animated television special *A Charlie Brown Christmas* premiered on CBS, enjoying both strong ratings and critical reviews. In figures that arguably had not been seen since the heyday of *I Love Lucy*, "almost half the people watching television in the United States tuned in—some fifteen and a half million households" (Michaelis 359). *A Charlie Brown Christmas* earned Schulz both an Emmy Award for Outstanding Individual Achievement and a Peabody Award for Excellence in Broadcasting. Moreover, the following year, a second animated *Peanuts* television special aired, *It's the Great Pumpkin, Charlie Brown*. Like its predecessor, the program was an instant classic. By the end of the decade, the first feature-length animated *Peanuts* movie hit theaters, *A Boy Named Charlie Brown* (1969). The musical comedy had its premiere at Radio City Music Hall and was a box office success. With a production cost of $1 million, *A Boy Named Charlie Brown* earned $12 million; it was also nominated for an Academy Award for Best Original Score.

Together with appearing on film and television during the 1960s, the *Peanuts* gang appeared on the stage. On March 7, 1967, the off-Broadway musical *You're a Good Man, Charlie Brown* debuted in New York City. The show quickly moved to Broadway, where it was performed 1,597 times before closing on February 14, 1971 ("You're a Good Man"). Additionally, the musical toured the United States, premiered in the West End in London, and was adapted as a television special. *You're a Good Man, Charlie Brown* remained exceedingly popular through the 1970s. By the 1990s, in fact, the show had become "the most performed musical in the history of American theatre" (Timeline).

Given *Peanuts*' appearance in musical theater, it is perhaps not surprising that the strip found its way to the nation's popular music. In November 1966, the Royal Guardsmen's song "Snoopy vs. the Red Baron" hit the airwaves. The tune, which narrated an encounter between the famous World War I Flying Ace and his nemesis, reached number two on the Hot 100 list. The song's success prompted the Royal Guardsmen to release a full-length *Peanuts*-themed album, *Snoopy and His Friends* (1967). The record was produced with Schulz's approval, and several of the songs were radio hits, including "Snoopy's Christmas" and "The Return of the Red Baron."

Snoopy permeated other walks of American life during the decade. In 1968, Schulz's strip commenced what would become its long-standing participation in the Macy's Thanksgiving Day parade, represented by a Snoopy balloon. That same year, Snoopy was chosen as official mascot for NASA's Apollo 10 mission (Kidd). The beagle, with Charlie Brown and other members of the comics cast, also appeared on the covers of major national publications, *Time* magazine (April 9, 1965) and *Life* (March 17, 1967). Given this prominence, it should perhaps come as no surprise that—as discussed in chapter 3—Snoopy was a write-in candidate for president of the United States in 1968 and again in 1972. The second "Snoopy for President" campaign garnered such widespread support that California passed a law making it "illegal to enter the name of a fictional character on the ballot" ("Snoopy for President").

Finally, and perhaps most visibly of all, the 1960s saw a veritable mountain of *Peanuts* merchandise. In a campaign initiated by Connie Boucher at Determined Productions, Schulz's characters appeared on seemingly every consumer product imaginable over the course of the decade: toys, clothes, home decor, jewelry, school supplies, sporting goods, stationary, health and beauty products, bedding, cookbooks, and games (Michaelis 337–39). As both Ann Patchett and Sarah Boxer have reflected, for young people growing up during this era, their childhoods were not merely surrounded by, but wholly immersed in, *Peanuts*. Schulz's characters were featured on kid's backpacks, lunchboxes, pajamas, bedsheets, T-shirts, plush toys, and more. Given this ubiquity, it is difficult to imagine a young person from this era not owning some *Peanuts*-themed item at some point during their youth. At the very least, they surely saw these items.

As even this brief overview indicates, *Peanuts* "had a profound influence on society and culture of its own time" (Inge, *Comics* 104). M. Thomas Inge made the following observation about the cultural force that the strip had attained by 1969: "No other American artist or writer in any other field of creative endeavor has ever been known to reach and earn the admiration of so many people simultaneously as Charles Schulz has done at such magic moments in his career" (*Comics* 106). When historians discuss influential happenings in American popular culture during the 1960s, they commonly mention events like the hippies, the miniskirt, and the British Invasion. Schulz's strip needs to be added to this list. In the same way that the decade was known for Beatlemania, it was also filled with *Peanuts*-mania.

GOOD GRIEF: THE SHARED EMOTIONAL REGISTERS OF *PEANUTS* AND *DYKES TO WATCH OUT FOR*

Not surprisingly, given the ubiquity of *Peanuts* during her childhood and also during the period when she was drawing *DTWOF*, Alison Bechdel was familiar with Schulz's strip. In fact, in an interview published in *Off Our Backs* in 1988, the cartoonist mentioned *Peanuts*. Discussing her early attempts at cartooning, she reflected: "I was also intimidated by trying to create real characters like Charlie Brown, Lucy, or Linus. It seems really scary to create genuine characters and then have to develop them in a believable way" (14). Then, a few questions later, when asked if *DTWOF* is sufficiently "universal" to be enjoyed by heterosexual readers, she asserts: "*We* do it every day. Any woman, any gay person, any person of any color whatsoever other than white picks up the daily paper and makes these incredible leaps of identity to understand *Peanuts, Garfield, The Phantom* and all that garbage" (14).

These few references aside, Bechdel has said little else about Schulz or *Peanuts*. In various articles and interviews, she has discussed a number of cartoonists whose style has influenced her own or whose work she admires. In a 2006 discussion with Hillary Chute, for example, Bechdel named Robert Crumb, Harvey Pekar, Harvey Kurtzman, Howard Cruse, and Art Spiegelman as important sources of inspiration (Bechdel, "Interview" 1012). Charles M. Schulz, however, was not among them. Likewise, Bechdel has also occasionally identified comics that she enjoyed as a young person. To that end, she has referenced her love for *Mad* magazine as an adolescent, along with her enjoyment of Little Lulu and Disney comics as a young child (1012). Once again, however, *Peanuts* has not been among them.

Although Bechdel has never directly mentioned Schulz's work as influencing her own, she was surely aware of it. Born on September 10, 1960, Bechdel came of age during an era that was saturated with *Peanuts* images, products, and paraphernalia. Indeed, her childhood took place amid what *Life* magazine rightly called "the Great *Peanuts* Craze." As the *Off Our Backs* interview reveals, even if Bechdel herself was not a daily reader of the strip, she was certainly familiar with it. Charlie Brown and company were everywhere when she was growing up and first began cartooning. Schulz's comic strip and characters appeared not just in the newspaper but on stage, screen, television, radio, clothing, toys, stationary, books, home decor, school supplies, and even the moon.

The ubiquity of *Peanuts* during Bechdel's coming of age calls for a consideration of the possible influence on, and an exploration of the potential affinities with, *DTWOF*. In features ranging from the plot and characters to the tone and themes, a number of suggestive echoes exist between the two comics. These points of correspondence between *DTWOF* and *Peanuts* are strong enough and numerous enough to suggest that Bechdel's early exposure to Schulz's work consciously or unconsciously shaped her own.

When we reexamine *DTWOF* in the context of *Peanuts*, a number of striking parallels arise. Even after one reads just a few of Schulz's strips, the general message or overall philosophy becomes clear: the comic explores how "we are flawed souls who occasionally have a redemptive experience, a moment of release, of joy, but then we revert to our old patterns and we suffer again" (DeLuca 301). Charlie Brown never kicks the football. Snoopy never finds a publisher for his novel. Linus never meets the Great Pumpkin. Instead, all the characters remain troubled by the same problems, flaws, and disappointments. Even when they try to change their attitudes or their actions, they cannot. Eventually they revert to their old ways. Charlie Brown may vow that he will never again believe Lucy's promise not to pull the football away at the last moment; however, time after time, he capitulates, demonstrating that we never really change.

This observation also accurately describes the world of *DTWOF*. All of Bechdel's characters follow this pattern. Mo remains the same high-strung, neurotic, panicky individual in comics that appeared in the 2000s as she was in ones that were published in the 1980s. Likewise, Clarice is the same idealistic workaholic that she was when we first met her in law school. Finally, and perhaps most vividly of all, even a bout with breast cancer doesn't change many aspects of Sydney's personality. As the "Cast Biographies" page on the *Dykes to Watch Out For* website indicates, Sydney's personality can still accurately be described as the "credit card debtor with a penchant for the theoretical and disdain for knee-jerk liberalism" (Bechdel, "Cast Biographies"). One of the features that made *Peanuts* not only so popular but so edgy during the 1950s and 1960s was that it incorporated the growing postwar interest in psychoanalysis. In the strip that appeared on March 27, 1959, Lucy opens a booth whose sign advertises its function: "Psychiatric Help 5¢." While Charlie Brown is her most frequent client, all the characters sit on the stool and talk with her at some point. As Geraldine DeLuca points out, however, "Therapy is not the route to salvation in *Peanuts*. Schulz's characters do not get over great losses. They do not change" (301). Indeed, even after numerous sessions over many decades, Charlie Brown remains the same depressive, luckless person he was before. In a feature that is difficult not to view as Schulz's commentary on the efficacy of psychoanalysis, Charlie Brown's therapy sessions with Lucy are repeatedly presented as fruitless at worst and absurd at best. The comic that appeared on May 30, 1969, offers an excellent case in point (fig. E.1). The strip shows Charlie Brown talking to Lucy at her psychiatric booth. "I don't know what to do," he says in the opening panel. "Sometimes I get so lonely I can hardly stand it. . . . Other times, I actually long to be completely alone" (Schulz, *1969 to 1970* 65). Her suggestion for how to solve this problem is thoroughly unhelpful. "Try to live in-between. . . . Five cents, please!" she tells Charlie Brown in the final panel, bringing the session to an abrupt close (65).

Therapy forms a recurring feature of Bechdel's strip as well. Numerous comics take place in the office of Mo's therapist as she discusses her worries

Figure E.1. *Peanuts* comic strip, May 30, 1969. Reprinted in *The Complete Peanuts: Dailies and Sundays, 1969 to 1970*, by Charles M. Schulz (Fantagraphics, 2008), 65. PEANUTS © Peanuts Worldwide LLC. Dist. by ANDREWS MCMEEL SYNDICATION. Reprinted with permission. All rights reserved.

and struggles. From the personal troubles that she is experiencing in her private life to the geopolitical problems plaguing the world at large, the topics of her sessions change, but this feature of the strip remains the same: Mo goes to therapy. Akin to Charlie Brown's interactions with Lucy, Mo's time talking with her therapist is not presented as psychologically productive, emotionally enlightening, or personally transformative. Although she frequently discusses problems such as anxiety and insecurity, she never makes much progress on these issues. Instead her experiences in therapy are often shown as unsatisfying. In the comic titled "The Soliloquy" from 1990, for example, Mo has ostensibly come to her therapist's office to discuss some difficulties in her relationship with Harriet (fig. E.2). But as both the thought bubbles and speech balloons reveal, Mo spends the bulk of the session wondering what her therapist thinks of her. After multiple panels engaging in private ruminations such as "I wonder if she **likes** me? After all, it's not her job to **like** me. . . . Still, **does** she?" Mo finally asks her therapist this question directly (Bechdel, *Sequel* 20; bold in original). The therapist's response is just as anticlimactic as the advice that Charlie Brown received from Lucy two decades earlier; moreover, it likewise signals the abrupt end of the session. "Of course I do!" Mo's therapist tells her in the final panel. "But I see our time is up now. Let's explore this further next week, shall we?" (21).

In addition to mirroring general events from Schulz's comic, *DTWOF* contains a variety of elements that embody even more specific instances of overlap. A frequent occurrence in *Peanuts* is when one character is experiencing a rare moment of happiness, pleasure, or joy, and another is quick to point out how this sentiment is fleeting, hollow, or foolish. For instance, in a strip that first appeared in the late 1950s and was reprinted in the 1970 paperback *Go Fly a Kite, Charlie Brown*, Snoopy is depicted in the opening panel doing his famous happy dance: his back feet are moving rapidly, his front paws are open wide, his head is thrown back, and there is a big smile on his upturned face (n.p.). An angry Lucy glowers at him as he approaches.

"The whole world could get blown up at any minute and all **you** think of is **dancing**!!" she complains (n.p.; bold in original).

Similar sentiments occur repeatedly in *DTWOF*. In the strip "High Anxiety" from 1987, Clarice and Toni encourage Mo to have more fun. Their pal is currently unemployed, and they urge her to use this period to "just take time out to do something you really enjoy" (Bechdel, *More* 36). Mo's response recalls that of Lucy upon seeing Snoopy gleefully dancing. In a series of panels, Mo wonders how anyone could possibly enjoy themselves when "out in the **real** world they're **bombing abortion** clinics . . . holding **Nazi** and **KKK** rallies . . . trying to **quarantine** people who might have **AIDS**" (37; bold in original). Mo makes strikingly similar remarks a few years later, in the 1992 strip "Mo Zone." The sequence opens with Clarice, Harriet, Toni, and the protagonist dining at their favorite local restaurant, Café Topaz. As Toni comments in the first panel, however, Mo is not enjoying her entrée. "How can I **eat?** An ozone hole could open up over our heads any minute now!" (Bechdel, *Spawn* 20; bold in original).

While the core cast of *Peanuts* remained the same, Schulz would also introduce new characters to the strip. From the birth of Charlie Brown's sister Sally in the late 1950s to the arrival of Rerun in the early 1970s, the cartoonist kept the strip fresh and interesting in part by adding fresh and interesting personalities. On August 22, 1966, a figure who would quickly become a beloved member of the *Peanuts* gang made her debut: Patricia Reichardt, better known as "Peppermint Patty." Schulz said that he added her to reflect the changing times (Timeline). With Patty's "distinct personality, athleticism, and trademark sandals" (Timeline), she reflected key social trends of the 1960s: the transformations happening to girlhood, the shifting style of national fashions, and the increasingly individualistic and even outspoken nature of American youth. Although Peppermint Patty is depicted as having a crush on Charlie Brown, she has commonly been seen as a lesbian character. As Vikki Reich, Heather Hogan, and Ben Saunders have all discussed, Patty possesses a variety of personal, behavioral, and sartorial traits that have long been associated with lesbians, from wearing Birkenstocks to playing softball (Reich, pars. 4–7; Hogan, pars. 3–12; Saunders 13–21). This association only strengthened when the character Marcie debuted on July 20, 1971. A shy and nerdy intellectual, Marcie follows Peppermint Patty around, calling her "Sir"—a trait that places their interactions in dialogue with butch/femme role play that emerged in lesbian bar culture during the twentieth century (Faderman 159–87). Peppermint Patty and Marcie quickly became icons of lesbian culture during the 1970s and 1980s (Reich, par. 3). Many queer women

Figure E.2. Alison Bechdel, "The Soliloquy." Image from *Off Our Backs* 20, no. 7 (July 1990): 24.

read the two as a same-sex couple or, at the least, as occupying a place on Adrienne Rich's "lesbian continuum" (Hogan).

This development has obvious resonance for *DTWOF*. Although Peppermint Patty was not the first character in American comics whom one could read as lesbian,[2] she was exceedingly well known. Peppermint Patty quickly became one of the core *Peanuts* characters, appearing frequently in the strips, playing a role in the animated television specials, and being featured on a bevy of merchandise. Alison Bechdel has often said that she created *DTWOF* out of a desire for increased queer visibility. As Adam R. Critchfield and Jack Pula write, "Syndicated in numerous gay and lesbian, feminist, or other alternative newspapers across the United States, the comic strip held up a rare mirror in which many lesbian, gay, bisexual, and transgender (LGBT) individuals could see themselves represented" (398). Before the appearance of *DTWOF*, Peppermint Patty largely occupied this role and served this function for the lesbian community. Indeed, Hogan, Reich, and Saunders have all made substantial claims for how this comics character both occupied an esteemed personal place among, and served an important cultural function for, queer women. Like Mo, Patty provided an important site of visibility. Peppermint Patty was then, and remains now, an iconic figure among lesbians, and especially white lesbians. Accordingly, it seems difficult to fully separate the significance of this character with that of Bechdel's comic. In many ways, in fact, Peppermint Patty was the most visible, beloved, and important comics character for lesbians in the United States before the appearance of *DTWOF*.

In a final area of overlap between the work of Bechdel and Schulz, the titles of several of the *Peanuts Philosophers* series of gift books (released from 1967 to 1969) are comments that could easily have been uttered by characters in *DTWOF*, especially Mo. The names of these volumes include *Everything I Do Makes Me Feel Guilty* (1969) and *We All Have Our Hangups* (1969). The same observation applies to the sentiments expressed by various *Peanuts* figures inside these books as well. In *We All Have Our Hangups*, for example, Lucy chastises Snoopy: "You wouldn't be so happy if you knew about all the troubles in this world!" (n.p.). One could easily imagine Bechdel's Mo making this exact remark. In many ways, in fact, she did precisely that in the scene from Café Topaz discussed earlier. In *Everything I Do Makes Me Feel Guilty*, Charlie Brown sits at a table writing a letter to his pencil-pal. "Did you have a nice summer?" he asks in scribbly cursive that appears above his head. Then, in the next panel, Charlie Brown reports on his own experiences: "Mine could have been better, but it could have been worse" (n.p.). Far from seeing this situation as a disappointment, he tells his pencil-pal: "For me, that's good." Once again, Bechdel's Mo would likely say the same thing.

THE PHILOSOPHER IN THE STRIPED SHIRT: LINUS VAN PELT AND MO TESTA

For decades, Mo Testa, the beloved protagonist of *DTWOF*, has been seen as an autobiographically inflected representation of Alison Bechdel. The two figures share a strong physical resemblance: both Mo and Bechdel sport short black hair, wear glasses, and have a lanky physique. In addition, they possess a variety of similar personality traits: as the cartoonist has commented, Mo reflects her tendency to be insecure, neurotic, and obsessive (Critchfield and Pula 399).

Mo Testa certainly functions as Bechdel's alter ego. However, in a feature that has been overlooked in previous criticism, this character also shares a variety of physical, behavioral, and personal traits with a central figure from *Peanuts*: Linus Van Pelt. As Charles M. Schulz once observed about Charlie Brown's best friend and Sally's "Sweet Babboo," "Linus, my serious side, is the house intellectual, bright, well-informed, which, I suppose, may contribute to his feelings of insecurity" ("Linus Van Pelt"). Linus is the character who offers philosophical commentary for the *Peanuts* gang. He is thoughtful, reflective, and exceedingly intelligent. Whereas figures like Charlie Brown, Lucy, and Peppermint Patty focus on individual events or specific details, Linus identifies the connections among and between these occurrences to see the larger social, cultural, and political ramifications. His perceptive nature, however, is precisely what makes him anxious and even somber. Linus knows enough about the world to recognize its awe-inspiring possibilities, but also to see its disheartening problems. This quality forms one of the reasons Linus is almost always carrying his trusty blue security blanket: he needs the comfort that it provides. Charlie Brown's sidekick is concerned with the ontological, theological, and epistemological implications of life events: What does it all mean? Why are we here? Is there a greater purpose? Not surprisingly, such weighty contemplations routinely leave Linus feeling unsettled or even melancholy.

The same sentiments, of course, could also be used to describe Mo. Many of her signature traits and hallmark qualities are ones that she shares with Linus: from her insecurity and intellectualism to her philosophical nature and her role as the reflective commentator (along with frequent killjoy) for the group. Furthermore, even Mo's penchant for striped clothing can be seen as taking a sartorial cue from Linus, who is always clad in a T-shirt with strikingly similar horizontal stripes (fig. E.3). These areas of physical, psychological, and personal overlap invite us to place these seemingly

Figure E.3. Side-by-side comparison of the sartorial style of Schulz's Linus Van Pelt and Bechdel's Mo Testa. *Peanuts* image is the final panel from the comic that appeared on February 22, 1982. The Bechdel image is a panel from the comic "Balm Blast," first published in 1999 and reprinted in *The Essential Dykes to Watch Out For* (Houghton Mifflin, 2008), 206. PEANUTS © Peanuts Worldwide LLC. Dist. by ANDREWS MCMEEL SYNDICATION. Reprinted with permission. All rights reserved.

disparate characters in dialogue with each other. However unexpected and even unlikely, Mo Testa can be seen as Mo Van Pelt in many ways.

Linus's contemplative, philosophical, and insecure nature is a recurring feature of the strip. While this character is sometimes presented as playing baseball with the rest of the gang, he is more frequently depicted thoughtfully ruminating, anxiously wondering, or sagely opining. "Lucy says that half of our heart is filled with hate and half is filled with love," Linus relays to Charlie Brown in a strip that was reprinted in a 1970 paperback, for example. He continues in the second panel: "And she says this hate and love are always fighting within us . . . always quarreling, battling, struggling" (Schulz, *Go*, n.p.). At this point, Linus has become completely unnerved by the situation. The third panel shows him in a state of anxious panic: he is clutching his stomach, his eyes are open wide in anxiety, and his whole body is trembling. Consumed with worry, Linus desperately shouts in the fourth and final panel: "**PEACE!**" (bold in original).

That said, it doesn't take weighty concerns about humanity's internal struggle with good and evil to send Linus into a panic. He is frequently driven there by far more quotidian events. For example, in a strip that was reprinted in *Good Ol' Charlie Brown* (1965), Linus strikes out at baseball. He returns to the bench, picks up his blanket, and begins sucking his thumb. The expression on his face is a mix of worry, sadness, and anxiety (n.p.). In a series of strips that appeared from late February to early March 1969, Linus becomes thoroughly outraged when his favorite teacher is dismissed at school (fig. E.4). "Do you ever have the feeling of impending doom?" he asks Charlie Brown

Figure E.4. Final panel from *Peanuts* comic strip, February 27, 1969. Reprinted in *The Complete Peanuts: Dailies and Sundays, 1969 to 1970*, by Charles M. Schulz (Fantagraphics, 2008), 26. PEANUTS © Peanuts Worldwide LLC. Dist. by ANDREWS MCMEEL SYNDICATION. Reprinted with permission. All rights reserved.

Figure E.5. *Peanuts* comic strip, March 1, 1969. Reprinted in *The Complete Peanuts: Dailies and Sundays, 1969 to 1970*, by Charles M. Schulz (Fantagraphics, 2008), 26. PEANUTS © Peanuts Worldwide LLC. Dist. by ANDREWS MCMEEL SYNDICATION. Reprinted with permission. All rights reserved.

after he reads him the newspaper story about the teacher's strike (Schulz, *1969 to 1970* 26). In the following day's strip, when Lucy breaks the news that his beloved teacher has been fired, Linus's looming unease turns to impassioned outrage. "FIRED! THAT CAN'T BE! THEY CAN'T FIRE MISS OTHMAR!" he erupts when Lucy informs him. "**SHE HAS A CONTRACT! SHE HAS TENURE! SHE HAS HER OWN PARKING PLACE!**" Linus exclaims even more stridently in the next panel (bold in original). Furthermore, far from being confined to this one episode, Linus sustains this level of outrage for several more strips (fig. E.5). "**I'LL WRITE A LETTER OF PROTEST! I'LL BLOW THIS THING WIDE OPEN!!**" he ardently vows in the next day's comic (Schulz, *1969 to 1970* 26; bold in original).

Bechdel's Mo, of course, is famous for her impassioned rants, moments of righteous outrage, and tendency to panic. Akin to Linus, these episodes are routinely sparked by everyday events in mundane settings. The strip "Angst in Right Field" from 1987 offers an excellent case in point (fig. E.6). As the exposition box that opens the strip relays, "It's softball season again, and Mo's having a touch of **Weltschmerz** in the last inning" (Bechdel, *More* 46; bold in original). The drawing that appears below these lines shows Mo standing

Figure E.6. Alison Bechdel, "Angst in Right Field." Image from "DTOWF Archive Episode #8," http://dykestowatchoutfor.com/dtwof-archive-episode-8.

in left field. A thought bubble reveals her ruminations: "It's so peaceful out here," she reflects. As with Linus, this moment of tranquil reflection quickly turns to more grandiose contemplations—and geopolitical concerns. "You'd never suspect that somewhere political prisoners are being **tortured**, people are **starving**, **chemicals** are spilling, **missiles** are piling up," Mo muses to herself in the next panel (bold in original). Over the next eight panels, she continues along the same lines, getting increasingly agitated as the softball game unfolds on the infield in front of her. Near the end of the strip, Mo's ruminations prompt her to exclaim aloud in a manner that recalls Linus's earlier exasperated eruptions: "How can we stand here paying **softball**? I mean, what's the **point?!?**" (47).

The *Peanuts Philosophers* series of gift books contains not one but two volumes dedicated to Linus: *Linus on Life* (1967) and *The Meditations of Linus* (1967). "There's no heavier burden than potential!" he announces in a strip collected in the former title (n.p.). In the latter book, Linus make observations about the absurdities of modern life, such as the following: "There's something symbolic about being run over by a portable TV while reading a book" (n.p.). As such remarks indicate, Linus is the member of the group who observes—and opines. Indeed, the official *Peanuts* character profile calls him "the most insecure but the smartest out of all the characters, with the most intellectualism; a philosopher and theologian."

This description could also apply to Mo. Her character bio on the *Dykes to Watch Out For* website, in fact, deems her a "worrier and kvetch extraordinaire" ("Character Bios"). When Mo is not philosophizing, she is panicking; when she is not fired up with righteous indignation, she is sinking into gloomy despair; when she is not fighting injustice, she is battling self-pity. In a strip that was reprinted in the paperback *Good Ol' Charlie Brown* (1965), Linus watches a leaf fall from a tree. Over the course of several panels, it flutters to the ground while he observes silently. Then, after the leaf has landed on the grass, Linus lets out a sigh. In the final panel, he offers the following glum takeaway about this event: "Nobody's happy where they are" (n.p.). Linus could easily be replaced by Mo in this sequence, and these events could easily serve as a *DTWOF* strip.[3]

LOCATING THE PAST IN THE PRESENT: CHILDHOOD, MEMORY, AND AUTOBIOGRAPHY IN *DTWOF*

Much has been written about the importance of childhood, memory, and autobiography in Alison Bechdel's *Fun Home* (2006). Ann Cvetkovich, for example, has explored "the role of child as witness" in the graphic memoir (111). Julia Watson has discussed "autobiographic disclosures and genealogies of desire" in the book (27). Finally, Jennifer Lemberg has detailed how memory serves as a mechanism for presenting "that which would otherwise remain unseen," in Bechdel's telling both of her own life story and that of her father (131).

Although the analyses by Cvetkovich, Watson, and Lemberg all have a different focus, they are united by their shared belief that Bechdel's book is inextricably connected to the past. *Fun Home* is not simply a memoir; it is also a cultural time capsule. The text is a rich historical archive about the cartoonist and her family. *Fun Home* contains drawings of photographs that were taken during Bechdel's youth, it reprints letters that her parents exchanged during their courtship, and it reconstructs entries from the journal that she kept as a girl. Accordingly, little has been written about *Fun Home* that does not mention childhood, memory, and autobiography. These issues are regarded not merely as the memoir's primary themes but as its foundational pivot points.

A significant portion of *Fun Home* takes place during Bechdel's childhood and is filled with references to popular culture from that era. In the opening chapter, for example, a panel shows her and her brother watching *Sesame Street* (14). On the facing page, another image shows the young Bechdel playing in her bedroom, where she has a trash can that has Harvey Ball's now-iconic yellow smiley face emblazoned on it (15). A sequence that takes place in the closing pages of the chapter shows a box of Quisp cereal sitting on the family's kitchen table; meanwhile, her father is wearing a necktie adorned with peace signs (18). The references to popular culture that permeate the opening chapter of *Fun Home* continue throughout the rest of the book. Indeed, when the cartoonist discusses the many differences between herself and her father in the opening pages, she identifies her interest in contemporaneous events as a key distinguishing feature. In the panel that contains the smiley face trash can, Bechdel says that she was "Modern to his Victorian" (15). As a child, she not only paid attention to popular culture but enjoyed and even identified with it.

Fun Home stands in marked contrast to common critical perspectives about *DTWOF* with regard to this topic. Whereas the cartoonist's graphic memoir is widely seen as being steeped in the past of her childhood, her serial comic strip is just as strongly associated with the contemporaneous present of her life as an adult. As Robin Bernstein and Susan Kirtley have each discussed, *DTWOF* routinely incorporated current events. The backdrop to the plot for many episodes, in fact, would be a recent sociopolitical occurrence: the Iran-Contra hearings in the 1980s, the passage of the Defense of Marriage Act in the 1990s, the war on terror in the early 2000s, and so on. The strip would detail what the characters thought about this event, how they were reacting to it, and the impact it was having on their lives. Accordingly, if *DTWOF* is seen as a form of life writing at all, then it is seen as being driven by events that were occurring during the time that Bechdel was drawing the strips.

The possible influence that *Peanuts* had on *DTWOF* changes this perception. More than simply being shaped by events that were occurring during the cartoonist's adulthood, the strip may also have been shaped by ones that transpired during her childhood. *DTWOF* has long been regarded as being rooted in the present, but the suggestive echoes that it possesses to Schulz's comic open up the possibility that it has equally strong ties with the past. Reading Mo Testa as Mo Van Pelt reveals that Bechdel's exploration of childhood, memory, and autobiography is not limited to *Fun Home*. Instead, these issues have played an important—but overlooked—role throughout her cartooning career.

"CHARLIE BROWN, SNOOPY, LINUS, LUCY . . . HOW CAN [WE] EVER FORGET THEM": THE DEATH OF CHARLES M. SCHULZ AND THE ONGOING LIFE OF *PEANUTS*

It is fitting that the elements of *Peanuts* that can be traced through *DTWOF* invite contemplation about memory and autobiography. Today, more than twenty years after Schulz's death and seventy years after the debut of his comic strip, issues like the passage of time, the function of memory, and the significance of a creative and cultural legacy loom large in the realm of *Peanuts*.

The story of Charles M. Schulz's death is almost as legendary as his life. On December 14, 1999, after years of declining health and mounting medical problems, the cartoonist announced that he would be retiring. In the previous month alone, Schulz had experienced a blocked abdominal aorta, suffered a series of small strokes, and learned that the colon cancer that he had been battling had metastasized (Michaelis 557–60). The chemotherapy for the cancer alone was extremely taxing. The treatments both nauseated the seventy-seven-year-old cartoonist and sapped his energy. Complicating matters further, the small strokes that he had suffered impaired his vision. As David Michaelis has relayed about Schulz's quality of life during this period, "He couldn't read, he couldn't draw, he couldn't drive a car" (559).

By early December, Schulz's poor health did not simply pose a challenge to drawing his daily comic strip; it had become an impediment to doing so. In a candid interview from his home for *The Today Show*, he revealed, "I never dreamed that this was what would happen to me. I always had the feeling that I would probably stay with the strip until I was in my early eighties. But all of a sudden it's gone. It's been taken away from me. I did not take this away from me" (Michaelis 561). The cartoonist announced that the final *Peanuts* strip would appear on February 13, 2000. The comic series that he had created and drawn every day for almost fifty years would come to a close.

Charles M. Schulz did not wish to end *Peanuts*, and in a fitting finale to both his life and his legacy, he did not live not see this moment happen: the cartoonist died in his sleep on February 12, 2000, the night before the final installment appeared in newspapers. The closing strip took the form of a short letter from the cartoonist to his fans. In it, he commented on the joy that drawing *Peanuts* had brought him ("It has been the fulfillment of my childhood ambition," he wrote); his gratitude to the readers, editors, and fans of the series over the years; and his sadness that he needed to bring it to a close. Schulz's text is surrounded by vignettes of some of the most beloved scenes from the comic strip series: Charlie Brown attempting to kick the football, Lucy sitting in her psychiatrist booth, Snoopy as the World War I Flying Ace, and others. Moreover, the entire episode is framed through another one of Snoopy's well-known activities: sitting atop his doghouse with his typewriter. Although Charlie Brown had long been regarded as the avatar for the cartoonist, Snoopy serves as his proxy persona in the final strip. In the second panel, the beagle types, "Dear Friends . . . ," which then segues into Schulz's letter, which opens with the same phrase.

Schulz closes his final comic with the following observation: "Charlie Brown, Snoopy, Linus, Lucy . . . how can I ever forget them." Of course, Schulz could not—and given that he died before the final comic appeared and the series officially ended, he need not. David Michaelis remarked, "To the very end, his life had been inseparable from his art" (566). For seven decades and counting, the cartoonist's art has been inseparable from American print, visual, and popular culture.

More than twenty years have now passed since Charles M. Schulz died and *Peanuts* ended. In the same way that the cartoonist wondered how he could ever forget characters like Charlie Brown, Snoopy, Linus, and Lucy, we might ponder the same issue. As the journalist David Gritten reflected in 2015, *Peanuts* ranks "among institutions that retain an unshakable hold on America's collective affections." Reprints of the strip still appear in the comics section of newspapers. Likewise, the animated television specials remain a cherished national tradition, with *It's the Great Pumpkin, Charlie Brown* (1966), *A Charlie Brown Thanksgiving* (1973), and *A Charlie Brown Christmas* (1965) airing annually. Additionally, beginning in 2004, the complete comic strip series was collected and released in book form. Spanning no fewer than twenty-six volumes, the final installment appeared in 2016. Far from merely an act of nostalgia, the release of *The Complete Peanuts* marked a resurgence of interest in the comic. In 2015, a new feature-length movie based on Schulz's comic strip arrived in theaters. Titled *The Peanuts Movie*, it received both critical acclaim and commercial success, earning nearly $250 million at the box office and also being nominated for a Golden Globe Award for Best Animated Feature.[4] The success of the movie inspired the launch of an animated *Peanuts* television series the following year. The second decade of the twenty-first century continues to see the release of new *Peanuts* programming. In 2021, "Apple TV+ debuted *The Snoopy Show*, six twenty-two-minute episodes that revolve around the famous beagle" (Daspin 5). The channel also "announced four specials celebrating Mother's Day, Earth Day, New Year's Eve, and going back to school" (5). These new programs appear to be in keeping with the now-iconic animated television specials from the 1960s and 1970s—only they are made for a new generation of young viewers.

Finally, but far from inconsequentially, merchandise featuring Schulz's characters remains ubiquitous in the United States.[5] From clothing and collectibles to home decor to school supplies, *Peanuts*-themed items can be found in nearly every shopping category or store department. The profits from these and other ventures have led to Schulz being "routinely ranked in the top five of *Forbes* magazine's 'Top Earning Dead Celebrities' list" (Lind x). Indeed, a special issue of *Life* magazine dedicated to *Peanuts* and released in 2021 offered specific details. "In 2020," it relayed, "the cartoonist, with $32.5 million in revenue, ranked number 3 on *Forbes*' list of wealthiest dead celebrities, just behind Michael Jackson and Theodor Seuss Geisel (Dr. Seuss)" ("Way More" 87).

This situation has not gone unnoticed by critics. As Jared Gardner and Ian Gordon remarked, Schulz's strip was "a hallmark of the second half of the twentieth century," and it "seems to be going through a period of growth in the twenty-first century" (3). Far from fading from American popular culture, *Peanuts* has experienced an increased presence in the years after the cartoonist's death.

Chip Kidd, in the foreword to *Only What's Necessary: Charles M. Schulz and the Art of Peanuts* (2015), observed: "Many books devoted to Mr. Schulz's *oeuvre* have come before this, and many more will follow, as well they should" (n.p.). *Blockheads, Beagles, and Sweet Babboos* affirms Kidd's prediction, but it certainly doesn't bring it to a close. These chapters give additional critical attention to the cartoonist and some of his most well-known characters, but they are anything but the final word about them. In the same way that my discussions have identified new ways of viewing, understanding, and interpreting Schulz's characters and comic, future readers and critics will surely do the same.

In numerous strips over the course of *Peanuts*, Snoopy receives feedback from a publisher about his latest manuscript. His response to such comments is generally the same. "I can't stand criticism," the World Famous Author declares in typical fashion in the strip from July 16, 1965, after kicking his typewriter off the top of his doghouse. Snoopy might rebuff analysis of his work, but—as *Blockheads, Beagles, and Sweet Babboos* has hopefully demonstrated—*Peanuts* continues to invite and reward it.

NOTES

CHAPTER 1. "SOMETIMES MY HAND SHAKES SO MUCH I HAVE TO HOLD MY WRIST TO DRAW": CHARLES M. SCHULZ AND DISABILITY

1. That said, in a series of strips that began in November 1965 and spanned the next few months, Sally is diagnosed with amblyopia—colloquially known as "lazy eye"—and wears an eye patch to correct it. One of Schulz's close friends in California was an ophthalmologist, which may have been the source of this plotline. Various strips explain Sally's condition, along with how it is treated. Moreover, some comics also discuss the difficulty that Sally experiences while wearing the eye patch. Not only does she feel self-conscious, but she faces stares and even teasing. Snoopy, for example, snatches her patch at one point and uses it to pretend that he is pirate. In 1968 a selection of these strips was reprinted as the booklet *Security Is an Eye Patch* by the US Department of Health, Education, and Welfare—presumably for use in ophthalmologists' offices. This plotline notwithstanding, though, Sally is not associated with amblyopia. Although she was diagnosed with this condition, it disappears from the comic after being treated. When readers think about Charlie Brown's little sister, a number of traits come to mind: her terrible book reports, her crush on Linus, her penchant for talking to the brick schoolhouse. However, the fact that she had lazy eye is not among them, which is why I mention this detail in a footnote. Neither the condition nor the taunting that she faced because of it became a permanent aspect of Sally's identity or of Schulz's strip.

2. I am indebted to an anonymous outside reader for pointing out the ways in which Charlie Brown, Snoopy, and Woodstock can be viewed through the lens of disability.

3. I am likewise indebted to an anonymous outside reader for pointing out that the muffled speech of the adults in the animated television specials can be viewed through the context of disability.

4. Of course, other modes of inquiry exist and are extant in comics criticism. For example, Foss, Gray, and Whalen, in the introduction to *Disability in Comic Books and Graphic Novels*, explain that some of the essays in their collection are interested in "reevaluations of comics theory through the lens of disability studies" (6). As they elaborate, "Using McCloud and other theorists more as a starting point, several contributors use the occasion of exploring disability to unpack the able-bodied assumptions underlying his theories" (7–8). That said, the two forms that I identify are the most common and pervasive.

5. Of course, comics are not the only aesthetic mode where corporeality plays a role. In the art forms of painting, dancing, acting, and singing—to name just a few—the physical

body of the creator is not simply a visible element but an influential one. Gardner's argument, as well as my point here, is that comics both incorporate and reveal the body in ways that prose-only modes of storytelling commonly do not.

CHAPTER 2. WHAT'S THE FREQUENCY, CHARLIE BROWN? SOUND WAVES, MUSIC, AND THE ZIGZAG SHIRT

1. This feature not only made Schulz's character distinctive but also became a source of some humor. In 2015, the cartoonist Dave Whamond satirized Charlie Brown's limited attire in his series *Reality Check*. The single-panel comic features a silhouette of the character Lucy. Above her head is a banner that reads "'Peanuts' Tell All." In a speech balloon that occupies a sizable portion of the panel, Lucy makes the following disclosure: "Sure, Pig-Pen was known for walking around in a cloud of dust, but Charlie Brown was stinky. He wore that same ugly zig-zag shirt every day since 1950!"

2. For more information about the use of classical music in *Peanuts*, see William Meredith's blog *Schulz's Beethoven* along with his article "Michaelis' Schulz, Schulz's Beethoven, and the Construction of Biography," *Beethoven Journal* 25, no. 2 (Winter 2008): 79–91.

3. Technically, the screech in Beck's "Beercan" is created by an artificial harmonic on an electric guitar, not by amplifying odd harmonics through sound mixing with triangle waves. Nonetheless, the end result is musical dissonance.

4. That said, Ian Hague points out that even ostensibly "silent" print-based comics that contain no speech balloons or indications of background noise still possess elements of sound: when the cover is opened, when the page is turned, when the spine is cracked, and so on. For more on this issue and its impact on our perception as well as experience of print-based sequential art, see Hague, *Comics and the Senses*.

CHAPTER 3. "WHY CAN'T I HAVE A NORMAL DOG LIKE EVERYONE ELSE?": SNOOPY AS CANINE—AND FELINE

1. Snoopy does publish some of his short stories. More specifically, in strips that appeared in 1974, his series of "Kitten Kaboodle" tales appear in *Playbeagle* magazine.

2. The one exception to this pattern is the World Famous Astronaut. Snoopy not only successfully lands on the moon in a series of strips that appeared in March 1969 but also beats the US astronauts there by several months.

3. This gag is repeated in the animated television special *A Charlie Brown Christmas* (1965), which aired later that year. This time, though, Snoopy licks her face during the play rehearsal.

CHAPTER 4. I LOVE LUCY: THE FUSSBUDGET AND THE FIRST LADY OF SITCOMS

1. Meredith Schulz was the daughter of Schulz's first wife from her previous marriage to Bill Lewis. As David Michaelis explains (in what can easily be described as a judgmental

tone), in 1948, nineteen-year-old Joyce Halverson "had run off to New Mexico, fallen in love with a cowboy, married, gotten pregnant, been abandoned by her husband, and come home to Minneapolis to have the child—all within twenty months" (223). Given the stigma of divorce at the time and especially the opprobrium directed at single mothers, the cartoonist and his wife hid this history. Soon after getting married, not only did Schulz legally adopt Meredith, but "he and Joyce lied about the year of their wedding (1951) in order to assimilate and protect Meredith's place in their marriage" (Michaelis 235). In the words of Michaelis once again, "Even in official notarized documents, they ever after gave April 18, 1949, as their nuptial day, placing Meredith's birth (on February 5, 1950) just within the bounds of propriety as Sparky's daughter" (235). Even Meredith was not aware of her paternity until she became an adult. Schulz and Joyce "maintained this fiction for the next eighteen years . . . hushing up any talk of Joyce's first marriage, to keep the truth from the public but also from Meredith herself, and perhaps even to keep her safe from such claims as might be made by Bill Lewis, who had never known that it was a daughter he had fathered" (Michaelis 236).

2. In the same way that Lucy Van Pelt's behavior was based on an actual person in Schulz's life, so too was her surname. Soon after Schulz and his first wife, Joyce, got married in April 1951, they moved to Colorado Springs. Among the first friends that the newlyweds made were Philip and Louanne Van Pelt. "The Van Pelts were an attractive, witty couple around whom laughter and conversation came easily" (Michaelis 252). Moreover, as Michaelis points out, "The Van Pelts were the happy exception to the Schulzes' mountain-town solitude" (253). The foursome spent as many as "three and sometimes four nights a week" together, having dinner, playing cards, and listening to music (253).

3. By my count, the following episodes contain plotlines about Lucy getting involved in show business: "The Diet" (ep. 3), "The Audition" (ep. 6), "Lucy Is Jealous of a Girl Singer" (ep. 10), "The Adagio" (ep. 12), "The Benefit" (ep. 13), "The Amateur Hour" (ep. 14), "Lucy Fakes an Illness" (ep. 16), "Lucy Writes a Play" (ep. 17), "The Ballet" (ep. 19), "The Young Fans" (ep. 20), "Cuban Pals" (ep. 28), and "Lucy Does a TV Commercial" (ep. 30).

4. Conversely, some lines of dialogue from *I Love Lucy* could have been uttered by one of Schulz's characters. In an episode from season 3, Lucy Ricardo's assertion "You can't tell people the truth. They think you're lying" sounds like something that Charlie Brown would say ("Lucy Tells the Truth"). So too does Lucy's lament to Ricky during season 1: "Here I am with all this talent bottled up inside of me and you're always sitting on the cork" ("The Ballet"). Far from being limited to one-liners from *I Love Lucy*, exchanges between the sitcom's characters also mirror exchanges between characters in Schulz's comic. For example, in an episode from season 1, Lucy complains, "There are just two things keeping me from dancing on that show," and Fred says matter-of-factly, "Your feet?" ("The Adagio"). Along the same lines, in a moment from season 2, Ethel remarks, "Ricky and Fred are cut out of the same mold." Without missing a beat—and akin to a character in *Peanuts*—Lucy retorts, "Yeah, and they're getting moldier" ("Vacation from Marriage").

5. The rise of television was not the only sociocultural factor that led to the decline of comic books in the United States. So too was Fredric Wertham's public crusade against them. Beginning in the late 1940s and accelerating rapidly in the opening years of the 1950s, the German-born psychiatrist wrote, lectured, and even testified before Congress about the damaging intellectual, moral, psychological, and social effects of comic books on young people. His efforts culminated in the passage of the Comics Code in 1954, a set of

publishing standards that were so restrictive that they all but shut down the industry. For more on these events, see David Hajdu, *The Ten-Cent Plague: The Great Comic-Book Scare and How It Changed America* (2008).

6. While *The Honeymooners* lasted only twelve issues ("Jackie Gleason"), *The Lone Ranger* enjoyed an impressive run of 145 issues released for nearly fifteen years ("*The Lone Ranger*").

7. To be clear, Beaty did not see this situation as necessarily positive. On the contrary, his introduction was a call in many ways for comics studies to push past its dependence on film and come into its own as a critical field.

CHAPTER 5. FRANKLIN AND PIG-PEN: THE AESTHETICS OF BLACKNESS AND DIRT

1. It should be noted that not all of Schulz's comments on this subject were so socially aware or politically enlightened. While the white cartoonist rightly realized his own limitations when it came to depicting the lives and experiences of racial groups to which he did not belong, he also said in the same interview, "I'm not out to grind a lot of axes." Although Schulz was talking somewhat more broadly about using comics to teach, instruct, or "stir things up" rather than just "to be funny" (Schulz, "Charles M. Schulz: An Interview"), these comments, which effectively liken challenging the all-white world of US comics to "grinding an axe," are obtuse at best and insulting at worst. At minimum, they are a poor choice of words that disappointingly undercut his other remarks on this topic.

2. It is worth noting that when any of the other white *Peanuts* characters get dirty—such as when Charlie Brown gets flattened by a line drive on the pitcher's mound—Schulz uses the same scribbly line shading as he does for Pig-Pen. So the cartoonist's presentation of dirt in this manner is not unique to Pig-Pen; it is uniform throughout the strip.

3. Far from being simply a relic of the past, such associations—as well as advertisements—still persist today. In October 2017, the soap brand Dove released a promotional GIF on social media in which "a black woman removes her brown shirt and—voila! Underneath is a white woman in a light shirt" (Astor, par. 1). The ad sparked immediate condemnation for the way that it "evoked a long-running racist trope in soap advertising: a 'dirty' black person cleansed into whiteness" (par. 3).

4. To this list, one could add the comic *Dateline: Danger!* Written by John Saunders and drawn by Al McWilliams, the strip appeared in 1968 and ran until 1974. *Dateline: Danger!* chronicled the adventures of two male undercover intelligence agents who were posing as reporters. Danny Raven, one of the protagonists, was the first African American character to have a lead role in a newspaper strip. That said, *Dateline: Danger!* features adult characters rather than juvenile ones. As a result, while it certainly participates in this important cultural moment in American comics, the strip also differs from *Wee Pals*, *Luther*, and *Quincy*.

5. I also spoke with Cesar Gallegos, archivist at the Charles M. Schulz Museum and Research Center, about this issue. He likewise did not know why Schulz chose to change from line hatching to screentone for shading Franklin, nor was he aware of any instance when the cartoonist commented on the change.

6. I am indebted to an anonymous outside reader for calling attention to this detail.

CHAPTER 6. CHIRPING 'BOUT MY GENERATION: WOODSTOCK, YOUTH CULTURE, AND INNOCENCE

1. To avoid confusion between the multiday concert Woodstock and Schulz's character Woodstock, I will refer to the music festival by this acronym.

2. The festival was officially slated to end on August 17. Like most everything else over the course of that weekend, however, this schedule did not go according to plan. Jimi Hendrix was the final performer at Woodstock. After various bands had played all through the night, Hendrix took the stage at 9 a.m. on Monday, August 18; he finished his now-iconic set at 11:10 a.m.

3. Since the event took place in an outdoor space that lacked numbered seating, and also since tickets were not collected, the official attendance at the WMAF is unknown; estimates generally range from 300,000 to 500,000. Additionally, "the New York State police suggest that a further 1.5 million people failed to get to the event because of traffic congestion on roads and highways leading to the festival site" (Bennett xiv).

4. That said, there were accidents, injuries, illnesses, and even two deaths at the WMAF: one attendee died from a drug overdose, and another perished after being accidently run over by a tractor. Additionally, there were dozens of broken bones, cuts, and assorted other medical problems. Personally, I also find it difficult to believe that no sexual assaults occurred at any point over the four days. The sheer number of attendees, combined with the widespread use of drugs that impaired an individual's ability to consent (assuming that consent was even sought), would suggest otherwise.

5. A critique of the limited race, gender, sexual, and socioeconomic dynamics of the hippie movement was not part of this criticism, either then or in many ways even now. While hippies advocated free love, it was limited to heterosexual couplings; the counterculture did not become allies with the nascent gay and lesbian liberation movement. Additionally, while hippies claimed to value and respect all individuals, "the counterculture movement was male-defined" (Miller xxiv). Women were regarded as little more than sex partners—"chicks" and "old ladies"—or as domestics who cooked, cleaned, and took care of the children on hippie communes (Miller 81). Given such attitudes, the counterculture movement was not influenced by, or even an advocate for, second-wave feminism. Finally, and perhaps most vividly of all, hippies claimed to welcome everyone, but their ranks were exceedingly homogeneous from a racial, ethnic, and socioeconomic standpoint. As William Rorabaugh has commented, "Hippies came from white middle-class families and grew up in suburbs, which were very white. So were crowds at Woodstock and other rock festivals. They had little experience with people of other races. . . . While hippies sneered at success, poor young blacks had to fight to join the mainstream that freaks rejected. . . . Young blacks craved consumer goods as signs of success and acceptance" (qtd. in Kelley). Hippies operated culturally parallel to, but politically separate from, the era's civil rights movement. In light of these issues, hippies may have claimed to reject and reimagine the nation's problematic social, political, and economic structure, but their commitment to social justice was limited at best and specious at worst. As John Anthony Moretta has written, the hippies can more accurately be seen to have engaged in a "quest for personal freedom rather than social justice" (3). For more on this issue, see also William Rorabaugh's *American Hippies* (Cambridge University Press, 2015).

6. Once again, I must call attention to the unspoken race, class, and sexual dynamics at play in this viewpoint. If a half-million young people who were largely nonwhite, queer, and working-class had gathered for a multiday festival that was marked by widespread drug use, nudity, and loud music that played all night, it is difficult to imagine the event being mythologized in this way. To be sure, it is difficult to imagine that an event with these demographic details would have been allowed to proceed, let alone permitted to effectively shut down a portion of upstate New York for an entire weekend.

7. Schulz generally did not publicly discuss or even reveal his political affiliations. As Stephen J. Lind has written, "Outside of the strip, Sparky's personal approach to politics was nuanced. 'Was Dad a Republican or a Democrat?' wondered his son Monte" (159). Even the Charles M. Schulz Museum and Research Center, which I queried for information on Schulz's party affiliation in the 1960s, does not know the cartoonist's full voting record, including for presidential elections.

8. To be fair, Schulz's son Monte said that his father came to regret this decision later in life. "'He confessed to me once,' Monte also remembered, 'that had he the opportunity to do it over again, he would have voted for Kennedy in 1960 instead of Nixon'" (Lind 156).

9. The group's name does not contain the possessive "s," even though it should grammatically. As the organization's official website famously says: "Yes, we know there is an apostrophe missing, but it is you who miss it. We don't" (FAQ).

10. I mention the race of the victim as well as of his killer because it played a role both in the use of lethal violence and especially in the trial that followed. Meredith Hunter did brandish a .22-caliber revolver during the fight that broke out in front of the stage. However, if he had been a white man instead of a Black one, he likely would not have been perceived as threatening to Passaro—or to those in the courtroom. Moreover, had Hunter been a white man, he would more likely have been seen as brandishing the weapon to protect himself and his girlfriend from the Hells Angels, rather than the other way around. Passaro was arrested and charged with murder but argued that he was acting self-defense. The jury agreed, and Passaro was acquitted. For more on the death of Meredith Hunter, see Saul Austerlitz's *Just a Shot Away: Peace, Love, and Tragedy with the Rolling Stones at Altamont* (2018).

11. I derived this number from a keyword search of *Peanuts* on the GoComics website, which contains the complete run of Schulz's strip. While this figure is not exact, it provides a reasonable estimate of the number of times that Woodstock appears in the series.

12. Admittedly, in strips that appeared over the next few days, Snoopy gets angry at Woodstock because he also colored in the grass and—even worse—the bunnies. Their rift is quickly mended, however, when Snoopy reveals in the strip on May 21, 1979, that he is getting Woodstock his own crayons and coloring books as gifts for his next birthday. Woodstock is so excited by this news that he jumps up and down, eventually falling off the top of the doghouse.

13. Michael Lang, arguably the most visible of the four young men who organized the WMAF, seemingly affirmed this viewpoint. In the 1980s, Lang began investing in real estate ventures, which prompted criticism that he had shifted from a hippie to a yuppie. The co-promoter of Woodstock responded by saying, "Hey, you have to grow up a little bit" (qtd. in Plasketes and Plasketes 43).

14. Woodstock does occasionally get angry and even physical. For example, he kicks Lucy on several occasions, such as after she criticizes Snoopy's work as the Head Beagle in the strip from March 2, 1970, and then again after she tells her little brother to stop patting birds

on the head in the strip from March 11, 1973. Moreover, on March 30, 1967, a Woodstock-like bird intentionally trips Lucy after she tells her little brother to stop patting birds on the head. These instances notwithstanding, it is difficult to imagine anyone characterizing Woodstock as violent or deeming him emotionally unstable.

15. Reexamining Woodstock in light of his namesake also shifts our perspective on one of his other, lesser-known traits. While the little bird is notoriously poor at flying on his own—looping in circles and crashing into things—he is a skilled helicopter pilot. When Snoopy whirls his ears like rotor blades and lifts off like a chopper, his feathered friend is usually sitting in his lap as the avian aviator. During a sequence that begins in late January 1977 and extends into February, Snoopy uses his helicopter skills to save Linus, who has gotten stranded on the icy roof of a barn. Woodstock, of course, serves as the pilot for the air rescue mission. In the comic on February 3, 1977, after Linus has successfully been plucked from atop the structure and is on his way to safety, he says to Woodstock: "You're a good pilot.... Where'd you learn to fly a chopper?" The little bird, of course, responds via inscrutable chicken scratch. Forming one of the rare moments when a character other than Snoopy understands Woodstock, Linus is surprised by what he learns. "Nam?" he says in the final panel. While this answer is meant to be humorous, it assumes symbolic significance given Woodstock's namesake. The war in Vietnam was a core issue both among the hippie countercultural movement and at the WMAF.

EPILOGUE. *PEANUTS* TO WATCH OUT FOR: LINUS VAN PELT, ALISON BECHDEL, AND THE LEGACY OF CHARLES M. SCHULZ

1. Bechdel suspended the strip in May 2008 so that she could give more attention to other comics projects, namely, her graphic memoirs *Fun Home* (2006) and *Are You My Mother?* (2012). On November 23, 2016, however, after Donald J. Trump was elected president, Bechdel released a new *DTWOF* strip titled "Pièce de Résistance." The posting of the strip on the cartoonist's website caused so much traffic that the site crashed (Bechdel Facebook). At the time of this writing in fall 2021, Bechdel has not resumed her former schedule of weekly *DTWOF* installments. Instead, as she has commented, she "draws single strips when inspiration strikes" (Bechdel, "New 'Dykes'").

2. Sanjak from Milton Caniff's *Terry and the Pirates* is commonly identified as the first lesbian character in American comics. She made her debut on February 12, 1939. That said, Caitlin McGurk has challenged this viewpoint in an essay about the strip, "Lucy and Sophie Say Goodbye" (1905). As McGurk argues, the coded interactions between these "previously unexamined early newspaper comic strip characters ... could lay the groundwork for queer comic studies" (336). For more on this issue, see McGurk, "Lovers, Enemies, Friends."

3. Bechdel and Schulz share connections beyond simply their creative work. Their backgrounds and personalities also overlap in a variety of compelling ways. Both cartoonists, for example, describe themselves as shy introverts who view the world with apprehension and even anxiety (DeLuca 301; Bechdel and Hall 15–21). Additionally, and even more powerfully, the lives of Schulz and Bechdel were shaped by the death of one of their parents when they were young adults: Schulz's mother died of cancer when he was twenty years old, and Bechdel's father died—likely from suicide, as she explores in *Fun Home*—when she was nineteen.

David Michaelis identifies the death of Schulz's mother as the single most important event in the cartoonist's life. The first chapter of Michaelis's biography of Schulz, in fact, describes this event. Michaelis presents it as changing Schulz irrevocably and thus being a key to understanding him and his personality (Michaelis 3–8). Similarly, Bechdel has discussed, both inside and outside the pages of *Fun Home*, how the death of her father—and her subsequent discovery of his secret homosexual liaisons—marked a profound turning point in her life. "Because of him," she remarked in an article in *Rolling Stone*, "I was determined to be very out and open about my queerness. My whole career has kind of spun out of that dynamic" (qtd. in Yarm, par. 3).

4. These accolades aside, *The Peanuts Movie* was also controversial for a variety of reasons. First, Schulz made it clear that he did not want anyone continuing his comic or even drawing his characters after he died. As Stephen J. Lind has documented, "When Sparky successfully renegotiated his contract with United Feature Syndicate in 1978 . . . his children insisted that they include a clause guaranteeing that no artist would be able to produce *Peanuts* after Sparky died" (Lind 223). The cartoonist reiterated this desire in his letter to fans that appeared in the final strip: "My family does not wish *Peanuts* to be continued by anyone else," he said about his impending retirement. Additionally, Schulz never liked the name "*Peanuts*"—which was chosen by his editors at United Feature Syndicate and not him—for his series. The cartoonist minimized or even avoided using this appellation as much as he could. In a powerful illustration of this phenomenon, none of the more than forty animated specials that were made about Schulz's comic and characters during his lifetime uses "*Peanuts*" in its title. Furthermore, the 2015 movie also showed the Little Red-Haired Girl—a character who, like the Great Pumpkin and all the adults, was never depicted during Schulz's lifetime. Finally, but far from insignificantly, *The Peanuts Movie* used 3D computer graphics, a style that is wholly out of step with the "limited animation (sparse character movement filmed with few frames per second)" that was employed during Schulz's lifetime (Lind 66). Beginning with *A Charlie Brown Christmas* in 1965, the cartoonist wanted the television specials to look like the comic strips. As a result, the animation style was flat and two-dimensional, showing the characters from only a few angles—generally from the side or facing forward—not fully in the round, let alone in 3D as in *The Peanuts Movie*.

5. Of course, this situation is also true in many countries around the world. *Peanuts* in general and Snoopy in particular are hugely popular in Japan, China, and Brazil, for instance. I say "the United States" here because that is the focus of my analysis—and my area of expertise. For more on the popularity of Schulz's comic and characters outside the United States, see the website for the Peanuts Global Artist Collective, https://www.peanutsglobalartistcollective.com, as well as Ian Gordon's "Charlie Brown Cafés and the Marketing of *Peanuts* in Asia."

WORKS CITED

ACKNOWLEDGMENTS

Patchett, Ann. "Snoopy Taught Me How to Be a Writer." *Washington Post*, 12 July 2012. https://www.washingtonpost.com/outlook/snoopy-taught-me-how-to-be-a-writer /2019/07/12/8db3ce3c-a31b-11e9-b7b4-95e30869bd15_story.html. Accessed 22 March 2020.

INTRODUCTION. CHARACTER STUDIES: THE *PEANUTS* GANG, RECONSIDERED

Ball, Blake Scott. *Charlie Brown's America: The Popular Politics of Peanuts.* Oxford UP, 2021.
Blauner, Andrew, editor. *The Peanuts Papers: Writers and Cartoonists on Charlie Brown, Snoopy, and the Gang, and the Meaning of Life.* Library of America, 2019.
Boxer, Sarah. "The Exemplary Narcissism of Snoopy." *The Atlantic*, November 2015.
A Boy Named Charlie Brown. Dir. Bill Melendez. Cinema Center, 1969.
Breines, Wini. *Young, White and Miserable: Growing Up Female in the Fifties.* Oxford UP, 1992.
Caputi, Mary. *A Kinder, Gentler America: Melancholy and the Mythical 1950s.* U of Minnesota P, 2005.
Caron, James E. "Review Essay: Everyone Deserves a Security Blanket." *Studies in American Humor*, vol. 3, no. 17, 2008, 145–55.
"Charles M. Schulz at the Louvre." *Big Bad Comics*, 2016. http://bigbadcomics.com/store/ charles-m-schulz-louvre-limited-edition-peanuts-poster. Accessed 3 July 2020.
A Charlie Brown Christmas. Dir. Bill Melendez. CBS, 9 December 1965.
A Charlie Brown Thanksgiving. Dir. Bill Melendez and Phil Roman. CBS, 30 November 1973.
Daspin, Eileen. "Life Itself." Special Issue, *Peanuts: The World's Greatest Comic Strip. Life*, 24 December 2021, 4–7.
Foreman, Joel. Introduction. *The "Other" Fifties: Interrogating Mid-century American Icons*, edited by Joel Foreman, U of Illinois P, 1997, 1–23.
Gardner, Jared, and Ian Gordon. Introduction. *The Comics of Charles Schulz: The Good Grief of Modern Life*, edited by Jared Gardner and Ian Gordon, UP of Mississippi, 2017, 3–9.
Halberstam, David. *The Fifties.* Random House, 1994.
Inge, M. Thomas, editor. *Charles M. Schulz: Conversations.* UP of Mississippi, 2000.

Inge, M. Thomas, editor. *Charles M. Schulz: My Life with Charlie Brown*. UP of Mississippi, 2010.
It's the Great Pumpkin, Charlie Brown. Dir. Bill Melendez. CBS, 27 October 1966.
Johnson, Rheta Grimsley. *Good Grief: The Story of Charles M. Schulz*. 1989. Andrews and McMeel, 1995.
Kidd, Chip. Foreword and preface. *Only What's Necessary: Charles M. Schulz and the Art of Peanuts*, edited by Chip Kidd, Abrams, 2015.
Laux, Cameron. "Good Grief! The Beguiling Philosophy of *Peanuts*." *The Guardian*, 13 November 2018. https://www.bbc.com/culture/article/20181112-good-grief-the-beguiling-philosophy-of-peanuts. Accessed 24 July 2022.
Lhamon, W. T., Jr. *Deliberate Speed: The Origins of Cultural Style in the American 1950s*. Smithsonian Institution Press, 1990.
Lind, Stephen J. *A Charlie Brown Religion: Exploring the Spiritual Life and Word of Charles M. Schulz*. UP of Mississippi, 2015.
Meyerowitz, Joanne. *Not June Cleaver: Women and Gender in Postwar America, 1945–1960*. Temple UP, 1994.
Michaelis, David. *Schulz and Peanuts: A Biography*. HarperCollins, 2007.
The Royal Guardsmen. "The Return of the Red Baron." *Snoopy and His Friends*, Laurie Records, 1967.
The Royal Guardsmen. *Snoopy and His Friends*. Laurie Records, 1967.
The Royal Guardsmen. "Snoopy's Christmas." *Snoopy and His Friends*, Laurie Records, 1967.
The Royal Guardsmen. "Snoopy vs. the Red Baron." Charles Fuller Productions, 1966.
Schulz, Charles M. *Happiness Is a Warm Puppy*. 1962. Penguin, 2019.
Schulz, Charles M. "My Life and Art with Charlie Brown and Others." *Charles M. Schulz: My Life with Charlie Brown*, edited by M. Thomas Inge, UP of Mississippi, 2010, 3–19.
Short, Robert L. *The Gospel according to Peanuts*. 1964. Westminster John Knox, 2000.
"Timeline: The Life of Charles M. Schulz." Charles M. Schulz Museum and Research Center. https://schulzmuseum.org/timeline. Accessed 10 July 2019.
Yee, Peter W. Y., editor. *Peanuts and American Culture: Essays on Charles M. Schulz's Iconic Comic Strip*. McFarland, 2019.
You're Good Man, Charlie Brown. Script by John Gordon and Charles M. Schulz. Music and Lyrics by Clark Gesner. Theatre 80, New York, NY, March 7, 1967.

CHAPTER 1. "SOMETIMES MY HAND SHAKES SO MUCH I HAVE TO HOLD MY WRIST TO DRAW": CHARLES M. SCHULZ AND DISABILITY

"About Essential Tremor." International Essential Tremor Foundation. https://www.essentialtremor.org. Accessed 10 July 2019.
Alaniz, José. *Death, Disability, and the Superhero: The Silver Age and Beyond*. UP of Mississippi, 2014.
"arthrology." *Merriam-Webster Medical Dictionary*. https://www.merriam-webster.com/medical/arthrology.

Baird, Robert M., Stuart E. Rosenbaum, and S. Kay Toombs. "The Disability Rights Movement: A Brief History." *Disability: The Social, Political, and Ethical Debate*, edited by Robert M. Baird, Stuart E. Rosenbaum, and S. Kay Toombs, Prometheus, 2009, 137–40.

Baynton, Douglas C. "Disability and the Justification of Inequality in American History." *The New Disability History: American Perspectives*, edited by Paul K. Longmore and Lauri Umansky, NYU Press, 2001, 33–57.

Boxer, Sarah. "Charles M. Schulz, 'Peanuts' Creator, Dies at 77." *New York Times*, 14 February 2000.

"Charles Schulz Was the Creator of the 'Peanuts' Cartoons and Had Essential Tremor." Diann Shaddox Foundation for Essential Tremor, 29 September 2014. https://www.diannshaddox foundation.org/dsf-blog/charles-schulz-was-the-creator-of-the-peanuts-cartoons-and -had-essential-tremor. Accessed 10 July 2019.

A Charlie Brown Christmas. Dir. Bill Melendez. CBS, 9 December 1965. Television special.

A Charlie Brown Thanksgiving. Dir. Bill Melendez and Phil Roman. CBS, 20 November 1973. Television special.

Chute, Hillary. "Comics Form and Narrating Lives." *Profession*, 2011, 107–17.

Crilley, Mariah. "Drawing Disability: Superman, Huntington's, and the Comic Form in *It's a Bird . . .*" *Disability in Comic Books and Graphic Narratives*, edited by Chris Foss, Jonathan W. Gray, and Zach Whalen. Palgrave Macmillan, 2016, 80–94.

Daspin, Eileen. "Life Itself." Special Issue, *Peanuts: The World's Greatest Comic Strip. Life*, 24 December 2021, 4–7.

Davis, Lennard. *Enabling Acts: The Hidden Story of How the Americans with Disabilities Act Gave the Largest US Minority Its Rights*. Beacon, 2015.

DeLuca, Geraldine. "'I Felt a Funeral in My Brain': The Fragile Comedy of Charles Schulz." *The Lion and the Unicorn*, vol. 25, no. 2, April 2001, 300–309.

Derrida, Jacques. *Of Grammatology*. 1976. Translated by Gayatri Chakravorty Spivak. Johns Hopkins UP, 1998.

Dolmage, Jay, and Dale Jacobs. "Mutable Articulations: Disability Rhetorics and the Comics Medium." *Disability in Comic Books and Graphic Narratives*, edited by Chris Foss, Jonathan W. Gray, and Zach Whalen, Palgrave Macmillan, 2016, 14–28.

"Essential Tremor." Mayo Clinic, 23 January 2019. https://www.mayoclinic.org/diseases -conditions/essential-tremor/symptoms-causes/syc-20350534. Accessed 10 July 2019.

Faderman, Lillian. *Odd Girls and Twilight Lovers: A History of Lesbian Life in Twentieth-Century America*. Columbia UP, 1991.

"Famous Cartoonists from the United States." Ranker.com, 2019. https://www.ranker.com/ list/famous-cartoonists-from-united-states-of-america/reference. Accessed 26 July 2019.

Galvan, Margaret. "Thinking Through Thea: Alison Bechdel's Representations of Disability." *Disability in Comic Books and Graphic Narratives*, edited by Chris Foss, Jonathan W. Gray, and Zach Whalen. Palgrave Macmillan, 2016, 187–202.

Gardner, Jared. "Storylines." *SubStance*, vol. 40, no. 1, 2011, 53–69.

Gardner, Jared, and Ian Gordon, editors. *The Comics of Charles Schulz: The Good Grief of Modern Life*. UP of Mississippi, 2017.

Garland-Thompson, Rosemarie. "Seeing the Disabled: Visual Rhetorics of Disability in Popular Photography." *The New Disability History: American Perspectives*, edited by Paul K. Longmore and Lauri Umansky, NYU Press, 2001, 335–74.

Gherman, Beverly. *Sparky: The Life and Art of Charles Schulz*. Chronicle Books, 2010.
Groensteen, Thierry. *The System of Comics*. Translated by Bart Beaty. UP of Mississippi, 2009.
Hogan, Heather. "Peppermint Patty and Marcie: BFFs and GFs?" *AfterEllen*, 24 June 2009. http://www.afterellen.com. Accessed 11 October 2017.
Inge, M. Thomas. Introduction. *Charles M. Schulz: My Life with Charlie Brown*, edited by M. Thomas Inge, UP of Mississippi, 2010, ix–xiv.
It's the Great Pumpkin, Charlie Brown. Dir. Bill Melendez. CBS, 27 October 1966. Television special.
Johnson, Rheta Grimsley. *Good Grief: The Story of Charles M. Schulz*. 1989. Andrews and McMeel, 1995.
Kafer, Alison. *Feminist, Crip, Queer*. Indiana UP, 2013.
Koch, Christina Maria. "'When you have no voice, you don't exist'? Envisioning Disability in David Small's *Stitches*." *Disability in Comic Books and Graphic Narratives*, edited by Chris Foss, Jonathan W. Gray, and Zach Whalen, Palgrave Macmillan, 2016, 29–43.
Linton, Simi. *Claiming Disability: Knowledge and Identity*. NYU Press, 1998.
Longmore, Paul K., and Lauri Umansky. "Disability History: From the Margins to the Mainstream." *The New Disability History: American Perspectives*, edited by Paul K. Longmore and Lauri Umansky, NYU Press, 2001, 1–29.
Martin, Jeffrey J. "Supercrip Identity." *Handbook of Disability Sport and Exercise Psychology*, Oxford UP, 2017, 139–49.
McRuer, Robert. *Crip Theory: Cultural Signs of Queerness and Disability*. NYU Press, 2006.
Michaelis, David. *Schulz and Peanuts: A Biography*. Harper Perennial, 2008.
Nielsen, Kim E. *A Disability History of the United States*. Beacon Press, 2012.
Phoenix, Woodrow. Review of *The Compete Peanuts, 1985–1986*. *The Slings and Arrows Graphic Novel Guide*. https://theslingsandarrows.com/the-complete-peanuts-1985-1986.
Reich, Vikki. "The Case of Peppermint Patty." *Up Popped a Fox*, 21 November 2012. http://www.vikkireich.com/blog/2012/11/the-case-of-peppermint-patty. Accessed 24 October 2019.
Saunders, Ben. "Peppermint Patty's Desire: Charles Schulz and the Queer Comics of Failure." *The Comics of Charles Schulz: The Good Grief of Modern Life*, edited by Jared Gardner and Ian Gordon, UP of Mississippi, 2017, 13–28.
Schulz, Charles M. *The Complete Peanuts, 1969 to 1970*. Fantagraphics, 2008.
Schulz, Charles M. *The Complete Peanuts, 1995 to 1996*. Fantagraphics, 2015.
Schulz, Charles M. *The Complete Peanuts, 1999 to 2000*. Fantagraphics, 2016.
Schulz, Charles M. "Creativity." *Charles M. Schulz: My Life with Charlie Brown*, edited by M. Thomas Inge, UP of Mississippi, 2010, 89–103.
Schulz, Charles M. "My Life and Art with Charlie Brown and Others." *Charles M. Schulz: My Life with Charlie Brown*, edited by M. Thomas Inge, UP of Mississippi, 2010, 3–19.
Siebers, Tobin. *Disability Theory*. U of Michigan P, 2008.
Spivak, Gayatri Chakravorty. Translator's preface. *Of Grammatology*, by Jacques Derrida, 1976, Johns Hopkins UP, 1998, ix–lxxx.
Thielman, Sam. "Peanuts Cartoonist Charles Schulz on the Necessity of Loserdom." *The Guardian*, 28 November 2015. https://www.theguardian.com/books/2015/nov/28/peanuts-movie-charles-schulz-charlie-brown-cartoon. Accessed 10 July 2019.
"Timeline: The Life of Charles M. Schulz." Charles M. Schulz Museum and Research Center. https://schulzmuseum.org/timeline. Accessed 10 July 2019.

Whalen, Zach, Chris Foss, and Jonathan W. Gray. "Introduction: From Feats of Clay to Narrative Prose/Thesis." *Disability in Comic Books and Graphic Narratives*, edited by Chris Foss, Jonathan W. Gray, and Zach Whalen, Palgrave Macmillan, 2016. 1–13.

CHAPTER 2. WHAT'S THE FREQUENCY, CHARLIE BROWN?
SOUND WAVES, MUSIC, AND THE ZIGZAG SHIRT

Brown, Kieron Michael. "Musical Sequences in Comics." *Comics Grid*, vol. 3, no. 1, 2013. https://www.comicsgrid.com/articles/10.5334/cg.aj. Accessed 29 December 2019.

Cook, Roy T. "Saying, Showing, and Schulz: The Typography of Notation in *Peanuts*." *The Comics of Charles Schulz: The Good Grief of Modern Life*, edited by Jared Gardner and Ian Gordon, UP of Mississippi, 2017, 42–62.

Cronin, Brian. "The 15 Most Iconic Comic Book Sound Effects." *Comic Book Resources*, 17 March 2017. https://www.cbr.com/the-15-most-iconic-comic-book-sound-effects/. Accessed 28 July 2022.

Gardner, Jared, and Ian Gordon. Introduction. *The Comics of Charles Schulz: The Good Grief of Modern Life*, edited by Jared Gardner and Ian Gordon, UP of Mississippi, 2017, 3–9.

Gherman, Beverly. *Sparky: The Life and Art of Charles Schulz*. Chronicle Books, 2010.

Hague, Ian. *Comics and the Senses: A Multisensory Approach to Comics and Graphic Novels*. Routledge, 2014.

Johnson, Rheta Grimsley. *Good Grief: The Story of Charles M. Schulz*. 1989. Andrews and McMeel, 1995.

Keightley, Keir. "Hogan's Tin Pan Alley: R. F. Outcault and Popular Sheet Music." *Musical Quarterly*, vol. 98, 2015, 29–56.

Khordoc, Catherine. "The Comic Book's Soundtrack: Visual Sound Effects in *Asterix*." *The Language of Comics: Word and Image*, edited by Robin Varnum and Christina T. Gibbons, UP of Mississippi, 2007, 156–73.

Kidd, Chip. *Only What's Necessary: Charles M. Schulz and the Art of Peanuts*. Abrams, 2015.

Kinney, Jeff. "Introduction." *Only What's Necessary: Charles M. Schulz and the Art of Peanuts*, edited by Chip Kidd, Abrams, 2015.

Kopin, Joshua Abraham. "'Wham, Bam, Pow!': An Introduction to the Seeing Sounds / Hearing Pictures Round Table." Seeing Sounds / Hearing Pictures—a Round Tale on Sound & Comics (part one), 9 April 2019. https://themiddlespaces.com/2019/04/09/seeing-sounds-part-one. Accessed 29 December 2019.

McCloud, Scott. *Understanding Comics: The Invisible Art*. William Morrow, 1993.

Meredith, William. "Greatest Hits." *Schulz's Beethoven*. http://absadmin.users.sonic.net/schulz/pages/page3.html. Accessed 29 December 2019.

Meredith, William. "Michaelis' Schulz, Schulz's Beethoven, and the Construction of Biography." *Beethoven Journal*, vol. 25, no. 2, Winter 2008, 79–91.

Michaelis, David. *Schulz and Peanuts: A Biography*. HarperCollins, 2007.

Oyola, Osvaldo. "'This Is Not a Sound': The Treachery of Sound in Comic Books." *Sounding Out! Sound Studies Blog*, 13 June 2011. https://soundstudiesblog.com/2011/06/13/this-is-not-a-sound-the-treachery-of-sound-in-comic-books. Accessed 29 December 2019.

Pilgrim, Caren. "What Color Is Charlie Brown's Shirt?—Collecting 101." *Collect Peanuts*, 21 March 2016. https://collectpeanuts.com/2016/03/21/what-color-is-charlie-browns-shirt. Accessed 29 December 2019.

Pino, Camilo Díaz. "Sound Affects: Visualizing Music, Musicians, and (Sub)Cultural Identity in BECK and Scott Pilgrim." *Studies in Comics*, vol. 6, no. 1, 2015, 85–108.

Prathapani, Nikhil. "Continuous Triangular Wave and Discrete Triangular Wave." MATLAB Central File Exchange. https://www.mathworks.com/matlabcentral/fileexchange/42721-continuous-triangular-wave-and-discrete-triangular-wave. Accessed 6 February 2020.

Rise, Scott. "Harmonics." The Synthesizer Academy. http://synthesizeracademy.com/harmonics. Accessed 15 January 2020.

Scheinin, Richard. "'Peanuts' and Beethoven." *Mercury News*, 24 April 2009. https://www.mercurynews.com/2009/04/24/peanuts-and-beethoven. Accessed 29 December 2019.

"Schroeder." *Peanuts* Wiki. Fandom. https://peanuts.fandom.com/wiki/Schroeder. Accessed 5 February 2020.

Schulz, Charles M. *The Complete Peanuts, 1950 to 1952*. Fantagraphics, 2004.

Schulz, Charles M. *The Complete Peanuts, 1967 to 1968*. Fantagraphics, 2008.

Schulz, Charles M. "Creativity." *Charles M. Schulz: My Life with Charlie Brown*, edited by M. Thomas Inge, UP of Mississippi, 2010, 89–103.

Schulz, Charles M. "My Life and Art with Charlie Brown and Others." 1975. *Charles M. Schulz: My Life with Charlie Brown*, edited by M. Thomas Inge, UP of Mississippi, 2010, 3–19.

Schulz, Charles M. "On Staying Power." 1986. *Charles M. Schulz: My Life with Charlie Brown*, edited by M. Thomas Inge, UP of Mississippi, 2010, 123–25.

Schulz, Jean. Foreword. *Only What's Necessary: Charles M. Schulz and the Art of Peanuts*, edited by Chip Kidd, Abrams, 2015.

Stewart, K. J. "21 Weirdest Examples of Comic Book Sounds Effects." *What Culture*, 14 February 2014. https://whatculture.com/comics/21-weirdest-examples-comic-book-sound-effects. Accessed 28 July 2022.

Thain, Douglas. "Simple Sound Library." CSE 20211: Fundamentals of Computing. Notre Dame University, Fall 2013. https://www3.nd.edu/~dthain/courses/cse20211/fall2013/wavfile. Accessed 4 February 2020.

Tisserand, Michael. "Footballs and Bottom Cliffs: Charlie Brown in Coconino." *The Comics of Charles Schulz: The Good Grief of Modern Life*, edited by Jared Gardner and Ian Gordon, UP of Mississippi, 2017, 111–20.

Uyeno, Greg. "KATCHOW! How to Write Sounds in Comics." *Slate*, 13 February 2013. https://slate.com/human-interest/2015/02/comic-sound-effects-comic-artists-lee-marrs-ryan-north-and-ben-towle-talk-how-they-write-down-unusual-sounds.html. Accessed 29 December 2019.

Whamond, Dave. "'Peanuts' Tell-All." *Reality Check*. Comic strip. Originally published December 12, 2015. Available on Go Comics, https://www.gocomics.com/realitycheck/2015/12/12.

"When 'I Love Lucy' Invented the Rerun." *The Barrel of Forty: TV, Life, and Other Stuff*, 9 July 2017. http://terrencemoss.blogspot.com/2017/07/when-i-love-lucy-invented-tv-rerun.html. Accessed 17 July 2020.

Whitehouse, Kieran. "Odd vs. Even Harmonic Distortion (What's the Difference?)." Producer Hive, 15 September 2019. https://producerhive.com/ask-the-hive/odd-vs-even-harmonic-distortion. Accessed 15 January 2020.

Whitted, Qiana J. "Sound and Silence in the Jim Crow South." *Hooded Utilitarian*, 19 April 2013. https://www.hoodedutilitarian.com/2013/04/sound-and-silence-in-the-jim-crow-south. Accessed 29 December 2019.

Zlabinger, Tom. "Listening to Charlie Brown: Musicians and Music Making as Cold War Critique." *Peanuts and American Culture: Essays on Charles M. Schulz's Iconic Comic Strip*, edited by Peter W. Y. Lee, McFarland, 2019, 49–81.

CHAPTER 3. "WHY CAN'T I HAVE A NORMAL DOG LIKE EVERYONE ELSE?": SNOOPY AS CANINE—AND FELINE

Boxer, Sarah. "The Exemplary Narcissism of Snoopy." *The Atlantic*, November 2015.

Brandt, Jessica K. "Cold War Snoopy, or, Do Beagles Dream of Electric Bunnies?" *Peanuts and American Culture: Essays on Charles M. Schulz's Iconic Comic Strip*, edited by Peter W. Y. Lee, McFarland, 2019, 178–97.

Caldwell, Christopher. "Against Snoopy." *New York Free Press*, 4 January 2000. http://www.nypress.com/news/against-snoopy-DXNP1020000104301049998. Accessed 16 February 2020.

A Charlie Brown Christmas. Dir. Bill Melendez. CBS, 9 December 1965.

Darling, Tim. "Charlie Brown's Guide to Welcoming Failure." Amnesta.net, June 2008. http://www.amnesta.net/other/peanuts. Accessed 1 March 2020.

Flagg, Gordon. "Snoopy: Cowabunga!" *Booklist*, 15 September 2013, 60.

Franzen, Jonathan. Foreword. *The Complete Peanuts, 1957 to 1958*. Fantagraphics, 2005, xi–iii.

Gherman, Beverly. *Sparky: The Life and Art of Charles Schulz*. Chronicle Books, 2010.

Johnson, Rheta Grimsley. *Good Grief: The Story of Charles M. Schulz*. 1989. Andrews and McMeel, 1995.

Mendelsohn, Daniel. "The Rejections." *New York Times*, 15 October 2006.

Patchett, Ann. "To the Doghouse." *The Peanuts Papers: Writers and Cartoonists on Charlie Brown, Snoopy and the Gang, and the Meaning of Life*, edited by Andrew Blauner, Library of America, 2019, 101–9.

Rivett-Carnac, Marc. "Snoopy Gets a Star on Hollywood's Walk of Fame." *Time*, 4 November 2015.

Schulz, Charles M. *Happiness Is a Warm Puppy*. 1962. Penguin, 2019.

Schulz, Charles M. *Peanuts Jubilee: My Life and Art with Charlie Brown and Others*. Ballantine Books, 1975.

Schulz, Charles M. "The Theme of Peanuts." *Charles M. Schulz: My Life with Charlie Brown*, edited by M. Thomas Inge, UP of Mississippi, 2010, 147–63.

"Snoopy." Macy's Balloon Characters. Fandom. https://macysthanksgiving.fandom.com/wiki/Snoopy. Accessed 24 February 2020.

"Snoopy for President." *Truth, Symmetry, Pleasure, Taste, Recognition*. https://tsptr.com/products/snoopy-for-president-sweatshirt. Accessed 19 February 2020.

Taube, Michael. "It's Time to Reconsider Snoopy's Bad Reputation." *New York Post*, 27 December 2015. https://nypost.com/2015/12/27/its-time-to-reconsider-snoopys-bad-reputation. Accessed 17 February 2020.

Wong, Kevin. "How Snoopy Killed *Peanuts*." *Kotaku*, 20 August 2015. https://kotaku.com/how-snoopy-killed-peanuts-1724269473. Accessed 1 March 2020.
"World Famous Tennis Player." *Peanuts* Wiki. Fandom. https://peanuts.fandom.com/wiki/World_Famous_Tennis_Player. Accessed 1 March 2020.

CHAPTER 4. I LOVE LUCY:
THE FUSSBUDGET AND THE FIRST LADY OF SITCOMS

All in the Family. Television series. CBS, 1971–79.
Andrews, Bart. *The "I Love Lucy" Book*. 1976. Doubleday, 1985.
"The Audition." *I Love Lucy*, season 1, ep. 6. CBS, 19 November 1951.
Austerlitz, Saul. *Sitcom: A History of 24 Episodes from "I Love Lucy" to "Community."* Chicago Review Press, 2014.
"The Ballet." *I Love Lucy*, season 1, ep. 19. CBS, 18 February 1952.
Beaty, Bart. "Introduction: Comics Studies; Fifty Years after Film." *Cinema Journal*, vol. 50, no. 3, 2011, 106–10.
Berman, Marc. "Timeless Appeal." *MediaWeek*, 11 September 2000, 58.
Bianculli, David. *The Platinum Age of Television: From "I Love Lucy" to "The Walking Dead," How TV Became Great*. Penguin Random House, 2016.
Boddy, William. "The History of Television." Oxford Bibliographies, 28 April 2017. https://www.oxfordbibliographies.com/view/document/obo-9780199791286/obo-9780199791286-0036.xml. Accessed 17 July 2020.
The Brady Bunch. Television series. ABC, 1969–74.
Bushmiller, Ernie. *Nancy*. Newspaper comic strip, 1938–present.
Caniff, Milton. *Terry and the Pirates*. Newspaper comic strip, 1934–73.
A Charlie Brown Christmas. Dir. Bill Melendez. CBS, 9 December 1965.
A Charlie Brown Thanksgiving. Dir. Bill Melendez and Phil Roman. CBS, 30 November 1973.
Clark, Benjamin. "FW: Research question." Email to Michelle Ann Abate, 24 April 2020.
Davis, Jim. *Garfield*. Newspaper comic strip, 1978–present.
Davis, Madelyn Pugh, and Bob Carroll. "Falling in Love with Lucy." *Time*, 31 March 2003, A28.
"The Diet." *I Love Lucy*, season 1, ep. 3. CBS, 29 October 1951.
Edwards, Elizabeth. *"I Love Lucy": Celebrating Fifty Years of Love and Laughter*. Running Press, 2001.
Edwards, Elizabeth. *"I Love Lucy": A Celebration of All Things Lucy*. Running Press, 2011.
Father Knows Best. Television series. NBC and CBS, 1954–60.
Fenton, Matthew McCann. "6. *I Love Lucy*: The Rubber-Faced Redhead's Comic Ballets Were Tutu Funny for Words." *Entertainment Weekly*, Fall 1998, 18.
Friends. Television series. NBC, 1994–2004.
Gaar, Gillian G. "Groundbreaking Lucy." *"I Love Lucy": Discovering America's Best-Loved Sitcom*, edited by Ben Nussbaum, Companion House Books, 2016, 44–51.
Gehring, Wes. "'I Love Lucy' Turns 50." *USA Today* magazine, September 2001.
Gilligan's Island. Television series. CBS, 1964–67.
Grace and Frankie. Television series. Netflix, 2015–present.
Gray, Harold. *Little Orphan Annie*. Newspaper comic strip, 1924–2010.

Groensteen, Thierry. *The System of Comics*. Translated by Bart Beaty and Nick Nguyen. UP of Mississippi, 2007.

Gunsmoke. Televisions series. CBS, 1955–75.

Hajdu, David. *The Ten-Cent Plague: The Great Comic-Book Scare and How It Changed America*. Macmillan, 2008.

"The Handcuffs." *I Love Lucy*, season 2, ep. 4. CBS, 6 October 1952.

Herriman, George. *Krazy Kat*. Newspaper comic strip, 1913–44.

The Honeymooners. Television series. CBS, 1955–56.

Hulse, E. "*I Love Lucy*: The Complete Second Season." *Video Librarian*, vol. 19, no. 6, November–December 2002, 38.

"*I Love Lucy* Comics." Grand Comics Database. https://www.comics.org/series/12581. Accessed 17 July 2020.

It's the Great Pumpkin, Charlie Brown. Dir. Bill Melendez. CBS, 27 October 1966.

"Job Switching." *I Love Lucy*, season 2, ep. 1. CBS, 15 September 1952.

Johnson-Carper Furniture Company. "Live Like Lucy (You'll Love It!)." Advertisement in *Life*, 6 April 1953.

Jordan, Elisa. "The Lucy Team." *"I Love Lucy": Discovering America's Best-Loved Sitcom*, edited by Ben Nussbaum, Companion House Books, 2016, 12–21.

Keogh, T. "I Love Lucy: The Complete Sixth Season." *Video Librarian*, vol. 21, no. 4, July–August 2006, 37.

"L.A. at Last." *I Love Lucy*, season 4, ep. 17. CBS, 7 February 1955.

Landay, Lori. *I Love Lucy* (TV Milestones series). Wayne State UP, 2010.

Landay, Lori. "*I Love Lucy*: Television and Gender in Postwar Ideology." *The Sitcom Reader: America Viewed and Skewed*, edited by Mary M. Dalton and Laura R. Linder, SUNY Press, 2005, 87–97.

Landay, Lori. "The Lucy Mystique." *"I Love Lucy": Discovering America's Best-Loved Sitcom*, edited by Ben Nussbaum, Companion House Books, 2016, 24–33.

Landay, Lori. "The Mirror of Performance: Kinaesthetics, Subjectivity, and the Body in Film, Television, and Virtual Worlds." *Cinema Journal*, vol. 51, no. 3, Spring 2012, 129–35.

Leave It to Beaver. Television series. CBS and ABC, 1957–63.

Lemoine, Chay. "Forever Lucy." *"I Love Lucy": Discovering America's Best-Loved Sitcom*, edited by Ben Nussbaum, Companion House Books, 2016, 5–9.

The Lone Ranger. Television series. ABC, 1949–57.

"The Lone Ranger." Grand Comics Database. https://www.comics.org/series/538. Accessed 30 April 2020.

Lopes, Paul. *Demanding Respect: The Evolution of the American Comic Book*. Temple UP, 2009.

"Lucy Does a TV Commercial." *I Love Lucy*, season 1, ep. 30. CBS, 5 May 1952.

"Lucy Is Enciente." *I Love Lucy*, season 2, ep. 10. CBS, 8 December 1952.

"Lucy Writes a Play." *I Love Lucy*, season 1, ep. 17. CBS, 4 February 1952.

"Lucy's Italian Movie." *I Love Lucy*, season 5, ep. 23. CBS, 16 April 1956.

McCay, Winsor. *Little Nemo in Slumberland*. Newspaper comic strip, 1905–27.

McClay, Michael. *I Love Lucy: The Complete Picture History of the Most Popular TV Show Ever*. Citadel Press, 1995.

McCloud, Scott. *Understanding Comics: The Invisible Art*. William Morrow, 1994.

McGruder, Aaron. *The Boondocks*. Newspaper comic strip, 1996–2006.

Michaelis, David. *Schulz and Peanuts: A Biography*. HarperCollins, 2007.
Miller, Stuart. "Pop! Goes the Culture." *Variety*, 17 October 2005, 141–70.
Morgan, Chris. "How *I Love Lucy* and Desilu Productions Defined the Modern Sitcom." *Paste*, 2 February 2016. https://www.pastemagazine.com. Accessed 17 April 2020.
My Favorite Husband. Radio program. CBS, 1948–51.
Nussbaum, Ben, editor. *"I Love Lucy": Discovering America's Best-Loved Sitcom*. Companion House Books, 2016.
Outcault, Robert. *Hogan's Alley*. Newspaper comic strip, 1895–98.
Ozzie and Harriet. Television series. ABC, 1952–66.
Parks and Recreation. Television series. NBC, 2009–15.
Perry Mason. Television series. CBS, 1957–66.
Pew Research Center. "Newspapers Fact Sheet." https://www.journalism.org/fact-sheet/newspapers. Accessed 9 April 2021.
Pitman, R. "*I Love Lucy*: Ultimate Season 2." *Video Librarian*, September–October 2015, 56.
Pittman, Alex. "Dis-assembly Lines: Gestures, Situations, and Surveillances." *Women and Performance: A Journal of Feminist History*, vol. 23, no. 2, 2013, 178–92.
"The Quiz Show." *I Love Lucy*, season 1, ep. 5. CBS, 12 November 1951.
Schulz, Charles M. *The Complete Peanuts, 1950 to 1952*. Fantagraphics, 2004.
Seinfeld. Television series. NBC, 1989–98.
Shales, Tom. "Lucy, Lost and Found." *Washington Post*, 18 December 1989. https://www.washingtonpost.com/archive/lifestyle/1989/12/18/lucy-lost-and-found/48e05657-de71-4b5c-9b9a-a09ff7fdd07c. Accessed 4 April 2020.
Three's Company. Television series. ABC, 1977–84.
Trudeau, Garry. *Doonesbury*. Newspaper comic strip, 1970–present.
Turner, Morrie. *Wee Pals*. Newspaper comic strip, 1965–2004.
The Twilight Zone. Television series. CBS, 1959–64.
VanDerWerff, Emily Todd. "Why Does Lucy Endure after All These Years?" *AV Club*, 9 April 2012. https://tv.avclub.com/why-does-i-love-lucy-endure-after-all-these-years-1798230734. Accessed 4 April 2020.
Wagner, Thomas. "The Redhead." *"I Love Lucy": Discovering America's Best-Loved Sitcom*, edited by Ben Nussbaum, Companion House Books, 2016, 59–67.
Walker, Mort. *Beetle Bailey*. Newspaper comic strip, 1950–2018.
Watterson, Bill. *Calvin and Hobbes*. Newspaper comic strip, 1985–95.
"When 'I Love Lucy' Invented the Rerun." *The Barrel of Forty: TV, Life, and Other Stuff*, 9 July 2017. http://terrencemoss.blogspot.com/2017/07/when-i-love-lucy-invented-tv-rerun.html. Accessed 17 July 2020.
Wright, Bradford. *Comic Book Nation: The Transformation of Youth Culture in America*. Johns Hopkins UP, 2003.

CHAPTER 5. FRANKLIN AND PIG-PEN:
THE AESTHETICS OF BLACKNESS AND DIRT

Akoukou, Nicole. "The Colorblind Millennial Generation and the Problem with Being Blind to Race." *Latin Post*, 27 June 2014. http://www.latinpost.com/articles/15663/20140627/

the-colorblind-millennial-generation-and-the-problem-with-being-blind-to-race.htm. Accessed 5 February 2018.

Astor, Maggie. "Dove Drops an Ad Accused of Racism." *New York Times*, 8 October 2017. https://www.nytimes.com/2017/10/08/business/dove-ad-racist.html. Accessed 5 February 2018.

Benson, Richard. *The Printed Picture*. Museum of Modern Art, 2009.

Bernstein, Robin. *Racial Innocence: Performing American Childhood from Slavery to Civil Rights*. NYU Press, 2011.

Brandon, Brumsic, Jr. *Luther*. Syndicated newspaper comic strip, 1968–86.

Cavna, Michael. "Franklin Integrated 'Peanuts' 47 Years Ago Today. Here's How a Teacher Changed Comics History." *Washington Post*, 31 July 2015.

"Charlie Brown." *Peanuts* Wiki. Fandom. http://peanuts.wikia.com/wiki/Charlie_Brown. Accessed 5 February 2018.

Entman, Robert M., and Andrew Rojecki. *The Black Image in the White Mind: Media and Race in America*. U of Chicago P, 2001.

Erickson, Christine. "How a Schoolteacher Helped Create the First Black Peanuts Character." *Mashable*, 26 November 2014. https://mashable.com/2014/11/26/franklin-black-peanuts-character-history/#7_RDhi9e.mqD. Accessed 1 February 2018.

Fanon, Frantz. "The Fact of Blackness." *Theories of Race and Racism: A Reader*, edited by Les Back and John Solomos, Routledge, 2000, 257–65.

Florido, Adrian. "How Franklin, the Black 'Peanuts' Character, Was Born." NPR, 6 November 2016. https://www.npr.org/sections/codeswitch/2015/11/06/454930010/how-franklin-the-black-peanuts-character-was-born.

"Franklin." *Peanuts* Wiki. Fandom. http://peanuts.wikia.com/wiki/Franklin. Accessed 5 February 2018.

Gardner, Jared. "Storylines." *SubStance*, vol. 40, no. 1, 2011, 53–69.

Gateward, Frances, and John Jennings. "Introduction: The Sweeter the Christmas." *The Blacker the Ink: Constructions of Black Identity in Comics and Sequential Art*, edited by Frances Gateward and John Jennings, Rutgers UP, 2015, 1–15.

Gurney, James. "Dead Tech: Zipatone." *Gurney Journey*, 31 May 2009. http://gurneyjourney.blogspot.com/2009/05/dead-tech-zipatone.html. Accessed 29 April 2021.

Ha, Thu-Huong. "The Sweet Story behind Peanuts' Groundbreaking First Black Character." *Quartz*, 11 December 2015. https://qz.com/571393/the-sweet-story-behind-peanuts-groundbreaking-first-black-character/. Accessed 1 February 2018.

Halliday, Ayun. "How Franklin Became Peanuts' First Black Character, Thanks to a Caring Schoolteacher." *Open Culture*, 17 July 2015.

Hébert, Paul. "'Welcome, You Dumb Honky.' Race in the Early *Doonesbury* Strips, Part II: Rufus." *Reading Doonesbury*, 10 May 2018. https://readingdoonesbury.com/tag/rufus. Accessed 3 October 2018.

Howard, Sheena C. "Brief History of the Black Comic Strip, Past and Present." *Black Comics: Politics of Race and Representation*, edited by Sheena C. Howard and Ronald L. Jackson III, Bloomsbury, 2013, 11–22.

Johnson, Jeff. "Happy Franklin Day: First Black 'Peanuts' Character Honored." *NBC News*, 31 July 2015. https://www.nbcnews.com/news/nbcblk/happy-franklin-day-first-black-peanuts-character-honored-n402041. Accessed 1 February 2018.

Kamp, David. "Guess Who's Coming to 'Peanuts.'" *New York Times*, 13 January 2018. https://www.nytimes.com/2018/01/13/opinion/sunday/peanuts-franklin-charlie-brown.html. Accessed 1 February 2018.

Kidd, Chip. *Only What's Necessary: Charles M. Schulz and the Art of Peanuts*. Abrams, 2015.

King, Martin Luther, Jr. "I Have a Dream." Speech. Originally delivered August 28, 1963. https://www.archives.gov/files/press/exhibits/dream-speech.pdf. Accessed 5 February 2018.

Lehman, Christopher P. "Franklin and the Early 1970s." *The Comics of Charles Schulz: The Good Grief of Modern Life*, edited by Jared Gardner and Ian Gordon, UP of Mississippi, 2017, 133–46.

McWhorter, John H. "Black Isn't a Personality Type." *Los Angeles Times*, 12 May 2002. http://articles.latimes.com/2002/may/12/opinion/op-mcwhorter. Accessed 5 February 2018.

Page, Clarence. "A 'Peanuts' Kid without Punchlines." *Chicago Tribune*, 16 February 2000. https://www.chicagotribune.com/news/ct-xpm-2000-02-16-0002160340-story.html. Accessed 26 April 2021.

"Pig-Pen." *Peanuts* Wiki. Fandom. http://peanuts.wikia.com/wiki/%22Pig-Pen%22. Accessed 5 February 2018.

Ross, Martha. "Morrie Turner: Pioneering 'Wee Pals' Cartoonist, Dies at 90." *Contra Costa Times* (California), 27 January 2014. https://www.eastbaytimes.com/2014/01/27/morrie-turner-pioneering-wee-pals-cartoonist-dies-at-90. Accessed 1 October 2018.

Saguisag, Lara. *Incorrigibles and Innocents: Constructing Childhood and Citizenship in Progressive Era Comics*. Rutgers UP, 2019.

Saunders, John, and Al McWilliams. *Dateline: Danger!* Newspaper comic strip, 1968–74.

Schulz, Charles M. "Charles M. Schulz: An Interview with Michael Barrier." Originally published in *Comics Buyers Guide*, no. 1473, February 8, 2001. Also available at www.michaelbarrier.com.

Schulz, Charles M. *The Complete Peanuts, 1953 to 1954*. Fantagraphics, 2014.

Schulz, Charles M. *The Complete Peanuts, 1959 to 1960*. Fantagraphics, 2006.

Schulz, Charles M. *The Complete Peanuts, 1967 to 1968*. Fantagraphics, 2008.

Schulz, Charles M. *The Complete Peanuts, 1969 to 1970*. Fantagraphics, 2008.

Shearer, Ted. *Quincy*. Syndicated newspaper comic strip, 1970–86.

Smith, Mychal Denzel. "White Millennials Are Products of a Failed Lesson in Colorblindness." *PBS NewsHour*, 26 March 2015.

Turner, Morrie. *Wee Pals*. Syndicated newspaper comic strip, 1965–present.

Tyree, Tia C. M. "Contemporary Representations of Black Females in Newspaper Comic Strips." *Black Comics: Politics of Race and Representation*, edited by Sheena C. Howard and Ronald L. Jackson III, Bloomsbury, 2013, 45–64.

Wanzo, Rebecca. *The Content of Our Caricature: African American Comic Art and Political Belonging*. NYU Press, 2019.

West, Traci C. *Wounds of the Spirit: Black Women, Violence, and Resistance Ethics*. NYU Press, 1999.

Wong, Kevin. "Franklin Broke *Peanuts*' Color Barrier in the Least Interesting Way Possible." *Kotaku*, 5 April 2017. https://kotaku.com/franklin-broke-peanuts-color-barrier-in-the-least-inter-1793843085. Accessed 5 February 2018.

CHAPTER 6. CHIRPING 'BOUT MY GENERATION: WOODSTOCK, YOUTH CULTURE, AND INNOCENCE

Austerlitz, Saul. *Just a Shot Away: Peace, Love, and Tragedy with the Rolling Stones at Altamont*. Thomas Dunne Books, 2018.

Begley, Sharon. "The Dark Side of Charles Schulz." *Newsweek*, 13 October 2007. https://www.newsweek.com/dark-side-charles-schulz-103889. Accessed 24 May 2020.

Bennett, Andy. Introduction. *Remembering Woodstock*, edited by Andy Bennett, Ashgate, 2004, xiv–xxi.

Brandt, Jessica K. "Cold War Snoopy, or, Do Beagles Dream of Electric Bunnies?" *Peanuts and American Culture: Essays on Charles M. Schulz's Iconic Comic Strip*, edited by Peter W. Y. Lee, McFarland, 2019, 178–97.

Burner, David. *Making Peace with the Sixties*. Princeton UP, 1996.

Cavna, Michael. "A Bird of Peace amid the Dogs of War." *Washington Post*, 15 August 2019, C01.

Clark, Benjamin. "RE: Another question." Email to Michelle Abate, 22 June 2020.

Clark, Benjamin. "RE: Exhibit question." Email to Michelle Abate, 19 May 2020.

Clark, Benjamin. "RE: Research question." Email to Michelle Abate, 27 April 2020.

Collier, Barnard L. "300,000 at Folk-Rock Fair Camp Out in Mud." *New York Times*, 16 August 1969, A1. https://www.nytimes.com/1969/08/17/archives/300000-at-folkrock-fair-camp-out-in-a-sea-of-mud-300000-at-music.html. Accessed 30 May 2020.

Combemale, Leslie. "Peanuts' Woodstock and the Woodstock Festival." Art Insights, 15 August 2019. https://artinsights.com/peanuts-woodstock-the-woodstock-festival-woodstock-production-art. Accessed 24 May 2020.

"Doctor Says Hippies Fear Role of Adult." *Chicago Tribune*, 5 March 1969, A5.

Eco, Umberto. "On *Krazy Kat* and *Peanuts*." 1985. *The Peanuts Papers: Writers and Cartoonists on Charlie Brown, Snoopy and the Gang, and the Meaning of Life*, edited by Andrew Blauner, Library of America, 2019.

Evans, Ron. *Chasing Woodstock: Finding the Cost of Freedom*. EupraxBooks, 2013.

Fass, Paula S. "The Child-Centered Family? New Rules in Postwar America." *Reinventing Childhood after World War II*, edited by Paula S. Fass and Michael Grossberg, U of Pennsylvania P, 2012, 1–18.

Fass, Paula S., and Michael Grossberg. Preface. *Reinventing Childhood after World War II*, edited by Paula S. Fass and Michael Grossberg, U of Pennsylvania P, 2012, ix–xiii.

FAQ. Hells Angels. https://hells-angels.com/faqcontact. Accessed 15 June 2020.

Fischer, Klaus P. *America in White, Black, and Gray: A History of the Stormy 1960s*. Continuum, 2006.

Greenblatt, Mike. *Woodstock: Back to Yasgur's Farm*. Krause Publications, 2019.

"The Hippies: Philosophy of a Subculture." *Time*, 7 July 1967, 18–22.

"Hippies and Violence." *Time*, 12 December 1969, 25.

Huntsinger, Gina. "*Peanuts* and Politics: New Exhibit at the Charles M. Schulz Museum." Press Release, 6 April 2016. https://schulzmuseum.org/wp-content/uploads/2016/04/Mr.-Schulz-Goes-to-Washington.pdf. Accessed 20 June 2020.

Kelley, Peter. "UW Historian William Rorabaugh Explores '60s Counterculture in 'American Hippies.'" *University of Washington News*, 17 August 2015. https://www.washington

.edu/news/2015/08/17/uw-historian-william-rorabaugh-explores-60s-counterculture-in-american-hippies. Accessed 15 June 2020.

Kneeland, Douglas E. "Coroner in Tate Case Shows Drawings of Wounds." *New York Times*, 25 August 1970, 27.

Kneeland, Douglas E. "Manson Trial Is Told Ms. LaBianca Was Stabbed 41 Times." *New York Times*, 29 August 1970, 22.

Lassonde, Stephen. "Ten Is the New Fourteen: Age Compression and 'Real' Childhood." *Reinventing Childhood after World War II*, edited by Paula S. Fass and Michael Grossberg, U of Pennsylvania P, 2012, 51–67.

Lewis, William. "'Wild, Useless' Generation, Supreme Court Hit by Adlow." *Boston Globe*, 21 October 1968, 54.

Life Special Edition: Woodstock Music Festival, 6 September 1969. https://frixos.files.wordpress.com/2016/01/life-magazine-special-edition-1969-woodstock.pdf. Accessed 20 June 2020.

Lind, Stephen J. *A Charlie Brown Religion: Exploring the Spiritual Life and Word of Charles M. Schulz*. UP of Mississippi, 2015.

Linder, Douglas O. "The Charles Manson (Tate-LaBianca Murder) Trial." Famous Trials, 2020. https://www.famous-trials.com/manson/243-home. Accessed 23 May 2020.

Lubas, Ken. "Hippie Increase Linked with 'New' Humanism." *Los Angeles Times*, 18 January 1970, A1.

Michaelis, David. *Schulz and "Peanuts": A Biography*. Harper, 2008.

Miller, Timothy. *The Hippies and American Values*. 1991. 2nd ed., U of Tennessee P, 2001.

Mintz, Steven. "The Changing Face of Children's Culture." *Reinventing Childhood after World War II*, edited by Paula S. Fass and Michael Grossberg, U of Pennsylvania P, 2012, 38–50.

Moretta, John Anthony. *The Hippies: A 1960s History*. McFarland, 2017.

"Morning After at Bethel." *New York Times*, 18 August 1969, 42.

"Nightmare in the Catskills." *New York Times*, 18 August 1969, 34.

Plasketes, George M., and Julie Grace Plasketes. "From Woodstock Nation to the Pepsi Generation: Reflections on Rock Culture and the State of Music, 1969–Present." *Popular Music and Society*, vol. 11, no. 2, 1987, 25–52.

Reagan, Ronald. Letter to Charles M. Schulz, 11 August 1980. *Reagan: A Life in Letters*, edited by Kiron K. Skinner, Annelise Anderson, and Martin Anderson, Simon and Schuster, 2004, 683.

Robinson, Douglas. "Jury Selection in Manson Case to Begin Today." *New York Times*, 16 June 1970. https://www.nytimes.com/1970/06/16/archives/jury-selection-in-manson-case-to-begin-today-up-to-300-candidates.html. Accessed 5 June 2020.

Rorabaugh, William. *American Hippies*. Cambridge UP, 2015.

Roszak, Theodore. "The Misunderstood Movement." *New York Times*, 3 December 1994, A23.

Sachs, Andrea. "An Interview with Manson Prosecutor Vincent Bugliosi." *Time*, 7 August 2009.

Schulz, Charles M. "Penthouse Interview." *Charles M. Schulz: Conversations*, edited by M. Thomas Inge, UP of Mississippi, 2000, 63–75.

Warner, Simon. "Reporting Woodstock: Some Contemporary Press Reflections on the Festival." *Remembering Woodstock*, edited by Andy Bennett, Ashgate, 2004, 55–74.

"Woodstock." *Peanuts* Wiki. Fandom. https://peanuts.fandom.com/wiki/Woodstock. Accessed 20 June 2020.

Woodstock: Three Days That Defined a Generation. Dir. Barak Goodman and Jamilia Ephron. Documentary series. Netflix, 2019.

Yasgur, Max. "These Kids Were Wonderful." *Life Special Edition: Woodstock Music Festival*, 6 September 1969.

Yusko, Dennis. "The Short Life and Tragic Death of Meredith Hunter." *Medium*, 17 April 2020. https://medium.com/@day4343/the-short-life-and-tragic-death-of-meredith-hunter-fb6eee23b5ad. Accessed 15 June 2020.

EPILOGUE: *PEANUTS* TO WATCH OUT FOR: LINUS VAN PELT, ALISON BECHDEL, AND THE LEGACY OF CHARLES M. SCHULZ

Back Cover. *Peanuts: The World's Greatest Comic Strip*. *Life*, 24 December 2021.

Bechdel, Alison. "Cast Biographies." *Dykes to Watch Out For*. http://dykestowatchoutfor.com/cast-biographies. Accessed 11 October 2017.

Bechdel, Alison. "Drawing on the Lesbian Continuum: An Interview with Alison Bechdel." Interview by June Thomas. *Off Our Backs*, vol. 18, no. 8, August–September 1988, 1, 14.

Bechdel, Alison. *Dykes to Watch Out For: The Sequel*. Firebrand Books, 1992.

Bechdel, Alison. *The Essential Dykes to Watch Out For*. Houghton Mifflin, 2008.

Bechdel, Alison. *Fun Home*. Houghton Mifflin, 2006.

Bechdel, Alison. Interview with Hillary Chute. *MFS: Modern Fiction Studies*, vol. 52, no. 4, Winter 2006, 1004–13.

Bechdel, Alison. *More Dykes to Watch Out For*. Firebrand Books, 1988.

Bechdel, Alison. "My website crashed from all the traffic to see my new DTWOF strip." Facebook post, 24 November 2016. https://www.facebook.com/alison.bechdel/posts/1152093518206545. Accessed 24 June 2020.

Bechdel, Alison. "New 'Dykes to Watch Out For' Tackles the Ides of Trump." *Seven Days*, 14 March 2017. https://www.sevendaysvt.com/vermont/new-dykes-to-watch-out-for-tackles-the-ides-of-trump/Content?oid=4598939. Accessed 24 June 2020.

Bechdel, Alison. *Spawn of Dykes to Watch Out For*. Firebrand Books, 1993.

Bechdel, Alison, and Marny Hall. "Ordinary Insurrections." *Journal of Lesbian Studies*, vol. 5, no. 3, 2001, 15–21.

Bernstein, Robin. "'I'm Very Happy to Be in the Reality-Based Community': Alison Bechdel's *Fun Home*, Digital Photography, and George W. Bush." *American Literature*, 89, no. 1, March 2017, 121–54.

Boxer, Sarah. "The Exemplary Narcissism of Snoopy." *The Atlantic*, November 2015.

Critchfield, Adam R., and Jack Pula. "On Psychotherapy, LGBTQ Identity, and Cultural Visibility: In Conversation with Alison Bechdel." *Journal of Gay and Lesbian Mental Health*, vol. 19, 2015, 397–412.

Cvetkovich, Ann. "Drawing the Archive in Alison Bechdel's *Fun Home*." *WSQ: Women's Studies Quarterly*, vol. 36, nos.1–2, Spring–Summer 2008, 111–28.

Daspin, Eileen. "Life Itself." Special Issue, *Peanuts: The World's Greatest Comic Strip*. *Life*, 24 December 2021, 4–7.

DeLuca, Geraldine. "'I Felt a Funeral in My Brain': The Fragile Comedy of Charles Schulz." *The Lion and the Unicorn*, vol. 25, no. 2, April 2001, 300–309.

"*The Essential Dykes to Watch Out For* [Book Review]." *Booklist*, vol. 105, no. 5, 2010, 32.

Faderman, Lillian. *Odd Girls and Twilight Lovers: A History of Lesbian Life in Twentieth-Century America*. Columbia UP, 1991.

Gardner, Jared, and Ian Gordon. Introduction. *The Comics of Charles Schulz: The Good Grief of Modern Life*, edited by Jared Gardner and Ian Gordon, UP of Mississippi, 2017, 3–9.

Garner, Dwight. "The Days of Their Lives: Lesbians Star in Funny Pages." *New York Times*, 2 December 2008.

Gordon, Ian. "Charlie Brown Cafés and the Marketing of *Peanuts* in Asia." *The Comics of Charles Schulz: The Good Grief of Modern Life*, edited by Jared Gardner and Ian Gordon, UP of Mississippi, 2017, 183–96.

Gritten, David. "*Peanuts*: The Legacy of Charlie Brown Creator Charles M. Schulz." *The Telegraph*, 4 December 2015. https://s.telegraph.co.uk/graphics/projects/peanuts-movie/index.html. Accessed 24 June 2020.

Hogan, Heather. "Peppermint Patty and Marcie: BFFs and GFs?" *AfterEllen*, 24 June 2009. http://www.afterellen.com. Accessed 11 October 2017.

Hunt, Fred. "Top 10 Comic Strips from Each Decade." Top Tenz, 26 March 2014. http://www.toptenz.net/top-10-comic-strips-from-each-decade.php.

Inge, M. Thomas. *Comics as Culture*. UP of Mississippi, 1990.

Inge, M. Thomas. Introduction. *Charles M. Schulz: My Life with Charlie Brown*, edited by M. Thomas Inge, UP of Mississippi, 2010, ix–xiv.

Kidd, Chip. *Only What's Necessary: Charles M. Schulz and the Art of Peanuts*. Abrams, 2015.

Kirtley, Susan. "The Political Is Personal: Dual Domesticity in *Dykes to Watch Out For*." *Inks: The Journal of the Comics Studies Society*, vol. 1, no. 1, Spring 2017, 40–55.

Lemberg, Jennifer. "Closing the Gap in Alison Bechdel's *Fun Home*." *WSQ: Women's Studies Quarterly*, vol. 36, nos. 1–2, Spring–Summer 2008, 129–40.

Liberator, Susan. (Reference librarian at the Billy Ireland Cartoon Library and Museum, and writing from the account cartoons@osu.edu.) "RE: Research question." Email to Michelle Abate, 19 April 2021.

Lind, Stephen J. *A Charlie Brown Religion: Exploring the Spiritual Life and Word of Charles M. Schulz*. UP of Mississippi, 2015.

"Linus Van Pelt." *Peanuts* Wiki. Fandom. http://peanuts.wikia.com/wiki/Linus_van_Pelt. Accessed 12 October 2017.

London, Lisa. "Dykes to Watch Out For." *Women's Review of Books*, vol. 21, no. 3, December 2003, 10–11.

Malinowitz, Harriet. "Keeping Tabs on the Dykegeist." *Women's Review of Books*, vol. 15, no. 2, November 1997, 6–7.

Mendelson, Lee. *Charlie Brown and Charles Schulz*. Signet, 1970.

McGurk, Caitlin. "Lovers, Enemies, Friends: The Complex and Coded Early History of Lesbian Comic Strip Characters." *Journal of Lesbian Studies*, vol. 22, no. 4, 2018, 336–53.

Michaelis, David. *Schulz and Peanuts: A Biography*. HarperCollins, 2007.

Obama, Barack. Foreword. *The Complete Peanuts, 1999 to 2000*. Fantagraphics, 2016.

Patchett, Ann. "Snoopy Taught Me How to Be a Writer." *Washington Post*, 12 July 2012. https://www.washingtonpost.com/outlook/snoopy-taught-me-how-to-be-a-writer/2019/07/12/8db3ce3c-a31b-11e9-b7b4-95e30869bd15_story.html. Accessed 22 March 2020.

"Peppermint Patty." *Peanuts* Wiki. Fandom. http://peanuts.wikia.com/wiki/Peppermint_Patty. Accessed 12 October 2017.

Queer Comics Database. "Dykes to Watch Out For (1983)." http://queercomicsdatabase.com/series/dykes-to-watch-out-for. Accessed 22 June 2020.

Reich, Vikki. "The Case of Peppermint Patty." *Up Popped a Fox*, 21 November 2012. http://www.vikkireich.com/blog/2012/11/the-case-of-peppermint-patty. Accessed 10 February 2018.

The Royal Guardsmen. "The Return of the Red Baron." *Snoopy and His Friends*, Laurie Records, 1967.

The Royal Guardsmen. *Snoopy and His Friends*. Laurie Records, 1967.

The Royal Guardsmen. "Snoopy's Christmas." *Snoopy and His Friends*, Laurie Records, 1967.

The Royal Guardsmen. "Snoopy vs. the Red Baron." Charles Fuller Productions, 1966.

Saunders, Ben. "Peppermint Patty's Desire: Charles Schulz and the Queer Comics of Failure." *The Comics of Charles Schulz: The Good Grief of Modern Life*, edited by Jared Gardner and Ian Gordon, UP of Mississippi, 2017, 13–28.

Schulz, Charles M. *The Complete Peanuts: Dailies and Sundays, 1967 to 1968*. Fantagraphics, 2008.

Schulz, Charles M. *The Complete Peanuts: Dailies and Sundays, 1969 to 1970*. Fantagraphics, 2008.

Schulz, Charles M. *Everything I Do Makes Me Feel Guilty: And Other Wisdom of Charlie Brown*. Hallmark, 1969.

Schulz, Charles M. *Go Fly a Kite, Charlie Brown*. 1959. Holt, Rinehart and Winston. 1970.

Schulz, Charles M. *Good Ol' Charlie Brown*. 1957. Holt, Rinehart and Winston, 1965.

Schulz, Charles M. *Linus on Life*. Hallmark, 1967[?].

Schulz, Charles M. *The Meditations of Linus*. Hallmark, 1967.

Schulz, Charles M. *We All Have Our Hangups: And Other Thoughts of Snoopy*. Hallmark, 1969.

Smith, Briana. "Watch Out! Alison Bechdel's Comics as Cultural Commentary." *Feminist Collections*, vol. 25, no. 2, Winter 2004, 1.

"Snoopy for President." *Truth, Symmetry, Pleasure, Taste, Recognition*. https://tsptr.com/products/snoopy-for-president-sweatshirt. Accessed 19 February 2020.

Street, John. "'This Is Your Woodstock': Popular Memories and Political Myths." *Remembering Woodstock*, edited by Andy Bennett, Ashgate, 2004, 29–42.

Timeline. About the Man. Charles M. Schulz Museum and Research Center. https://schulzmuseum.org/timeline. Accessed 10 October 2017.

"Timeline of Charles M. Schulz and Peanuts." Charles M. Schulz Museum and Research Center. https://schulzmuseum.org/wp-content/uploads/2020/05/Timeline-of-Charles-M-Schulz-and-Peanuts.pdf. Accessed 18 April 2021.

Watson, Julia. "Autographic Disclosures and Genealogies of Desire in Alison Bechdel's *Fun Home*." *Biography*, vol. 31, no. 1, Winter 2008, 27–58.

"Way More Than Peanuts." Special Issue, *Peanuts: The World's Greatest Comic Strip. Life*, 24 December 2021, 87–92.

Yarm, Mark. "Alison Bechdel on Her Genius Grant and Family Secrets." *Rolling Stone*, 5 December 2010. http://www.rollingstone.com/culture/features/alison-bechdel-on-her-genius-grant-and-family-secrets-20141205. Accessed 9 October 2017.

You're a Good Man, Charlie Brown. Masterworks Broadway. https://www.masterworksbroadway.com/music/youre-a-good-man-charlie-brown-broadway-revival-cast-recording-1999. Accessed 10 July 2020.

INDEX

References to illustrations appear in **bold**.

Adventures of Ozzie and Harriet, 85
Aesop, 115
Akoukou, Nicole, 127
Alaniz, José, 28
Alice's Adventures in Wonderland, 70
All in the Family, 99
Altamont Concert. *See* Rolling Stones
Altamont Speedway, 140, 141
Alther, Lisa, 153
American Cancer Society, 24
Americans with Disabilities Act, 22–23
Andrews, Bart, 83, 101
Archie (comic strip), 24, 54
Architectural Barriers Act, 21
Apollo 10 space mission, 4, 21, 156
Armstrong, Franklin, 8, 10, 12, 23, 36, 105, 106–29, **111, 113, 118**, 130, 136, 150, 177; and baseball, 106, 110; and Charlie Brown, 106; debut, 10, 23, 106, 107–8, 111, 112; line shading, 10, 105, 111, 112–13, 123–24, 177; personality, 109–11; and Pig-Pen, 10, 105, 106, 111–13; reactions in the South, 108–9; and screentone, 123–24, 177
Armstrong, Louis, 105
Arnaz, Desi, 83, 84, **87**, 92, 101
Austerlitz, Saul, 85, 88, 89, 100, 101, 179

Baby Boomers, 127, 147
Bach, Johann Sebastian, 40
Baez, Joan, 132
Baird, Robert M., 21, 22, 23
Baldwin, Alec, 152
Ball, Blake Scott, 8
Ball, Harvey, 169
Ball, Lucille, 83, 84, 86, 87, **87, 89**, 90, 95, 101, **103**, 101, 104; Emmy Awards, 84; and facial expressions, 86–87; and pregnancy, 95; and slapstick/physical comedy, 90, 101; and vaudeville, 101
Ballard, David, 120
Barrier, Michael, 107
Batman, 98
Baynton, Douglas, 32
Beatlemania, 157
Beaty, Bart, 104, 105, 177
Bechdel, Alison, 11, 28, 151, 153, 180; *Are You My Mother?*, 180; biographical details, 11, 155, 157–58, 164, 168–70, 180–81; and Charles M. Schulz, 157–58, 180–81; *Dykes to Watch Out For* (*DTWOF*), 11, 151, 153–54, 157–70, 180; *Fun Home*, 168–70, 180; as Mo, 11, 164; and *Peanuts*, 157–58
Beck (musician), 43, 175
Beethoven, Ludwig van, 40, 49, 50, 51, 52, **52**, 53, 94, 175
Beetle Bailey (Walker), 99, 125
Begley, Sharon, 149
Bell, Cece, 29

Belle (*Peanuts* character), 4, 22
Bennett, Andy, 133
Bernstein, Robin, 113, 154, 169
Bethel, NY, 132
Bianculli, David, 85
Björk, 43
Blauner, Andrew, 7
Boddy, William, 101
Boondocks, The, 100
Boucher, Connie, 4, 157
Boxer, Sarah, 57, 58, 59, 79, 157
Boy Named Charlie Brown, A, 4, 77, 156
Brady Bunch, The, 100
Brandon, Brumsic, Jr., 121, 124
Brandon-Croft, Barbara, 108
British Invasion (music), 157
Brown, Charlie, viii, 3, 8, 12, **15, 16**, 16, 24, 32, 33–40, **35, 46, 48, 49, 50, 51, 52**, 57–80, **61, 63, 64, 65, 66, 67, 68, 69**, 72, 79, 81, 88, 89, 90, **91**, 94, 96, 97, 102, 104, 106, 112, 125, 146, 149, 150, 152, 153, 156, 158, 159, 160, **160**, 161, 165, **166**, 168, 170, 171, 172, 174, 175, 176, 177, 181; and baseball, 44, 52–53, 77, 94, 100, 104, 106, 177; birthday, viii; and football, 24, 44, 77, 81, 90–91, 159, 171; and Franklin, 106; and kite flying, 43, 77; and Linus, 11; and Lucy, 77, 81; and mental health, 26, 146, 159; and music, 47–51; and pencil-pal, 163; and Schroeder, 50–53; and Snoopy, 56, 57–80; and Valentine's Day, 77; zigzag shirt, 9, 12, 32, 33–53, 55–56, 80, 125, 129, 152
Brown, Kieron Michael, 55
Brown, Rita Mae, 153
Brown, Sally, 5, 73, **74, 75**, 138, 161, 164, 174; and amblyopia ("lazy eye"), 174; and book reports, 174; debut, 161; and interactions with brick schoolhouse, 174; and Linus/Sweet Babboo, 5, 164; and Snoopy, 73, 75
Bugliosi, Vincent, 140
Bushmiller, Ernie, 101
Buster Brown (Outcault), 115
butch/femme, 27, 161

Caldwell, Christopher, 79–80, 155
Calvin and Hobbes (Watterson), 99
Camp Snoopy, 57
Caniff, Milton, 99, 180
Caron, James E., 5
Catterall, Claire, 5
Cavna, Michael, 109, 131, 136
CBS (television broadcasting company), 82, 85, 95, 101, 104, 156
Cedar Point Amusement Park (Ohio), 57
Charles M. Schulz Museum and Research Center, viii, 96, 130, 136, 177
Charlie Brown Christmas, A, 3, 26, 104, 156, 172, 175, 181
Charlie Brown Thanksgiving, A, 4, 22, 104, 172
Cheshire Cat, 70
Chicago, IL, 83
Chute, Hilary, 30, 158
Civil Rights Act, 22, 137
Clarice (character in *Dykes to Watch Out For*), 159, 161, **167**
Clark, Benjamin, viii, 96, 130, 131, 136
Cocker, Joe, 132
Collier, Barnard L., 135
comic books, 97–98, 100, 101, 176; and adults, 98; and children, 98; and Comics Code Authority, 176–77; and Fredric Wertham, 176; and television, 98, 99, 100, 176; and World War II, 98
Comics Code Authority (CCA), 176–77
Cook, Roy T., 40, 41, 42
Creedence Clearwater Revival, 132
Crilley, Mariah, 25
Critchfield, Adam R., 163
Cronin, Brian, 54
Cronkite, Walter, 152
Crosby, Stills, Nash & Young, 132, 141
Crumb, Robert, 158
Cruse, Howard, 158
Cvetkovich, Ann, 168–69

Daisy Hill Puppy Farm, 137
Daredevil (character), 28
Darling, Tim, 77

Daspin, Eileen, 5, 23
Dateline: Danger!, 124, 177
David B. (cartoonist), 28
Davis, Jim, 100
Davis, Lennard, 25
DeLuca, Geraldine, 6, 180
Democratic National Convention (1968), 138
Demonakos, Jim, 55
Dennis the Menace (comic strip), 24, 119
Derrida, Jacques, 29
Determined Productions, 4, 157
Diann Shaddox Foundation, 19
Dick Tracy, 98, 99
Ding Dong School (television show), 96
Dirks, Rudolph, 115
disability, 8–9, 11, 18, 25, 27, 32, 33, 174; and ableism, 25, 26, 27, 32; Americans with Disabilities Act, 22–23; Architectural Barriers Act, 21; in comics, 28–31; crips, 27; disability rights movement, 21–23; Education for All Handicapped Children Act, 22; and graphic medicine, 28–29; Individuals with Disabilities Education Act (IDEA), 22; medical model, 18; in *Peanuts* animated specials, 24, 26; in *Peanuts* comics, 26, 29–31; Physically Disabled Students Program (UC Berkeley), 21; President's Committee on the Employment of the Handicapped, 22; social model, 18; socio-somatic model, 18; supercrip, 20–21
Dolly Madison bakery, 5
Dolmage, Jay, 29
Doonesbury, 100
Dove soap, 177
Dykes to Watch Out For (*DTWOF*), 11, 28, 151, 153, 158, 159, **165**, **167**, 180; and AIDS crisis, 154, 161; Café Topaz, 161; Clarice, 159, 161, **167**; debut, 153; and environmentalism, 153; and gender fluidity, 154; Harriet, 160, 161, **167**; and homonormativity, 153; and Iran-Contra hearings, 170; and laissez-faire capitalism, 154; Lois, **167**; and marriage equality/Defense of Marriage Act, 154, 170; Mo Testa, 11, 152, 159, **162**; and partisan politics, 153; and *Peanuts*, 11, 151, 153–54, 157–70; and polyamory, 153; and racism/white supremacy, 161; Sydney, 159; Thea, 28; Toni, 161; and trans issues, 154; and US military-industrial complex, 153; and vegetarianism, 153; and war on terror, 154, 170; and women's reproductive rights, 154, 161

East Village (New York City), 141
Eco, Umberto, 7, 149
Education for All Handicapped Children Act, 22
Edwards, Elizabeth, 89, 101
Eisenhower, Dwight, 84
Eisner, Will, 119
El Deafo (Bell), 29
Entman, Robert M., 111
Epileptic (David B.), 28
Erickson, Christine, 108
essential tremor, 17, 18. *See also under* Schulz, Charles M.

Faderman, Lillian, 27, 161
Fanon, Frantz, 113
Fantastic Four, 28
Faron (*Peanuts* character), 75–76
Fass, Paula S., 147, 149
Father Knows Best (television show), 85
feminism, 23, 93, 153, 163, 178
Fenton, Matthew McCann, 83
Finch, Stuart, 146
Flagg, Gordon, 60
Flap, Lt. Jackson (*Beetle Bailey*), 125
Florido, Adrian, 108
Folger, Abigail, 140
Ford, Gerald, 22
Foss, Chris, 28, 174
Franklin. *See* Armstrong, Franklin
Franzen, Jonathan, 7, 58, 152
Frawley, William, 84
Frieda (*Peanuts* character), 73, 76

Friedan, Betty, 93
Friends, 100
Frykowski, Wojciech, 140
Fun Home (Bechdel), 168–70, 180

Gaar, Gillian G., 95
Gallaudet University, 22
Gallegos, Cesar, 177
Galvan, Margaret, 28
Gardner, Jared, 6, 7, 24, 30, 37, 91, 122, 125, 126, 128, 152, 172, 174
Garfield, 100, 158
Garland, Judy, **117**
Garland-Thompson, Rosemarie, 21, 27, 29
Gateward, Frances, 119, 121
Gehring, Wes, 82, 83, 87
Geisel, Theodor Seuss (Dr. Seuss), 172
gender, 7, 23, 25, 32, 93, 149, 154, 163, 178. See also sexuality
Generation X, 127
Gherman, Beverly, 14, 18, 23, 37
Gilburt, Harry, 38
Gilligan's Island, 99
Glass, Ira, 7
Gleason, Ralph, 141
Glickman, Harriet, 107, 108, 120, 126, 128
Goldberg, Whoopi, 152
Gordon, Ian, 6, 7, 24, 37, 91, 152, 172, 181
Gospel According to Peanuts, The, 3, 155
Grace and Frankie, 99
Grateful Dead, 132, 141
Gray, Harold, 101
Gray, Jonathan W., 28, 174
Great Depression, 147
Great Pumpkin, 4, 24, 77, 81, 104, 139, 156, 159, 172, 181; *It's the Great Pumpkin, Charlie Brown*, 4, 104, 156, 172; and Linus, 24, 77, 81
Greenblatt, Mike, 135
Gritten, David, 171
Groenig, Matt, 152
Groensteen, Thierry, 31, 104
Grossberg, Michael, 147
Groth, Gary, 7
Gunsmoke, 85

Ha, Thu-Huong, 106, 107
Hague, Ian, 175
Haight-Ashbury (San Francisco), 141
Hajdu, David, 97, 177
Halliday, Ayun, 106, 107, 109, 111
Happiness Is a Warm Puppy, 3, 21, 47, 80, 155
Harriet (character in *Dykes to Watch Out For*), 160, 161, **167**
Hébert, Paul, 125
Hells Angels, 141, 179
Hendrix, Jimi, 132, 178
Hernandez, Jaime, 54
Herriman, George, 39, 100
hippies, 132–36, 138–42, 146–48, 150, 157, 178, 179, 180; and civil rights movement, 178; and gay and lesbian liberation movement, 178; and gender roles, 178, 179; and heterosexuality, 178, 179; and *Peanuts*, 137–39; and Peppermint Patty, 161; and racial composition, 178, 179; and second-wave feminism, 178; and socioeconomic class, 178, 179; and whiteness, 178, 179; and Woodstock (*Peanuts* character), 138–39, **138**, **139**; and Woodstock Music and Arts Festival (WMAF), 132–36, 138–42, 146–48, 150, 157, 178, 179, 180
Hogan, Heather, 26, 27, 161, 163
Hogan's Alley (Outcault), 53, 54, 99
Holden, William, 84
Honeymooners, The, 85, 95, 101, 102, 177
Howard, Sheena C., 119
Hulse, E., 90
Hunt, Fred, 152
Hunter, Meredith, 141, 179

Ignatz Mouse (*Krazy Kat*), 100
I Love Lucy, 8, 9, 10, 81–85, 176; "The Adagio," 176; "The Amateur Hour," 176; "The Audition," 92, 93, 101, 176; awards and award nominations, 84; "Babalu" (song), 92; "The Ballet," 90, 176; "The Benefit," 176; comic book, 102, **103**; "Cuban Pals," 176; debut, 82; "The Diet," 176; and feminism/gender

roles, 93; "The Handcuffs," 90; "Job Switching," 84; "L.A. at Last," 84; "Lucy Does a TV Commercial," 84, 176; "Lucy Fakes an Illness," 176; "Lucy Goes to the Hospital," 84; "Lucy Is Enciente," 92; "Lucy Is Jealous of a Girl Singer," 176; "Lucy's Italian Movie," 84, 90; "Lucy Writes a Play," 93, 176; "The Marriage License," 83; merchandising, 84, 86; and *Peanuts*, 176; and pregnancy, 84, 95; "The Quiz Show," 90, 95; and radio, 101; and ratings, 84; and slapstick, 90; and the sitcom, 85; and Television Hall of Fame, 85; and television history, 84–85; Tropicana Club, 92, 93; "Vacation from Marriage," 176; and vaudeville, 101; Vitameatavegamin, 84, 86, **87**, 93; "We're Having a Baby" (song), 92; "The Young Fans," 176

Individuals with Disabilities Education Act (IDEA), 22

Inge, M. Thomas, 6, 7, 20, 91, 152, 157, 182, 183, 185, 187, 188, 194, 195, 197

It's a Bird (Seagle), 28

It's the Great Pumpkin, Charlie Brown, 4, 104, 156, 172, 183, 185, 190

Jackson (character in *Dennis the Menace*), 119
Jackson, Michael, 172
Jacobs, Dale, 29
Janice (character in *Why, Charlie Brown, Why?*), 24
Jefferson Airplane, 141
Jennings, John, 119, 121
Johnson, Donna. *See* Wold, Donna Johnson
Johnson, Rheta Grimsley, 5, 17, 18, 19, 20, 33, 38, 107
Johnston, Lynn, 152
Joplin, Janice, 132
Jordan, Elisa, 89

Kafer, Alison, 27
Kamp, David, 107, 108
Karasik, Paul and Judy, 28

Katzenjammer Kids, The, 115
Keightley, Keir, 54
Keillor, Garrison, 152
Kelly, Kenneth C., 108
Kennedy, John F., 136, 179
Kennedy, Robert F., 138
Keogh, T., 89
Khordoc, Catherine, 54
Kidd, Chip, 3, 4, 37, 121, 172–73
Kiddy Land (Tokyo), 58
Kinflicks, 153
King, Billie Jean, 23, 152
King, Martin Luther, Jr., 23, 126–28; assassination, 126; and colorblindness, 126–28; "I Have a Dream" speech, 126–28; March on Washington, 126
Kirtley, Susan, 169
Kneeland, Douglas E., 140
Knott's Berry Farm, 57
Koch, Christina Maria, 28
Kopin, Joshua Abraham, 53
Krall, Diana, 152
Krazy Kat, 39, 100
Kurtzman, Harvey, 158

LaBianca, Leno, 140
LaBianca, Rosemary, 140
Landay, Lori, 82, 93
Lassonde, Stephen, 149
Leary, Timothy, 133
Leave It to Beaver, 100
Lee, Peter W. Y., 7
Lehman, Christopher P., 106, 109, 110, 120
Lemberg, Jennifer, 169
Lemoine, Chay, 84, 86, 88
Lewis, John, 55
Liberator, Susan, 155
Lila (character in *Snoopy Come Home*), 24
Lind, Stephen J., 7, 179, 181
Linton, Simi, 18, 21
Linus. *See* Van Pelt, Linus
Little Lulu, 158
Little Nemo in Slumberland (McCay), 99, 101
Little Orphan Annie (comic), 101

Little Red-Haired Girl, 38, 76, 97, 181
Lois (character in *Dykes to Watch Out For*), **167**
Lone Ranger, The, 101, 102, 177, 190
Long, Mark, 55
Longmore, Paul K., 18, 22
Lopes, Paul, 97
Los Angeles, CA, 140
Los Feliz, CA, 140
Louvre Museum, 4–5
Lucy. *See* Van Pelt, Lucy
"Lucy and Sophie Say Goodbye" (1905 comic), 180
Luther, 121, 124, 177

Macy's Thanksgiving Day parade, 5, 58, 156
Mad magazine, 158
Mall of America, 57
Manson, Charles, 140, 142, 195
Manson Family, 140, 141, 146, 147
Marbles (Forney), 29
March, 55
Marcie, 27, 39, 130, 161, 185; and butch/femme, 27, 161; debut, 27, 161; and lesbianism, 27, 161, 163; and Peppermint Patty, 27, 39, 130, 161, 163
Marshall Field's (department store), 83
Martin, Jeffrey J., 21
Marvel Comics Universe, 6
Matlin, Leonard, 7
Mayo Clinic, 17
McCay, Winsor, 99, 101
McClay, Michael, 86
McCloud, Scott, 55, 104, 174
McDonnell, Patrick, 39
McGurk, Caitlin, 180
McRuer, Robert, 25, 27
McWhorter, John H., 109
McWilliams, Al, 124, 177
Melendez, Bill, 152
Mendelsohn, Daniel, 79
Meredith, William, 40, 41, 51, 175
Mertz, Ethel, 82, 83, 84, 86, 94, 176
Mertz, Fred, 82, 83, 176
MetLife, 5

Michaelis, David, ix, 3, 4, 5, 7, 17, 23, 39, 85, 94, 96, 97, 137, 155, 156, 157, 170, 171, 175, 176, 181
Miller, Timothy, 150, 177
Mintz, Steven, 149
Miss Frances (children's television host), 96
Mo (from *Dykes to Watch Out For*). *See* Testa, Mo
Moretta, John Anthony, 132, 133, 135, 140, 178
Morgan, Chris, 85
My Favorite Husband (radio show), 101

Nancy (comic strip), 24, 101
Narvaez, Alfonso, 135
National Aeronautics and Space Administration (NASA), 4, 21, 136, 156
Nielsen, Kim, 23, 31, 32
Nielsen ratings, 84
Nixon, Richard M., 136, 179
Nussbaum, Ben, 84

Obama, Barack, 152
Off Our Backs, 157
Of Grammatology (Derrida), 29
onomatopoeia in comics, 54
Oppenheimer, Jess, 95
Outcault, Richard, 53, 54, 99, 115, 119
Oyola, Osvaldo, 56

Page, Clarence, 106, 110
Parks and Recreation, 100
Passaro, Alan, 179
Patchett, Ann, ix, 157, 182, 188, 197
Patty (*Peanuts* character), **35**, 45, 48, **48**, 51, **51**, 101, 104, 116, **116**, 149
Peanuts: in advertising, 5; and American childhood, viii, 10–11, 132, 171; animated specials, 3, 4, 5, 171; and baseball, 38, 44, 53, 56, 77, 94, 100, 104, 106, 107, 110, 144, 165; and bean bag chair, 104; Belle (*see* Belle); and bird characters before Woodstock, 130, 137–39; Charlie Brown (*see* Brown, Charlie); comic strip, 3, 5, 6, 14, 16, 155; as commentary on US children and childhood, 132, 149–50,

158–59, 163; *The Complete Peanuts* volumes, 7, 58, 152; debut, 3, 10, 24, 35, 111–12, 132, 149, 152, 170; and *Dykes to Watch Out For (DTWOF)*, 11, 151, 153–54, 157–70; and failure (theme), 57, 58–59, 77–79; fashion show, 4–5, 22; final strip, 170, 171; Franklin (*see* Armstrong, Franklin); Golden Age, 155; kite flying, 44, 47, 77, 107, 160; Linus (*see* Van Pelt, Linus); Lucy (*see* Van Pelt, Lucy); in Macy's Thanksgiving Day parade, 5, 58; Marcie (*see* Marcie); merchandising, viii, 4, 5, 12, 57, 157, 172; and music, 34, 39–42; paperback reprints, viii, 3, 4, 5, 155, 160, 165, 168; Patty (*see* Patty); *Peanuts Philosophers* series, 163–64, 168; Peppermint Patty (*see* Peppermint Patty); perceived decline in quality, 59–60; Rerun (*see* Van Pelt, Rerun); Sally (*see* Brown, Sally); Schroeder (*see* Schroeder); Shermy (*see* Shermy); Snoopy (*see* Snoopy); Spike (*see* Spike); and television, 96–97, 102, 104; theatrical productions, 4, 77; Woodstock (*see* Woodstock)

Peanuts Movie, The, 58, 172, 181

Peanuts Philosophers series, 163–64, 168; *Everything I Do Makes Me Feel Guilty*, 163; *Linus on Life*, 168; *The Meditations of Linus*, 168; *We All Have Our Hangups*, 163

Pears Soap, 114, **115**

Pekar, Harvey, 54, 158

Peppermint Patty, 26, 27, 36, 39, 78, **79**, 100, **111**, **113**, **118**, 130, 136, 161, 163, 164, 185; and Birkenstock sandals, 136, 161; and butch/femme, 26–27, 161; and Charlie Brown, 26, 161; debut, 26, 161; and lesbianism, 26–27, 161, 163; and Marcie, 27, 130, 161, 163; as Patricia Reichardt (actual name), 161; and possible learning disability, 26

Perry Mason, 85

Phantom, The (Falk), 158

Phoenix, Woodrow, 19

Physically Disabled Students Program (UC Berkeley), 21

Pig-Pen, 8, 10, 12, 105, 106–29, **113**, **116**, **117**, 150, 175, 177; debut, 112; and Franklin, 106, 107, 111–13

Pilgrim, Caren, 33

Pino, Camilo Díaz, 54, 55

Pitman, R., 84, 90

Playbeagle magazine, 175

Polanski, Roman, 140

Prathapani, Nikhil, 34

President's Committee on the Employment of the Handicapped, 22

Quincy, 121, 124, 177

Quisp (cereal), 169

race, 10, 25, 32, 105, 106–29; in *Beetle Bailey*, 125; blackface minstrelsy, 117–18, 119; blackness, 10, 23, 105, 106, 107, 113–18, 177; in *Buster Brown* (comic), 115; civil rights movement, 110, 126–28; and colorblindness, 126–28; in comics, 10, 23, 106, 107, 113–18, 119, 121, 177; in *Dennis the Menace*, 119; in *Doonesbury*, 125; and *Dykes to Watch Out For (DTWOF)*, 153, 154; and Franklin, 10, 23, 106–29; and hippies, 178, 179; in *The Katzenjammer Kids*, 117; and *Luther*, 121; March on Washington, 126; and Martin Luther King Jr., 126–28; racism, 10, 23, 105, 113–18, 119; in Richard F. Outcault, 119; and *Quincy*, 121; and Pig-Pen, 106–29; school desegregation, 23, 109; segregation and integration, 106, 126–28; in *The Spirit* (Eisner), 119; and *Wee Pals*, 119–21; whiteness, 10, 23, 106, 107–8, 177, 178, 179; and Woodstock Music and Arts Festival (WMAF), 133, 141, 147, 148, 178, 179; and the Yellow Kid (Outcault), 119

Rachmaninoff, Sergei Vasilyevich, 40, 51

Radio City Music Hall, 156

Reality Check (Whamond), 175

Red Baron, 4, 71, 78, 100, 156; "The Return of the Red Baron," 4, 156; and Royal

Guardsmen, 4, 156; and Snoopy, 71, 78, 100; *Snoopy and His Friends*, 4, 156; "Snoopy's Christmas," 4, 156; "Snoopy vs. the Red Baron," 4, 156
Redding, Otis, 55
Reich, Vikki, 26, 27, 161, 163
religion, 3, 7, 25, 155
Rerun. *See* Van Pelt, Rerun
Ricardo, Little Ricky, 84, 93
Ricardo, Lucy, 8, 9, 10, 80–90, **87**, **88**, 92–95, 97, 99, 101, **103**, 105, 176; and Lucy Van Pelt, 80, 82, 85, 86, 88–97, 99, 104, 152; pregnancy, 84, 95
Ricardo, Ricky, 81, 82, 83, 84, **87**, 90, 92, 93, 94, 176; as musician, 92–93
Rich, Adrienne, 25, 27, 163
Ride Together, The (Karasik and Karasik), 28
Rise, Scott, 42
Roberts, Ed, 21
Rock the Vote, 5
Rockwell, Norman, 149
Rojecki, Andrew, 111
Roker, Al, 152
Rolling Stones, 140–41, 179, 194; concert at Altamont Speedway, 140, 141, 146, 179, 194; and Hells Angels, 141, 179
Rorabaugh, William, 178
Rosenbaum, Stuart E., 21, 22, 23
Ross, Martha, 119
Roszak, Theodore, 146
Royal Guardsmen, 4, 156; "The Return of the Red Baron," 4, 156; *Snoopy and His Friends*, 4, 156; "Snoopy's Christmas," 4, 156; "Snoopy vs. the Red Baron," 4, 156
Rubyfruit Jungle, 153

Sachs, Andrea, 140
Saguisag, Lara, 115
Sally. *See* Brown, Sally
Sanjak (character from *Terry and the Pirates*), 180
Santana, 132, 141
Saunders, Ben, 26, 27, 161, 163
Saunders, John, 177

Scheinin, Richard, 40
Schroeder, 13, 33, 35, 39, 40, **41**, 45, 48, 50, **51**, **52**, 53, 77, 93, 94, 130; and baseball, 52, 53; and Charlie Brown, 50–53; debut, 50; and Lucy, 13, 40, 41, 93–94, 130; and music, 13, 33, 35, 39, 40, 41, 50–53
Schulz, Charles M.: and Alison Bechdel, 180–81; awards, accolades, and honors, 3, 4, 5, 14, 24, 156; biographical details, 5, 8, 14, 18, 20, 23, 37, 38, 57, 136, 137, 139–40, 152, 170–71, 174, 176, 179, 180–81, 185, 186; biographical details in comics, 23, 38; birthday, viii; and California, 136, 139–40, 174; and Colorado Springs, 176; culinary tastes, ix; death, 5, 6, 18, 37, 152, 170–71; drawing style, 8–9, 10, 11, 12, 29, 36, 37, 107, 111, 118, 123–24, 126; earnings and income, 5; as Eisenhower Republican, 136; essential tremor (ET), 8–9, 12, 14–25, 27, 29–31, 33, 34, 44, 45; health problems, 17, 170–71; on Hollywood Walk of Fame, 58; and ice hockey, 14; and John F. Kennedy, 136, 179; legacy, 154, 170–72; as midwesterner, 6, 14; and Minnesota, 57; and Morrie Turner, 119–20, 121; and mother, ix, 23, 181; and musical tastes, 136; and Nancy Reagan, 136; and Philip and Louanne Van Pelt, 176; and political views, 136, 179; posthumous earnings, 172; and Richard M. Nixon, 136, 179; and Ronald Reagan, 136; and screentone, 123–24; as Sparky (nickname), 18, 37, 136, 176, 179, 181; studio fire, 23; as supercrip, 20–21; and television, 96–97; and Woodstock Music and Arts Festival, 130, 134; work habits, 20; World War II veteran, 14, 137; zigzag shirt, 37–38
Schulz, Jean, 37, 187
Schulz, Joyce (née Halverson), 23, 136, 176
Schulz, Meredith, 23, 41, 85–86, 175–76
Schulz, Monte, 179
Scott Pilgrim series, 55
screentone, 123–24; Zip-A-Tone, 123
Seagle, Steven T., 28

Security Is an Eye Patch, 174
Seinfeld, 99
Sesame Street, 169
sexuality, 25, 27, 32, 93; compulsory heterosexuality, 25, 27; and disability, 27; heterosexuality, 93, 154; and hippies, 133, 178; lesbian continuum, 27, 161, 163; and "Lucy and Sophie Say Goodbye" (1905 comic), 180; and Marcie, 27, 130; non-heternormativity/queerness, 25, 27, 161, 180; and Peppermint Patty, 26–27, 130, 161, 163; and postwar era, 93; and Sanjak (*Terry and the Pirates*), 180
Shearer, Ted, 121, 124
Shermy, 45, 50, 60
Shore, Peter, 5
Short, Robert L., 3, 155
Siebers, Tobin, 21
Silence of Our Friends, The, 55
Simpsons, The, 6
Skippy (comic strip), 24
Small, David, 29
Smith, Mychal Denzel, 127
Snoopy, vii–viii, **vii**, 8, 9, 12, 22, 23, 33, 36, 40, 41, **41**, **46**, **49**, 52, 57–80, **61**, **62**, **63**, **64**, **65**, **66**, **67**, **68**, **69**, 72, 81, 110, 125, 129, 130, 137, 138, **138**, 139, **142**, **143**, **144**, **145**, 148, 150, 152, 171, 174; anthropomorphism, 59–60; as astronaut, 70; and baseball, 56; in Brazil, 181; and cat next door, 76; and Charlie Brown, 49, 56, 57–80; in China, 181; as college student, 60; and Daisy Hill Puppy Farm, 137; debut, 57; doghouse, vii, **vii**, ix, 9, 23, 33, 56, 58, 59, 60, 62, **62**, **63**, **64**, **65**, **66**, **67**, **68**, 69, **69**, 71, 72, **72**, 75, 76, 78, 79, 101, 104, 130, 137, 138, **138**, 139, 144, 145, 171, 172, 173, 179; doghouse fire, 23, 71; as Easter Beagle, 58, 74; in Europe, 58; and failure, 58, 59; and Faron, 75–76; feline qualities, 9, 56, 57–80, 129; and food, 63–67; and the happy dance, 160–61; as Head Beagle, 59, 74, 179; on Hollywood Walk of Fame, 58; in Japan (Tokyo), 58, 181; as Joe Cool, 58, 59, 60; and "Kitten Kaboodle" stories, 175; as legal beagle, 71; and Lucy, 80; and Macy's Thanksgiving Day parade, 58, 156; as mascot for NASA's Apollo space program, 137, 156; and mental health, 26, 58, 62, 67, 71, 79, 146; and merchandising, 57; and National Dog Day, 74; and *Playbeagle* magazine, 175; as presidential candidate, 57, 136, 157; and the Red Baron, 71, 78, 100; and Sopwith Camel, viii, 71, 144; and Vietnam War, 137; and Woodstock, 10, 130–33, 142–14, 145, 146, 148, 179; as World Famous Astronaut, 71, 175; as World Famous Attorney, 60, 71, 78; as World Famous Author, vii–viii, **vii**, 24, 58, 60, 69, 70, 71, 77, 78, 172, 175; as World Famous Flying Ace, 57, 58, 60, 70, 78, 137, 156, 171; as World Famous Hockey Player, 60, 71, 78; as World Famous Surgeon, 71; as World Famous Tennis Player, 60, 71, 78
Snoopy Come Home, 24
Snoopy Show, The, 172
Snoopy Town (Tokyo), 58
Sopwith Camel, viii, 71, 144
sound in comics, 54–55
speech balloons, 54, 55
Spiegelman, Art, 158
Spike (*Peanuts* character), 23
Spirit, The (Eisner), 119
Spivak, Gayatri Chakravorty, 29
Stanley Cup (ice hockey), 78
Star Wars, 6
Stewart, K. J., 54
Stitches (Small), 29
Summer of Love (1969), 134, 136, 146
Superman, 98
Sydney (character in *Dykes to Watch Out For*), 159

Tate, Sharon, 140
Tate-LaBianca Murders (1969), 140–42, 195
Taube, Michael, 71

television, 83–85, 176; and comic books, 98, 99, 100, 176; and newspaper comics, 99, 100, 101; in postwar era, 83–85, 176
Terry and the Pirates (Caniff), 99, 180
Testa, Mo, 11, 153, **162**, **165**, **167**; and Linus Van Pelt, 11, 164–68, 170; and softball, **167**, 168; and talk therapy, 159, **162**
Thain, Douglas, 43
Thea (character from *Dykes to Watch Out For*), 28
Thielman, Sam, 19
Three's Company, 100
Tiber, Elliot, 135
Tiny Tots concerts, 39
Tisserand, Michael, 39
Toni (character in *Dykes to Watch Out For*), 161
Toombs, S. Kay, 21, 22, 23
triangle wave, 9, 33, **33**, 39, 42, 44, 47, 53, 55, 152; in electronic power transmission, 33; and even harmonics, 43; and odd harmonics, 9, 33, 43, 44, 47; in radio technology, 33; in sound engineering, 9, 33, 34, 42–43, 47
Trudeau, Garry, 7, 125
Trump, Donald J., 180
Turner, Morrie, 99, 119–20, 121; and Charles Schulz, 119–20
Twilight Zone, The, 85

Umansky, Lauri, 18, 22
Understanding Comics (McCloud), 55
United Feature Syndicate, 5, 38, 109, 181
University of California, Berkeley, 21
US Department of Education, 21
Uyeno, Greg, 54

Vance, Vivian, 84; Emmy Award, 84
VanDerWerff, Emily Todd, 85, 88, 90, 95
Van Gogh, Vincent, 71, 72
Van Pelt, Linus, 8, 11, 12, 33, 44, 53, **69**, 70, 71, 72, **75**, 77, 81, 89, 94, 95, 96, 104, 110, 130, 138, **139**, 149, 150, 151, 159, 164, **165**, **166**, 168, 171, 179, 180; and baseball, 165; and Charlie Brown, 11, 151, 165; and Great Pumpkin, 24, 77, 81, 139, 159; and lisp/speech impediment, 26; and Lucy, 81, 89, 94; and Miss Othmar (teacher), 165–66; and Mo Testa, 11, 164–68, 170; security blanket, 5, 11, 33, 76, 81, 130, 155, 164, 165; and Snoopy, 69, 70, 71, 72, 75, **75**; as Sweet Babboo, 5, 164
Van Pelt, Louanne, 176
Van Pelt, Lucy, 5, 8, 12, 13, 23, 26, 36, 40, 52, **75**, 77, 80, 81–82, 85–86, 88, **88**, 89–97, 91, **92**, 104, 105, 110, 130, 150, 152, 159, **160**, 163, 164, 165, **166**, 171, 175, 176, 179–80; and blue dress, 81, 88; as bully, 26, 81, 89, 146, 160–61, 179–80; debut, 5, 81; and football, 24, 44, 77, 81, 90–91, 159, 171; as fussbudget, 9, 80, 81, 82, 83, 85, 86, 87, 89, 91, 93, 95, 97, 99, 101, 103, 105, 175; and Lucy Ricardo, 5, 9, 80, 82, 85, 86, 88–97, 99, 104, 152; and psychiatry booth, 7, 77, 94, 97, 159, **160**, 171; and Rerun, 95–96; and saddle shoes, 81, 88; and Schroeder, 13, 40, 41, 93–94, 130; and slapstick comedy, 81, 91–92; and Snoopy, 80; as toddler, 81, 88, 89, 90
Van Pelt, Philip, 176
Van Pelt, Rerun, 73, **74**, 95–96, 105, 161; and Snoopy, 73–74
Vinolia Soap, 114, **114**
Violet, **46**, 52, 53, 77
Vitameatavegamin, 84, 86, **87**, 93

Wagner, Thomas, 105
Walker, Mort, 99, 125
Wallkill, NY, 134
Wanzo, Rebecca, 119, 122
Ware, Chris, 7
Warner, Simon, 148
"Washing the Blackamoor White" (Aesop), 115
Watson, Julia, 169
Watterson, Bill, 7, 99
Wee Pals (Turner), 99, 119–21, 177
Wertham, Fredric, 176
West, Traci S., 113
Whalen, Zach, 28, 174

Whamond, Dave, 175
White, Ebony, 119
Whitehouse, Kieran, 43, 46
Whitted, Qiana J., 55
Who, The, 132
Why, Charlie Brown, Why?, 24
Wilco, 43
Wold, Donna Johnson, 38, 97
Wong, Kevin, 58, 59, 106, 109, 110
Woodstock (*Peanuts* character), vi, 8, 10, 11, 12, 16, 26, 41, **41**, 57, 58, 128–29, 130–33, 135–39, 138, 141–51, **142**, **143**, **144**, **145**, 174, 178, 179, 180; as "bird hippie," 138–39, **138**, **139**; as childlike, 142–43, 144, 145, 146; debut, 10, 130; as female character, 131; as helicopter pilot, 180; as mechanic for Snoopy's Sopwith Camel, 130, 144; and music festival, 128–29; name, 130, 142; and neurodivergence, 26; as participant in bird protests and demonstrations, 137–38; and Snoopy, 10, 130–33, 142–14, 145, 146, 148, 179; as Snoopy's secretary, 130, 144; speech patterns, 16, 26, 147, 148; and Vietnam, 180; and Woodstock Generation, 132, 144, 146
Woodstock Music and Art Festival (WMAF), 8, 10, 128–29, 130, 131, 132–36, 139–42, 147–49, 178, 179, 180; accidents, injuries, and deaths at, 178; attendance, 178; and Bethel, NY, 132, 134–35; and class, 178; community resistance,

objections, and threats toward, 134–35; and Creedence Clearwater Revival, 132; and Crosby, Stills, Nash & Young, 132; and the Grateful Dead, 132; and hippies, 132–36, 138–42, 146–48, 150, 157, 178, 179, 180, 194, 195; and Janis Joplin, 132; and Jimi Hendrix, 132, 178; and Joan Baez, 132; and Joe Cocker, 132; legacy, 130, 132–33, 135; and Max Yasgur, 132, 134, 135, 147, 194, 196; negative press reviews, 135; origins, 130–31; performers, 132, 178; poster, 131; and race, 178; and Santana, 132; and sexuality, 178; and Wallkill, NY, 134; and The Who, 132; and youth counterculture, 132, 133, 134, 139, 140, 141, 146, 147, 150, 178
Wright, Bradford, 97, 98, 101
Wyeth, Andrew, 71

X-Men, 28

Yablonsky, Lewis, 141, 142
Yasgur, Max, 132, 134–35, 147
Yellow Kid (Outcault), 53, 119
You're a Good Man, Charlie Brown, 4, 156
youth counterculture (1960s), 132, 133, 134, 139, 140, 141, 146, 147, 150, 178
Yusko, Dennis, 141

Zip-A-Tone, 123
Zlabinger, Tom, 39, 40

ABOUT THE AUTHOR

Michelle Ann Abate is professor of literature for children and young adults at The Ohio State University. She has published six books and dozens of essays on a wide range of topics in US popular culture, comics and graphic novels, LGBTQ studies, and literature for young readers.

www.ingramcontent.com/pod-product-compliance
Lightning Source LLC
Chambersburg PA
CBHW030108170426
43198CB00009B/538